INTENSIFYING MATHEMATICS INTERVENTIONS FOR STRUGGLING STUDENTS

The Guilford Series on Intensive Instruction
Sharon Vaughn, Editor

This series presents innovative ways to improve learning outcomes for K–12 students with challenging academic and behavioral needs. Books in the series explain the principles of intensive intervention and provide evidence-based teaching practices for learners who require differentiated instruction. Grounded in current research, volumes include user-friendly features such as sample lessons, examples of daily schedules, case studies, classroom vignettes, and reproducible tools.

Essentials of Intensive Intervention
Rebecca Zumeta Edmonds, Allison Gruner Gandhi,
and Louis Danielson

Intensive Reading Interventions for the Elementary Grades
Jeanne Wanzek, Stephanie Al Otaiba, and Kristen L. McMaster

Intensifying Mathematics Interventions for Struggling Students
Edited by Diane Pedrotty Bryant

*Literacy Coaching in the Secondary Grades:
Helping Teachers Meet the Needs of All Students*
Jade Wexler, Elizabeth A. Swanson, and Alexandra Shelton

INTENSIFYING MATHEMATICS INTERVENTIONS
for Struggling Students

EDITED BY

Diane Pedrotty Bryant

Series Editor's Note by Sharon Vaughn

THE GUILFORD PRESS
New York   London

Library of Congress Cataloging-in-Publication Data

Names: Bryant, Diane Pedrotty, editor.
Title: Intensifying mathematics interventions for struggling students / edited by
   Diane Pedrotty Bryant.
Description: New York : The Guilford Press, [2021] | Series: The Guilford series on
   intensive instruction | Includes bibliographical references and index.
Identifiers: LCCN 2020042181 | ISBN 9781462546190 (paperback) |
   ISBN 9781462546206 (cloth)
Subjects: LCSH: Mathematics—Study and teaching. | Response to intervention
   (Learning disabled children) | Effective teaching.
Classification: LCC QA20.R47 I58 2021 | DDC 372.7—dc23
LC record available at *https://lccn.loc.gov/2020042181*

About the Editor

Diane Pedrotty Bryant, PhD, is the Mollie Villeret Davis Professor in Learning Disabilities in the Department of Special Education at The University of Texas at Austin. She is also Project Director of the Mathematics and Science Institute for Students with Special Needs at the Meadows Center for Preventing Educational Risk. Dr. Bryant has published numerous articles on instructional strategies for students with mathematics difficulties. She is Editor-in-Chief of *Learning Disability Quarterly* and coauthor of educational tests, an early numeracy intervention, and textbooks on methods for teaching struggling students.

Contributors

Brian R. Bryant, PhD (deceased), Meadows Center for Preventing Educational Risk, The University of Texas at Austin, Austin, Texas

Diane Pedrotty Bryant, PhD, Meadows Center for Preventing Educational Risk, The University of Texas at Austin, Austin, Texas

Benjamin S. Clarke, PhD, Special Education and Clinical Services, University of Oregon, Eugene, Oregon

Christian T. Doabler, PhD, Department of Special Education, The University of Texas at Austin, Austin, Texas

Barbara J. Dougherty, PhD, Curriculum Research and Development Group, University of Hawai'i at Mānoa, Honolulu, Hawaii

Melissa K. Driver, PhD, Department of Inclusive Education, Kennesaw State University, Kennesaw, Georgia

Suzanne R. Forsyth, MA, Cameron Independent School District, Cameron, Texas

Douglas Fuchs, PhD, Department of Special Education, Vanderbilt University, Nashville, Tennessee

Lynn S. Fuchs, PhD, Department of Special Education, Vanderbilt University, Nashville, Tennessee

Jessica H. Hunt, PhD, College of Education, North Carolina State University, Raleigh, North Carolina

Asha K. Jitendra, PhD, Graduate School of Education, University of California, Riverside, Riverside, California

Elisheba W. Kiru, PhD, Topeka Public Schools, Topeka, Kansas

Jennifer Krawec, PhD, Department of Teaching and Learning, University of Miami, Coral Gables, Florida

Jihyun Lee, PhD, School of Counseling, Leadership, Advocacy, and Design, University of Wyoming, Laramie, Wyoming

Katherine E. Lewis, PhD, College of Education, University of Washington, Seattle, Washington

Maryam Nozari, PhD, Department of Special Education, University of Hawaii at Manoa, Honolulu, Hawaii

Min Wook Ok, PhD, Department of Special Education, Daegu University, Gyeongsangbuk-do, South Korea

Sarah R. Powell, PhD, Department of Special Education, The University of Texas at Austin, Austin, Texas

Pamela M. Seethaler, PhD, Department of Special Education, Vanderbilt University, Nashville, Tennessee

Mikyung Shin, PhD, Department of Education, West Texas A&M University, Canyon, Texas

Marissa P. Suhr, MS, Special Education and Clinical Services, University of Oregon, Eugene, Oregon

Marah Sutherland, MS, Special Education and Clinical Services, University of Oregon, Eugene, Oregon

Series Editor's Note

When you think about intensive instruction for students, what instructional problems come to mind? You likely think about your students with reading, writing, and spelling problems; however, I imagine you also think about students with intensive mathematics difficulties. Many teachers perceive that there are inadequate resources to guide them on how to provide intensive instruction to youngsters with significant problems in mathematics. Fortunately, this book by Bryant and colleagues thoroughly addresses this issue. Within the book you will learn about the characteristics of students with math difficulties, how to use data for progress monitoring, how to intensify interventions, and specific evidence-based practices for addressing early numeracy, time and money, whole numbers, rational numbers, word-problem-solving strategies, algebra, and even technology.

Intensive Mathematics Interventions for Struggling Students provides thorough background knowledge about mathematics difficulties across the grade span. Even more valuable to educators, this book provides user-friendly guidance on how to address all of the elements of mathematics difficulties from preschool to secondary grades. Each topic provides clear guidance to support decision making about intensive instruction, including examples, ideas, practices, and suggestions.

Are you wondering what you might do as a school leader to ensure that all of your students are making adequate gains in mathematics? This book defines the plan to address that question. As a teacher, are you perplexed as to what else you could do to enhance your instruction in the foundation skills of mathematics, such as early numeracy, time, money, and whole numbers? This book not only enhances your background knowledge but also provides you with highly specific guidance that you can implement immediately in your classroom. What about problem solving—for which it is always a challenge to develop appropriately intensive instruction? This book provides an entire chapter dedicated to improving your practices for intensifying instruction in problem-solving mathematics. Perhaps one of the most challenging areas in mathematics is how to use data-based informed instruction for progress monitoring students' response to intensive instruction. Good news! This book provides an entire chapter specifying how to proceed.

The methods, activities, and guidelines included here will increase your confidence and skills across all of the essential areas related to intensive instruction in mathematics.

As series editor for The Guilford Series on Intensive Instruction, I am particularly excited about *Intensive Mathematics Interventions for Struggling Students*, written by the team of outstanding research-to-practice authors and edited by Diane Bryant. This book reflects the extraordinary evidence-based knowledge of the author team as well as their classroom expertise. In addition to the instructional approaches described and the assessment and instructional practices provided, these individuals share expertise on how to differentiate instruction for the range of learners across a range of grade spans. This is the third book in the Intensive Instruction series, and it successfully achieves the high bar of providing very specific guidance for educators and administrators on how to implement evidence-based practices to effectively meet the needs of students who require intensive instruction. It is also an outstanding, comprehensive source for educational leaders and scholars about the research-to-practice knowledge on intensive interventions in mathematics and should be a useful resource for preservice training.

The knowledge, practices, and lessons in this book achieve the goal of helping educators as well as educational leaders to improve outcomes for the many students struggling to learn mathematics, as well as those who require research-based mathematics intensive instruction to help them reach grade-level expectations. This book provides guidance for teachers who are instructing the many students with the most severe mathematics difficulties who do not make adequate progress through standard mathematics instruction and require more intensive instruction to achieve sufficient growth. Also provided is guidance on the specialized instruction needed to implement an intensive intervention to make significant progress. The authors focus on the ways in which teachers can intensify interventions for students for whom current mathematics interventions are not sufficient.

This volume is a perfect addition to The Guilford Series on Intensive Instruction. All of the books in the series present innovative ways to improve learning outcomes for students with challenging academic and behavioral needs. As with this volume, they provide evidence-based teaching practices for learners who require differentiated instruction and include user-friendly features, such as sample lessons, classroom vignettes, and reproducible tools. Additional features include valuable case studies to better understand the application of the practices specified. These enable you to align the learning and behavior difficulties of the individuals in the book to those in your own classroom or school. I suspect that many of you will return often to this book, as I know I will, to expand my knowledge of key mathematics practices and to seek out its lessons for improving instruction.

Get ready to learn about instructing students with significant mathematics problems.

SHARON VAUGHN, PhD

Preface

The purpose of *Intensifying Mathematics Interventions for Struggling Students* is to provide classroom teachers and special educators in grades K–12, school administrators, and teacher educators with an understanding of the reasons students at the elementary, middle, and high school levels have difficulties with mathematics. Additionally, practical techniques for intensifying mathematics interventions are included. These interventions are evidence based and aimed at improving the mathematics performance of students, including those with mathematics disabilities.

The book is organized according to several themes and features that are integrated across the chapters. These themes and features include (1) the Common Core State Standards for Mathematics, (2) important mathematical vocabulary, and (3) common student misconceptions about mathematical ideas and concepts. Mathematical misconceptions result from students' faulty and incorrect ideas about a mathematical idea or concept.

The primary focus of this book is on presenting information and ideas about intensifying mathematics interventions. Included is a discussion of a multi-tiered system of instructional support, with an emphasis on Tier 2 and Tier 3, and how interventions can be intensified to meet different student instructional needs. The ADAPT model is discussed in terms of how to make adaptations or modifications to instructional delivery and content to promote student access to the general education curriculum.

The book's 10 chapters describe the characteristics of struggling students, including those with mathematics disabilities (dyscalculia). Key instructional ideas for intensifying interventions are introduced, including mathematical learning progressions. Effective instructional practices such as using multiple representations to illustrate a concept, having students explain their understanding of mathematics, and employing questioning techniques are included. Content includes early numeracy, time and money, whole number and rational number computation, word-problem-solving strategies, algebra, and technology applications that enable readers to learn about techniques pertinent to mathematical topics taught at the elementary and secondary levels. Reproducible materials are included to provide teachers with more available tools for instruction.

I hope readers enjoy this book and identify within it strategies that they can implement with their students.

Contents

Purchasers of this book can download and print enlarged copies
of the reproducible figures at *www.guilford.com/bryant2-forms* for personal use
or use with students (see copyright page for details).

CHAPTER 1

Mathematics Interventions

DIANE PEDROTTY BRYANT, BRIAN R. BRYANT, and MIKYUNG SHIN

LEARNING OUTCOMES

After studying this chapter, you will be able to answer the following questions:

1. What are the Common Core State Standards for Mathematics?
2. Who are students with mathematics difficulties and mathematics learning disabilities?
3. What are multi-tiered systems of support and response to intervention?
4. How can mathematics interventions be intensified in Tiers 2 and 3 for students with mathematics difficulties and mathematics learning disabilities?

Mathematics is an important part of the curriculum for preschool through 12th grade and extends into postsecondary education as a means for preparing students to be competitive in today's workforce. Not only is mathematics knowledge important for work in many professions, but we know that the ability to reason mathematically and apply mathematics knowledge is critical for students to address daily living tasks that we all encounter. In fact, mathematics is such an important part of the curriculum and everyday living that professional organizations have provided information to help us better understand what mathematical literacy means in today's society.

Mathematical literacy is a term that describes the ability to reason and communicate about mathematics to solve problems in the classroom and everyday life (National Mathematics Advisory Panel [NMAP], 2008). Moreover, mathematical literacy refers to the ability to formulate, apply, and translate mathematical understandings in different situations including everyday life using mathematical concepts, procedures, and tools (Organization for Economic Co-operation and Development [OECD], 2012). The National Council of Teachers of Mathematics (NCTM, 2000) stressed the urgency in better preparing our children and adolescents for the "real world," where the translation of mathematical literacy abilities is critical. NCTM noted, "The need to understand and be able to use mathematics in everyday life and in the workplace has never been greater and will continue to increase" (p. 4); "those who understand and can do mathematics will have significantly enhanced opportunities and options for shaping their futures. A lack of mathematical competence keeps those doors closed" (p. 5).

Consider for a moment how and when you use your mathematics knowledge in everyday life. What ideas did you identify where you use mathematics to help? If you identified the use of mathematics for managing your finances, purchasing household items, paying taxes, computing a tip, cooking with recipes, and using different types of measurement, as examples, then it is clear we all need a solid understanding in mathematical literacy to navigate school, work, and daily living.

Even in our technologically advanced society that will only continue to provide ways to use technology in schools, work, and home, we must still understand the mathematics to be sure our solutions to problems are reasonable mathematically. For instance, when using a calculator to compute a tip, you need to know how to enter numbers into the tool and the operation to select to calculate the tip; this sounds simple to do. But translating the tip percentage into a decimal equivalence and clicking the correct operation are necessary prerequisite skills to easily calculate the tip. Or perhaps you prefer to round the total bill and then compute the tip percentage. Even if the bill has percentage options, such as a 15% or 20% tip, you still have to use addition to calculate the final amount.

Just this one task alone, computing the tip on a restaurant bill, involves various mathematics abilities, illustrating how important mathematics literacy is for all of us. For students with mathematics difficulties, being mathematically literate is not easy because of the problems they experience with understanding mathematics concepts and using mathematics procedures to solve problems.

We can see that a focus on the mathematics abilities and challenges of all students is paramount for educators to ensure children and adolescents are prepared to meet future demands of the workforce and daily living. Unfortunately, consider the following results from international and national mathematics assessments. At the international level, the Program for International Student Assessment (PISA; OECD, 2012) is a measure given every 3 years to 15-year-old students across multiple countries to assess their application of mathematics to real-world problems. U.S. students' average score was 481 on a scale of 0–1,000; the 2012 average score showed U.S. students ranking 31st out of 34 OECD countries and 31 partner countries (OECD, 2012).

At the national level, on the National Assessment of Educational Progress (NAEP), average grade 4 mathematics scores for students with disabilities showed a decrease of 4 points compared to the 2015 findings. For grade 8, results showed no significant score change from the 2015 findings. For students with and without disabilities, results indicated that on average, only 49% of fourth graders with disabilities compared to 84% of students without disabilities scored at or above the *Basic* level (National Center for Education Statistics [NCES], 2017). In eighth grade, average scores of students with and without disabilities were even more alarming with 31% and 75%, respectively, scoring at or above the *Basic* level.

Taken together, it is evident that, in general, U.S. students' mathematics performance is disconcerting compared to other industrialized countries and U.S. students with disabilities are at a decided disadvantage compared to their peers without disabilities. It is easy to conclude that the development and application of mathematical literacy at school and in daily living are important for all students, including those students with mathematics difficulties (MD) and mathematics learning disabilities (MLD). But as can be seen in the international and national assessment results, gaps in our students' mathematical knowledge and performance are evident. These gaps are not acceptable and cause major concern among educators and policy makers. Therefore, educators must be equipped to address the issues students with MD and MLD show in their classroom mathematics activities related to their district's and state's standards and assessments. Specifically, students with MD and MLD must receive intensive mathematics interventions in mathematical domains if they are to stand a chance of succeeding in school and beyond.

Thus, the purpose of this book is to provide readers with content in several mathematics areas that are deemed to be the most critical aspects of mathematics interventions for students with MD and MLD. Researchers who work in developing and validating mathematics interventions have contributed chapters to this book in areas that educators must teach to students with MD and MLD.

What will you read about in the chapters in this book? First, you will find descriptions and explanations of mathematics areas. You will also learn about evidence-based practices for teaching the various mathematics areas. Collectively, the chapters will include connections to the Common Core State Standards for Mathematics (CCSSM; National Governors Association [NGA] Center for Best Practices & Council of Chief State School Officers [CCSSO], 2010), information about MD and MLD as they relate to each chapter, and examples of how each chapter's content can be operationalized within a response-to-intervention (RTI) model that can be used to intensify mathematics interventions for struggling students. Misconceptions and vocabulary associated with specific content knowledge is presented. Finally, in each chapter, you will find a reproducible of specific content that you can use in your classroom to plan interventions. Now, take a moment to review the table of contents for this book to find out which mathematics areas are most critical for struggling students to learn. Note that the last chapter, "Use of Technology for Intensifying Mathematics Intervention," contains information that can be used with the mathematics areas in the other chapters.

To get started, in this chapter, as a foundation for reading the remaining chapters in this book, we provide information about the characteristics of students with mathematics difficulties. Let's begin with learning more about the CCSSM as the framework for content in this book.

Common Core State Standards for Mathematics

In 2010, the NGA and CCSSO published the CCSSM. Aware of how U.S. students were performing commensurate to their U.S. and international peers on national (e.g., NAEP) and international (e.g., PISA, Trends in International Mathematics and Science Study [TIMSS]) assessments, the CCSSM authors recognized that a more "focused and coherent" mathematics curriculum in U.S. schools could be informed with Standards that tap the most critical concepts and skills needed at each grade level. Well over half of the states and the District of Columbia have adopted the CCSSM; the remaining states that have not adopted the CCSSM have their own standards or have implemented an adapted version.

So, what are the CCSSM? The CCSSM are evidence based and incorporate "learning progressions" or "learning trajectories" of important mathematics domains and topics. A learning progression or learning trajectory is evidence based regarding the typical developmental progression of mathematical concepts and skills across the grades, representing what we know about how mathematics concepts and skills build on each grade level's content (Confrey, Maloney, Nguyen, Mojica, & Myers, 2009). Learning trajectories are empirically supported "descriptions of children's thinking as they learn to achieve specific goals in a mathematical domain" (Sarama & Clements, 2009, p. ix). The CCSSM provide guidance about what students should know and be able to apply at the end of each grade; that is, the CCSSM offer grade-level expectations. The CCSSM also were designed with the idea that upon graduating from high school, students would possess important concepts and skills needed for postsecondary education, work requirements, and life activities. Today, we think about the CCSSM as being "college readiness" standards.

Take a moment to locate the CCSSM at *www.corestandards.org/wp-content/uploads/Math_Standards1.pdf*. In examining the CCSSM, you will find two major areas. The first area is "Mathematical Content" across the grade levels. Notice that the standards consist of domains, standards, and clusters of related standards for mathematical content. As noted in the CCSSM, "Domains are larger groups of related standards, standards define what students should understand and be able to do, and clusters are groups of related standards" (NGA & CCSSO, 2010, p. 5). Let's look at an example from the fourth-grade CCSSM. One domain is called "Number and Operations—Fractions," and this domain has three standards, each with clusters of related standards. Look at the first standard, "Extend understanding of fraction equivalence and ordering" (p. 30). Notice that for this standard, fraction models are recommended to represent fraction equivalence and fraction comparisons. Both of these concepts, equivalence and comparisons, are critical for students to understand and be able to represent, because these concepts are two critical cornerstones for more advanced work with fractions.

The second area is "Mathematical Practice." Students are expected to understand Mathematical Content with opportunities to connect Mathematical Practice with the content knowledge. Mathematical Practice stems from the NCTM process standards and an important publication, *Adding It Up* (National Research Council, 2001), which focuses on adaptive reasoning, strategic competence, and conceptual understanding, procedural fluency, and productive disposition" (NGA & CCSSO, 2010, p. 6). The Mathematical Content and Mathematical Practice become the intersection for understanding, modeling, and reasoning about concepts and for developing proficiencies in mathematical fluency. Table 1.1 shows the CCSSM (NGA & CCSSO, 2010) Mathematical Content and Mathematical Practice.

TABLE 1.1. CCSSM Mathematical Content and Mathematical Practice for Kindergarten through High School

Mathematical Content	Mathematical Practice
• Counting and Cardinality • Operations and Algebraic Thinking • Number and Operations in Base Ten • Number and Operations—Fractions • Measurement and Data • Geometry • Ratios and Proportional Relationships • The Number System • Expressions and Equations • Statistics and Probability • Number and Quantity • Algebra • Functions • Modeling	1. Make sense of problems and persevere in solving them. 2. Reason abstractly and quantitatively. 3. Construct viable arguments and critique the reasoning of others. 4. Model with mathematics. 5. Use appropriate tools strategically. 6. Attend to precision. 7. Look for and make use of structure. 8. Look for and express regularity in repeated reasoning.

Note. From National Governors Association Center for Best Practices and Council of Chief State School Officers (2010). Copyright © 2010. All rights reserved.

Taken together, the CCSSM information can assist state and school district leaders in making decisions about next steps for identifying their mathematics curriculum, assessments, and instruction and helping students with MD and MLD improve their mathematics achievement. We know that, because of the hierarchical nature of mathematics meaning, later grade content knowledge is based on earlier grade knowledge, and that students with MD and MLD are disadvantaged because of the "holes" in their knowledge and understanding of CCSSM concepts and skills.

Students with MD and MLD

Information about students with MD and MLD frame the content of each chapter because it is for these students that we present our content. Let's find out more about some of the characteristics of students with MD and MLD. It is important to note that both groups of students will have similar learning characteristics associated with mathematics; however, students with MLD will exhibit more persistent, chronic mathematics difficulties throughout their lives due to the associated learning disability in mathematics.

MD refers to those children and adolescents who have learning problems that make it challenging for them to understand mathematics instruction. Although these students are not diagnosed with MLD, they often seem perplexed with simple mathematics areas, thus requiring more deliberate instruction on challenging areas. Sometimes, the MD group of students is referred to as low achievers, and they are usually identified as scoring between the 11th and 25th percentiles on mathematics assessments. For example, elementary-level students might struggle with understanding whole-number concepts, place value, and number combinations; secondary-level (middle and high school) students likely find ratios and proportional thinking and algebra difficult to understand. Even at the preschool and kindergarten levels, parents and teachers realize that some young children have problems with basic skills such as counting from 1 to 10, learning number names, and comparing one quantity to another quantity with counters to tell which is "more than," "less than," or if they are "the same." Thus, it is not surprising that students with MD demonstrate low achievement in mathematics with whole-number concepts in the elementary grades and rational numbers and algebra in later grades.

We also know that there is another group of students who have *developmental dyscalculia,* another name for MLD. This group of students typically scores at or below the 10th percentile on mathematics performance measures, which implies that these students have very low mathematics performance compared to their peers. Dyscalculia refers to difficulties in learning arithmetic, including problems such as understanding number, doing arithmetical calculations, and computing number combination facts in mathematics. Students may also have challenges with telling time on an analog clock, counting money and making change, learning and remembering procedures for solving problems, and identifying and knowing the meaning of symbols (Butterworth, 2010). Unfortunately, this pattern of chronic very low mathematics performance continues across the grade levels and into adulthood. Dyscalculia and MLD are often used interchangeably; in this book, we use the term MLD because it is more commonly used in schools. In Table 1.2, you can find a list of signs of dyscalculia at different ages (Understood, 2014–2019).

So, how pervasive are MD and MLD? Did you know that about 5–6% of the school-age population is diagnosed as having MLD in one or more mathematical areas? Also, about 10% of the school-age population is identified as having chronic mathematics difficulties, but these children are not diagnosed as having MLD. Thus, when looking at these percentages, we can see that a substantial number of children and adolescents have poor mathematics performance, which is persistent and pervasive across the grades and will likely extend into postsecondary mathematics courses and adulthood mathematics-related activities (Geary, 2011; Shalev, Manor, & Gross-Tsur, 2005; Swanson, 2006).

Additional information is available about the ramifications of students with MD and MLD experiencing chronic problems learning the mathematics curriculum. For example, research findings have shown that persistent mathematics learning problems contribute to a mathematics achievement performance gap between students with MD and MLD and their typically achieving peer group. Findings indicated that the achievement gap continues to widen as students fall further behind because these struggling students do not master important foundational and conceptual knowledge, which supports their mathematics learning in higher grades (Aunola, Leskinen, Lerkkanen, & Nurmi, 2004; Morgan, Farkas, & Wu, 2011). Students with MD and MLD have difficulties with processing numerical relations (e.g., 53 > 49) quickly, retrieving (remembering) solutions for number combinations (i.e., basic facts), and solving word problems. These problems hinder students' ability to "catch up" to their typically achieving peers (Geary, Hoard, Nugent, & Bailey, 2012).

The good news is that, in recent years, much more research attention has focused on students who have MD and MLD in the earlier grades (Bryant et al., 2011; Clarke et al., 2014; Dyson, Jordan, & Glutting, 2013) and the secondary grades (Dougherty, Bryant, Bryant, & Shin, 2017; Krawec, 2014). Researchers are learning about the effects of carefully designed studies to determine what practices can be identified as making a difference with student understanding of and performance in mathematics. Researchers are studying instructional components and programs that teachers and interventionists can use with their students with MD and MLD, usually in special education or under the multi-tiered systems of support (MTSS) and RTI models. Now, let's turn our attention to a brief overview about MTSS and RTI, and how mathematics instruction can occur for struggling students, including those with MD and MLD.

TABLE 1.2. Signs of Dyscalculia at Different Ages

Signs of Dyscalculia in Preschool

- Has trouble learning to count and skips over numbers long after kids the same age can remember numbers in the right order.
- Doesn't seem to understand the meaning of counting. For example, when you ask for five blocks, she or he just hands you a large group of blocks, rather than counting them out.
- Struggles to recognize patterns, like smallest to largest or tallest to shortest.
- Has trouble understanding number symbols, like making the connection between "7" and the word *seven*.
- Struggles to connect a number to an object, such as knowing that "3" applies to groups of things like 3 cookies, 3 cars, or 3 kids.

Signs of Dyscalculia in Elementary School

- Has difficulty learning and recalling basic math facts, such as 2 + 4 = 6.
- Still uses fingers to count instead of using more advanced strategies (like mental math).
- Struggles to identify math signs like + and – and to use them correctly.
- Has a tough time understanding math phrases, like greater than and less than.
- Has trouble with place value, often putting numbers in the wrong column.

Signs of Dyscalculia in Middle School

- Struggles with math concepts like commutativity (3 + 5 is the same as 5 + 3) and inversion (being able to solve 3 + 26 – 26 without calculating).
- Has a tough time understanding math language and coming up with a plan to solve a math problem.
- Has trouble keeping score in sports games and gym activities.
- Has difficulty figuring out the total cost of things and often runs out of money on his or her lunch account.
- May avoid situations that require understanding numbers, like playing games that involve math.

Signs of Dyscalculia in High School

- Struggles to understand information on charts and graphs.
- Has trouble applying math concepts to money, such as making exact change and figuring out a tip.
- Has trouble measuring things like ingredients in a simple recipe or liquids in a bottle.
- Lacks confidence in activities that require understanding speed, distance, and directions, and may get lost easily.
- Has trouble finding different approaches to a math problem, such as adding the length and width of a rectangle and doubling the answer to solve for the perimeter (rather than adding all the sides).

Note. Adapted from Understood For All, Inc. (2014–2019).

MTSS and RTI Models

The content in our chapters is based on the idea that the MTSS and RTI models provide a way to think about how to intensify interventions for struggling students. We focus on three tiers of instruction, anticipating that you will see how instruction is intensified depending on the needs of students.

The MTSS and RTI models consist of evidence-based interventions and progress monitoring measures to provide important supports to students who have MD or MLD. The goal is to reduce inappropriate referrals to special education due to poor instruction and to improve student achievement. According to the Every Student Succeeds Act (2015), the term *MTSS* refers to "a comprehensive continuum of evidence-based, systemic practices to support a rapid response to students' needs, with regular observation to facilitate data-based instructional decision-making" (§ 7801[33]). MTSS models focus on preventing student difficulties and providing services within tiered and increasingly intensive levels of support (Kilgus & Eklund, 2016). MTSS is a broader framework including the RTI approach for differentiating instruction and intensifying interventions for students who, in this case, struggle with learning and remembering key mathematical content across the grades.

RTI models are based on screening for at-risk students; providing high-quality, research-based instruction in general core education; conducting progress monitoring; and providing multi-tiered intensive instruction to those in need (e.g., Memorandum to Chief State School Officers, 2008). RTI is usually characterized as having three tiers, Tier 1, Tier 2, and Tier 3, of prevention and intervention. Tier 1 is thought of as core or general education mathematics instruction, aligned with state or national standards for *all* students, including students with MD and MLD. In Tier 1, specific practices are recommended for elementary- and secondary-level mathematics core concepts and skills to ensure high-quality mathematics instruction for all students. Table 1.3 shows a list of recommended policies and practices that teachers should plan on incorporating into their daily mathematics instruction.

Tier 1 also features differentiated instruction for those students who are struggling in mathematics and includes, for example, providing adaptations to instruction through the use of different instructional materials and ways of presenting concepts. In Tier 2 (about 15% of school-age students) and in Tier 3 (about 5% of school-aged students), a universal screening process is used at the beginning of the year to identify these struggling students. Students may then be assigned to receive Tier 2 intervention, which is supplemental to core mathematics instruction, or to Tier 3, which focuses on more intensified intervention aimed at individual learning needs. Teachers and mathematics interventionists can provide intensified interventions to these groups of students to address their specific learning needs. For these smaller percentages of students, interventions in critical mathematical content occurs across the school year with smaller groups, adapted instruction, and frequent progress monitoring. Now we examine how teachers can intensify mathematics interventions to address the needs of their students with MD or MLD who are receiving Tier 2 or Tier 3 interventions.

TABLE 1.3. 10 Key Policies and Practices for Elementary and Secondary Mathematics

All students can become proficient in mathematics when:

1. Students are fluent with addition, subtraction, multiplication, and division number combinations. Students know the 390 mathematics facts.
2. Students master key algebraic-readiness concepts for fractions, decimals, integers, ratios and proportions, and expressions and equations.
3. Students learn effective problem-solving strategies for different types of word-problem structures. Teachers present "real life" word problems for students to solve on a daily basis.
4. Teachers differentiate mathematics instruction for diverse learners.
5. Teachers use explicit instruction. Teachers verbalize explanations of concepts and steps for solving problems.
6. Teachers provide multiple opportunities for practice and promote student engagement.
7. Students make their mathematics thinking visible by talking about their solution process, drawing a picture, or making a graph using mathematically correct vocabulary.
8. Teachers help students to solve mathematics problems using manipulatives and models to bridge concrete to symbolic understandings of mathematics.
9. Students are given solved problems (correctly and incorrectly solved with misconceptions) to discuss how the problems were solved.
10. Teachers collect data regularly to determine whether their students are benefiting from instruction and use the data to make instructional decisions for subsequent lessons.

Note. Adapted from the Meadows Center for Preventing Educational Risk (2017).

Intensifying Mathematics Tiers 2 and 3 Interventions for Students' MD and MLD

The primary focus of this book across the chapters is on how interventions can be planned for and intensified for Tier 2 and Tier 3 students. The challenge is to determine how we can provide quality instruction to help students with MD and MLD become more successful with mathematics learning. We provide a summary of important ways instruction can be intensified so it is responsive to struggling students. Additionally, you will read about many of these ways in subsequent chapters; here we provide an overview.

To begin, we ask the questions "Who needs intensive mathematics interventions?" and "What key ingredients are possible for intensifying interventions?" Students with persistent, chronic low mathematics performance in core or Tier 1 instruction are good candidates for intensive interventions. One key ingredient involves using cognitive strategies that support cognitive processing, such as strategies to support remembering steps and procedures for finding solutions to problems and solving basic facts. Self-regulation strategies, such as asking oneself to recall word-problem-solving procedures or using a checklist when steps are used, can be useful to regulate one's own learning in conjunction with cognitive strategies (Vaughn, Wanzek, Murray, & Roberts, 2012). Another key ingredient is using explicit, systematic instruction, which is described in this section. Yet another key ingredient is to control task difficulty starting with smaller "chunks" of content to reduce overload on students' memory. Now we turn our attention to examples of ways to intensify interventions for Tier 2 and Tier 3 for students who have MD and MLD. We discuss universal screening to identify struggling students, evidence-based practices for interventions, progress monitoring to determine student response to the intervention, vocabulary knowledge, mathematical misconceptions, and finally the ADAPT framework, which represents a process for identifying appropriate ways to adapt or change instruction to better address an individual student's needs.

Universal Screening for Mathematics Identification

Universal screening is an important feature of the RTI model because this process is used to identify students at risk for academic difficulties through the use of brief assessment measures (Jenkins, Hudson, & Johnson, 2007). Students whose scores on mathematics screeners fall below a designated "cut score" such as below the 25th percentile, that is, below average performance, are identified as in need of intensive intervention, which may be Tier 2 or Tier 3 depending on each student's individual performance and mathematics problems.

Evidence-Based Practices

Evidence-based practices (EBPs) refer to the continuous use of effective instructional routines, which have been shown through carefully constructed research studies to improve the mathematics performance of students with MD and MLD. A great deal of research has been conducted for many years on EBPs, and now we see these EBPs incorporated into Tier 2 and Tier 3 mathematics interventions. For example, Gersten and his colleagues (2009) conducted reviews of literature to determine those EBPs that held the most promise for improving the mathematics performance of students with MD and MLD. The EBPs they identified included (1) explicit and systematic instruction, consisting of the teacher's verbalizations (thinking aloud) of his or her thinking process for solving problems for students to hear, guided practice, corrective feedback, and frequent cumulative review; (2) word-problem-solving instruction based on common underlying structures or types of schema; (3) practice opportunities with the use of representations of mathematical ideas; and (4) 10 minutes of daily practice for students to develop fluent retrieval of basic facts (number combinations).

In another classic review of the literature on practices for students with MLD, Swanson, Hoskyn, and Lee (1999) found that, in addition to explicit, systematic instruction, cognitive strategy instruction (CSI) is effective for teaching, for example, basic facts and word-problem solving. CSI consists of cognitive strategies (steps or a routine for solving problems) and metacognitive strategies (self-questioning) for the learner to check his or her understanding of the instructional steps or routine (Montague & Dietz, 2009).

Finally, Swanson and his colleagues (1999) found the following instructional practices to be effective, and thus they are included in many interventions for students with MD and MLD: (1) breaking down tasks and providing step-by-step prompts, (2) asking process or content questions of students, (3) sequencing tasks from easy to difficult and teaching prerequisite skills, (4) delivering instruction via multimedia, (5) delivering instruction to a small group, and (6) reminding students to use strategies. We know a great deal about what constitutes EBPs; intensive interventions include many of these practices, as you will read about in the remaining chapters.

Progress Monitoring

Progress monitoring (PM) is also an essential feature of RTI, as it measures students' mathematics responsiveness to interventions. PM measures can assess students' understanding of lessons' objectives and content and can show students' mathematical misconceptions. There are three key features of PM to determine student responsiveness to mathematics interventions. First, specific skills that are being taught are measured. Second, the procedures are systematic, meaning that administration of PM measures is done the same way each time they are given. Third, PM measures are given consistently and frequently. For instance, Tier 2 students might receive a PM measure weekly, whereas Tier 3 students might receive PM twice a week. These PM measures can be implemented in a small group. Particular attention should be given to selecting evidence-based PM measures and to administering the measures as intended (e.g., following administration and scoring guidelines).

Vocabulary

Vocabulary knowledge is central to making sense of mathematics (NGA & CCSSO, 2010). The lack of vocabulary knowledge can negatively affect students' learning of new content (Fisher & Frey, 2008; Powell & Nelson, 2017). Because mathematics terms are unlikely to be used during daily conversation, they are challenging to learn. Therefore, explicitly teaching vocabulary terms is highly recommended so that when students encounter the terms they can understand their meaning and how they are associated with the mathematics (Dunston & Tyminski, 2013). Developing mathematical vocabulary knowledge allows struggling learners to expand their abstract algebraic reasoning and move beyond mathematical operations to solve word problems.

In the *Principles and Standards for School Mathematics* (NCTM, 2000), it was noted that the ability to communicate mathematically should be addressed in all areas of assessment and instruction. Clearly vocabulary, or the knowledge of words and their meanings, is a critical component of mathematics communication (Monroe, 2006). Many years ago, yet still relevant for today, Wiig and Semel (1984) commented that mathematics is "conceptually dense," meaning that students must comprehend the meaning of terms and mathematical symbols because, unlike in reading, there are few context clues to help aid in meaning. Other researchers agree (Miller, 1993; Schell, 1982), noting that mathematics language is complex and particularly abstract.

Several authorities (Miller, 1993; Monroe & Orme, 2002) have noted that unfamiliar vocabulary is a leading cause of mathematics difficulties. Bryant, Bryant, and Hammill (2000) identified difficulties with the language of mathematics as a distinguishing characteristic of MLD. Capps and Cox (1991) suggested that the language of mathematics must be directly taught during the course of a mathematics lesson. Monroe (1998) agreed, noting that mathematics vocabulary cannot be taught incidentally.

Misconceptions

Mathematical *misconceptions* are faulty and incorrect ideas resulting from students' misunderstanding about a mathematical idea or concept. In some cases, the term *errors* is used as a way to suggest that student thinking is faulty, but not all errors are misconceptions; rather, errors could be attributed to careless work, a solution that is lacking a step, or incorrect recall of the solution to a basic fact (e.g., 4 + 9 = 13 and not 12).

Misconceptions are usually based on faulty thinking about generalizations or rules or misunderstanding about the structure of the mathematics. For example, when multiplying two numbers (e.g., 40 • 6 = ?) where the multiplicand has a 0 in the unit place, sometimes students are told to multiply the 2 nonzero numbers, in this case 4 and 6, and then to "bring down the zero." Although this procedure might yield the correct solution, the procedure does not help students learn about place value for multiplying numbers with a 0 in the ones place. Despite teachers' best intentions, the "tricks" or "shortcuts" they teach contribute to students' misconceptions.

For students with MD and MLD, interventions must be mathematically correct with both teachers and students using mathematically precise language. For example, a rhombus is not a diamond and the alligator's opened mouth pointing in a specific direction does not convey the mathematically accurate use of the "greater than" or "less than" signs. Moreover, incorrect use of representations, such as manipulatives, does not automatically mean students conceptually grasp the problems for which the manipulatives are being used. Rather, students should be able to describe their use of the manipulatives to represent a problem or concept.

As another example, misconceptions about the meaning of the equal sign as an operator symbol rather than as a relational symbol leads to errors. For instance, when given nontraditional equations such as 6 = _____ + 2, students might think that the answer is "8" because 6 + 2 = 8.

These are but a few of the many mathematical misconceptions that students who struggle with mathematics exhibit. Teachers must understand what misconceptions exist for the content they teach and avoid tricks or shortcuts that could be causing misconceptions to fester. In fact, students often have to be explicitly taught ways to think about the mathematics that reduce or prevent misconceptions (Bamberger & Oberdorf, 2010).

ADAPT Framework

Adaptations help students with MD and MLD participate in classroom discussions and learn mathematical skills and concepts, which are emphasized in the CCSSM (NGA & CCSSO, 2010). We define adaptations as any alterations that are made to a lesson or scaffolds that are added to a lesson to account for (1) a lack of prerequisite skills necessary to learn new concepts and skills being taught or (2) struggles that students encounter during a lesson. For struggling students, teachers and mathematics interventionists must be aware of their students' mathematical strengths and struggles, so that they can plan ways to provide much-needed support. This support can occur in the form of making adaptations to instructional delivery, instructional activities, instructional content, and instructional materials.

By way of illustration, at the beginning of any new work we do in mathematics research, we usually conduct at least one focus group meeting with teachers and/or conduct teacher interviews. There are many purposes of such meetings and interviews, but perhaps the most important information we receive has to do with teachers' perceptions of the students they work with, specifically, how their students struggle with the grade-level content being taught. What we hear most often is that there are usually several students in their classes (more if there are students with MLD in the class) who do not have the skills that the teacher feels are needed to learn the content that is being taught; that is, they are ill prepared to meet the demands of the assignments.

The skills at the primary grade are foundational, such as having basic number sense, including numeral recognition, knowledge of magnitude, number sequences, place value, and so forth. At the upper elementary level, some students may still struggle with components of number sense, but they may also have difficulty with number combinations or anything having to do with rational numbers. At the middle and high school levels, earlier concepts and skills such as fractions, and ratios and proportions, may be lacking, which can impede the ability to be successful with more advanced mathematics. Teachers share with us that the students in their classes who do not have the basic mathematics prerequisites have little chance of being successful mastering the new skills and concepts being taught. Thus, the ADAPT framework can be a useful tool to promote understanding and knowledge.

The steps of the ADAPT framework are easy to follow. First, teachers <u>A</u>sk, "What am I requiring the student to do?" For example, the teacher thinks, "The students have to solve five computation problems written on the board that involve adding two 2-digit numbers with regrouping to the tens place." Second, the teacher <u>D</u>etermines the prerequisite skills of the task. In our example, students typically have to listen to the teacher's explanations (i.e., attend to what is being said), see the items on the board, follow the teacher's instructions concerning what to do, have the fine motor skills needed to write the problems on a sheet of paper with proper alignment, know number combinations, add single digits for each place value (ones, tens), regroup from the ones to the tens place, and retrace (check their work). Certainly, as you read this, you may be able to add a few prerequisites of your own.

Next, teachers <u>A</u>nalyze the student's strengths and struggles, specifically as they relate to the noted prerequisite skills. Which of the skills can the student accomplish readily (strengths), and which will impede their ability to do the task (struggles)? If any of the prerequisite skills are designated as struggles, the lesson will pose problems for the student and some changes (i.e., instructional adaptations) need to be made. To continue with our example, let's say that the student has difficulties or struggles with the concept of regrouping ten ones to a group of ten so that the two 2-digit numbers can be added correctly. But the student knows his number combinations, which is a strength.

Adaptations take place in the fourth step, which is Propose and implement adaptations from among the four adaptations categories. Those categories are Instructional Content (WHAT is being taught, the skills and concepts that are the focus of teaching and learning), Instructional Delivery (HOW the lesson is being taught, that is, the procedures and routines used to teach the lesson), Instructional Materials (TOOLS used during teaching and learning, such as supplemental aids used to teach and reinforce skills and concepts), and Instructional Activity (OTHER lessons that can be used to meet the same objective). With our example, the teacher decides to work with the student on regrouping using base-ten models or base-ten blocks, which is an example of an instructional material to show addition of the two 2-digit numbers beginning in

TABLE 1.4. ADAPT Framework: Ways to Intensify Mathematics Interventions

Tier 2	➡ Tier 3
Instruction—Modeling/think-aloud: Conducted as part of instructional lessons initially (ID)	➡ **Instruction**—Modeling/think-aloud: Conducted as part of instructional lessons *throughout a unit of lessons* (ID)
Instruction—Practice: Opportunities to say, show, and write solutions; practice built into lessons (ID)	➡ **Instruction**—Practice: Increased opportunities to say, show, and write solutions; more practice built into lessons; game formats to increase practice opportunities and increase motivation (ID)
Grouping: Five to six students with one teacher (ID)	➡ **Grouping:** One to three students with one teacher (ID)
Dosage: 3 days per week, 25- to 30-minute sessions (ID)	➡ **Dosage:** 5 days per week, 45- to 60-minute sessions (ID)
Instructional content: Task analyzed (IC)	➡ **Instructional content:** More task analyzed; smaller instructional steps for teaching whole-number computation; facts taught in smaller groups—just +0, just +1, +0 and +1 together (IC)
Vocabulary: Math terms reviewed within context of lesson (IC)	➡ **Vocabulary:** Math terms explicitly taught using vocabulary strategies (e.g., word mapping); connections between student language and math language: "plus" means "add" (IC)
Representations: Concrete–pictorial–abstract; move away from concrete and emphasize more pictorial/abstract/symbolic (IM)	➡ **Representations:** Concrete–pictorial–abstract/symbolic; remain with the three levels; gradually fade concrete (IM)
Progress monitoring: Weekly	➡ **Progress monitoring:** Two times per week

Note. ID, instructional delivery; IC, instructional content; IM, instructional material.

the ones place and regrouping a group of ten to the tens place. The teacher models the calculation process using the base-ten models, and the student practices along with the teacher. The problem to be worked is 36 + 48 = ? The following steps show how the teacher proceeds with modeling the calculation using base-ten models: 6 + 8 = 14, regroup one group of ten ones to the tens place, which leaves four ones in the ones place, 3 tens + 4 tens + 1 ten = 8 tens, 36 + 48 = 84.

Finally, after adaptations have been implemented, the teacher administers a Test to determine if the adaptations helped the student to accomplish the task. To finish our example, the teacher decides to give the student five problems, two digits + two digits with regrouping, to see if the student can now do the calculations correctly. In Table 1.4, we provide examples of how interventions can be intensified using the ADAPT framework in terms of instructional delivery, instructional content, and instructional materials. An example of adapting progress monitoring frequency is also provided. Examples of how to implement the ADAPT framework are presented in Chapters 5, 9, and 10. For the remaining chapters, think about how you can apply the ADAPT framework to some of the activities.

To summarize, some students in classrooms bring challenges that may be disability related or content specific. As teachers, we often incorrectly assume that all of the students in our classroom have the prerequisite skills needed to address the daily tasks we assign to them. However, we know through teacher focus-group meetings and teacher interviews that this is not always the case; one or two students (or more) face challenges that interfere with their ability to perform a lesson's task as prepared and delivered.

Conclusion

In conclusion, across the elementary and secondary grade levels, universal screening procedures, ongoing interventions utilizing EBPs, vocabulary instruction, and PM measures can be used to help struggling students improve their mathematics performance in Tier 2 and Tier 3 and reduce or eliminate their misconceptions about concepts and procedures. A tiered system can provide differentiated support, such as in Tier 1, and intensified interventions for Tier 2 and Tier 3, to students identified as having MD or MLD. As you read the remaining chapters in this book, consider how authors of the other chapters apply the content described in this chapter to their mathematics topic. We hope you enjoy the book!

ACKNOWLEDGMENTS

Research described in this chapter was supported in part by Grant Nos. R324B070164 and R324A160042 from the Institute of Education Sciences in the U.S. Department of Education to The University of Texas at Austin. The content is solely the responsibility of the authors and does not necessarily represent the official views of the Institute of Education Sciences and the U.S. Department of Education.

REFERENCES

Aunola, K., Leskinen, E., Lerkkanen, M.-K., & Nurmi, J.-E. (2004). Developmental dynamics of math performance from preschool to grade 2. *Journal of Educational Psychology, 96*(4), 699–713.

Bamberger, H. J., & Oberdorf, C. (2010). *Activities to undo math misconceptions.* Portsmouth, NH: Heinemann.

Bryant, D. P., Bryant, B. R., & Hammill, D. D. (2000). Characteristic behaviors of students with learning disabilities who have teacher-identified math weaknesses. *Journal of Learning Disabilities, 33*(2), 168–177, 199.

Bryant, D. P., Bryant, B. R., Roberts, G., Vaughn, S., Hughes, K., Porterfield, J., & Gersten, R. (2011). Effects of an early numeracy intervention on the performance of first-grade students with mathematics difficulties. *Exceptional Children, 78*(1), 7–23.

Butterworth, B. (2010). Foundational numerical capacities and the origins of dyscalculia. *Trends in Cognitive Sciences, 14*(12), 534–541.

Capps, L. R., & Cox, L. S. (1991). Improving the learning of mathematics in our schools. *Focus on Exceptional Children, 23*(9), 1–8.

Clarke, B., Doabler, C. T., Cary, M. S., Kosty, D., Baker, S., Fien, H., & Smolkowski, K. (2014). Preliminary evaluation of a Tier 2 mathematics intervention for first-grade students: Using a theory of change to guide formative evaluation activities. *School Psychology Review, 43*(2), 160–177.

Confrey, J., Maloney, A., Nguyen, K., Mojica, G., & Myers, M. (2009). Equipartitioning/splitting as a foundation of rational number reasoning. In M. Tzekaki, M. Kaldrimidou, & C. Sakonidis (Eds.), *Proceedings of the 33rd conference of the International Group for the Psychology of Mathematics Education*, Thessaloniki, Greece.

Dougherty, B., Bryant, D. P., Bryant, B. R., & Shin, M. (2017). Promoting understanding of ratios and proportional reasoning for middle school students with persistent mathematics difficulties. *Teaching Exceptional Children, 49*(2), 96–105.

Dunston, P. J., & Tyminski, A. M. (2013). What's the big deal about vocabulary? *Mathematics Teaching in the Middle School, 19*(1), 38–45.

Dyson, N. L., Jordan, N. C., & Glutting, J. (2013). A number sense intervention for low-income kindergartners at risk for mathematics difficulties. *Journal of Learning Disabilities, 46*(2), 166–181.

Every Student Succeeds Act, 20 U.S.C. §§ 6301 *et seq.* (2015).

Fisher, D., & Frey, N. (2008). *Word wise and content rich, grades 7–12: Five essential steps to teaching academic vocabulary.* Portsmouth, NH: Heinemann.

Geary, D. C. (2011). Consequences, characteristics, and causes of mathematical learning disabilities and persistent low achievement in mathematics. *Journal of Developmental and Behavioral Pediatrics, 33*(30), 250–263.

Geary, D. C., Hoard, M. K., Nugent, L., & Bailey, D. H. (2012). Mathematical cognition deficits in children with learning disabilities and persistent low achievement: A five-year prospective study. *Journal of Educational Psychology, 104*(1), 206–223.

Gersten, R., Beckmann, S., Clarke, B., Foegen, A., Marsh, L., Star, J. R., & Witzel, B. (2009). *Assisting students struggling with mathematics: Response to Intervention (RtI) for elementary and middle schools* (NCEE 2009-4060). Washington, DC: National Center for Education Evaluation and Regional Assistance, Institute of Education Sciences, U.S. Department of Education.

Jenkins, J. R., Hudson, R. F., & Johnson, E. S. (2007). Screening for service delivery in an RTI framework: Candidate measures. *School Psychology Review, 36*, 582–599.

Kilgus, S. P., & Eklund, K. R. (2016). Consideration of base rates within universal screening for behavioral and emotional risk: A novel procedural framework. *School Psychology Forum, 10*(1), 120–130.

Krawec, J. L. (2014). Problem representation and mathematical problem solving of students of varying math ability. *Journal of Learning Disabilities, 47*(2), 103–115.

Meadows Center for Preventing Educational Risk. (2017). *10 key math practices for all middle and high schools with strong evidence of effectiveness from high-quality research.* Austin, TX: Author.

Memorandum to Chief State School Officers, 51 IDELR ¶ 49 (2008).

Miller, S. (1993). Mnemonics: Enhancing the mathematics performance of students with learning difficulties. *Intervention in School and Clinic, 29*(2), 78–82.

Monroe, E. E. (1998). Using graphic organizers to teach vocabulary: Does available research inform mathematics instruction? *Education, 188*(4), 538–540.

Monroe, E. E. (2006). *Math dictionary: The easy, simple, fun guide to help math phobics become math lovers.* Honesdale, PA: Boyds Mills Press.

Monroe, E. E., & Orme, M. P. (2002). Developing mathematical vocabulary. *Preventing School Failure, 46*(3), 139–142.

Montague, M., & Dietz, S. (2009). Evaluating the evidence base for cognitive strategy instruction and mathematical problem solving. *Exceptional Children, 75,* 285–302.

Morgan, P. L., Farkas, G., & Wu, Q. (2011). Kindergarten children's growth trajectories in reading and mathematics: Who falls increasingly behind? *Journal of Learning Disabilities, 44*(5), 472–488.

National Center for Education Statistics (NCES). (2017). *The nation's report card: 2017 mathematics and reading.* Washington, DC: Institute of Education Sciences, U.S. Department of Education.

National Council of Teachers of Mathematics (NCTM). (2000). *Principles and standards for school mathematics.* Reston, VA: Author.

National Governors Association (NGA) Center for Best Practices & Council of Chief State School Officers (CCSSO). (2010). *Common Core State Standards for mathematics.* Washington, DC: Authors.

National Mathematics Advisory Panel (NMAP). (2008). *Foundations for success: The final report of the National Mathematics Advisory Panel.* Washington, DC: U.S. Department of Education.

National Research Council. (2001). *Adding it up: Helping children learn mathematics.* Washington, DC: Mathematics Learning Study Committee.

Organization for Economic Co-operation and Development (OECD). (2012). *PISA 2012.* Paris: Author.

Powell, S. R., & Nelson, G. (2017). An investigation of the mathematics-vocabulary knowledge of first-grade students. *Elementary School Journal, 117*(4), 664–686.

Sarama, J., & Clements, D. H. (2009). *Early childhood mathematics education research: Learning trajectories for young children.* New York: Routledge.

Schell, V. J. (1982). Learning partners: Reading and mathematics. *The Reading Teacher, 35*(5), 544–548.

Shalev, R., Manor, O., & Gross-Tsur, V. (2005). Developmental dyscalculia: A prospective six-year follow-up. *Developmental Medicine and Child Neurology, 47,* 121–125.

Swanson, H. L. (2006). Cognitive processes that underlie mathematical precociousness in young children. *Journal of Experimental Child Psychology, 93,* 239–264.

Swanson, H. L., Hoskyn, M., & Lee, C. (1999). *Interventions for students with learning disabilities: A meta-analysis of treatment outcomes.* New York: Guilford Press.

Understood For All. (2014–2019). Signs of dyscalculia at different ages. Retrieved from *www.*

understood.org/en/learning-attention-issues/signs-symptoms/could-your-child-have/signs-of-dyscalculia-in-children.

Vaughn, S., Wanzek, J., Murray, C. S., & Roberts, G. (2012). *Intensive interventions for students struggling in reading and mathematics: A practice guide.* Portsmouth, NH: RMC Research Corporation, Center on Instruction.

Wiig, E. H., & Semel, E. M. (1984). *Language assessment and intervention for the learning disabled* (2nd ed.). New York: Macmillan.

CHAPTER 2

Effective Mathematical Practices for Mathematics Instruction and Developing Mathematical Reasoning

BARBARA J. DOUGHERTY

LEARNING OUTCOMES

After studying this chapter, you will be able to answer the following questions:

1. What are multiple representations, and how can they be used to teach mathematics concepts?
2. What tasks support mathematics reasoning?
3. What questioning techniques can be used to engage students with the mathematics?

What is *mathematical reasoning*? The National Council of Teachers of Mathematics wrote that students using mathematical reasoning "tend to note patterns, structure, or regularities in both real-world situations and symbolic objects; they ask if those patterns are accidental or if they occur for a reason; and they conjecture and prove" (2000, p. 55). Furthermore, Russell (1999) pointed to active mathematical reasoning as the development, *justification* (to explain a conclusion, process, or answer so that it convinces your audience of its accuracy and appropriateness), and use of *generalizations* (a pattern that can be applied across all related cases). She continued by indicating that "mathematical reasoning leads to an interconnected web of mathematical knowledge within a mathematical domain" (p. 1). Thus, the focus of instruction should be to develop mathematical reasoning that includes ways in which students with mathematics learning disabilities (MLD) and students with mathematics difficulties (MD) can see connections within and across concepts and skills and then use those connections to build strong generalizations. For example, addition and subtraction are related but are often taught separately, causing students with MLD and MD to think of them as separate computations with no connections. However, if they are taught together, students with MLD and MD can see the relationships, including seeing them as inverse operations or see-ing the opportunity to solve a subtraction computation by using addition.

In this chapter, you will consider ways in which the Standards for Mathematical Practice (SMP) in the Common Core State Standards for Mathematics (CCSSM; National Governors Association [NGA] Center for Best Practices & Council of Chief State School Officers [CCSSO], 2010) can support students with MLD and MD in their development of reasoning. You will also read about misconceptions that may occur pertaining to mathematical reasoning. Because mathematical reasoning is critical for students to develop about mathematical topics, a chapter is devoted to this important aspect of mathematics instruction.

What are ways that mathematical reasoning can be developed with students with MLD and MD? What strategies can be used to deepen their understanding? The fol-lowing are strategies that can be employed in the classroom and in Tier 2 and Tier 3 mathematics interventions on a regular basis to support this robust understanding, including the use of multiple representations, the selection of good tasks, and question-ing techniques. Each strategy will be discussed in the following sections.

Multiple Representations

The forms in which ideas, concepts, or relationships can be expressed are an impor-tant component of mathematics. The same mathematical idea can be shown in multiple ways. For example, the number 48 can be written with numerals, modeled with base-ten blocks, pictured as a drawing of base-ten blocks, and written in words as *forty-eight*. These are called *multiple representations*.

When we think about mathematics, we often think that the topics have to be presented in a linear, very sequential manner. In some ways, this is true. Concepts and skills build one on another. For example, before students work with multidigit numbers such as 6,453, they should understand place value of two-digit numbers and the relationship between the positions of the digits. In this sense, mathematics is linear so that students can build on their previous understandings.

The linear and sequential notion may extend into the use of different representa-tions of mathematical ideas based on Piaget's seminal work (Piaget, 1954). His ideas are often interpreted as a structured pathway where students are moved from concrete to pictorial to abstract representations and thinking. This progression is aligned with the concrete–semiconcrete–abstract continuum where students begin with physical materi-als and then progress through the other two representational systems. However, better connections can be formed among these representations when they are presented con-currently (Dougherty, 2008). See the example in Figure 2.1.

When students see the three representations at the same time, they form deeper connections across them and understand the meaning of the more formal algorithm. In Figure 2.1, students see that it is not possible to describe the joining of ¼ and ½ without changing the fractions to a common denominator. Otherwise, you would not be able to assign a quantity or numerical value to the resulting area or physical model. When

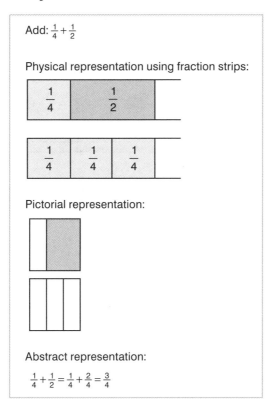

FIGURE 2.1. Concurrent representations for adding fractions.

all the fractions are represented by fourths, it is clear that the sum is ¾. This provides a strong rationale for the algorithm that will be developed as the instructional sequence moves forward (SMP 2; NGA & CCSSO, 2010).

You may also note that these representations show different ways of thinking about a problem. Some students may fluently use each of these representations while others are drawn to particular ones as they try to make sense of a problem (Sternberg, 1999). By using multiple representations, you help students form images in their minds that connect ideas. The connections across and within topics solidify the learning and promote stronger retention of concepts and skills.

Even though multiple representations are important in building student understanding, they must be chosen wisely. Some representations better model the mathematical ideas than others do. For example, a number line is often used to model any computation. For whole-number addition as in Figure 2.2 or subtraction, it appears to be very straightforward in how it models the operation.

From the model in Figure 2.2, the lengths of the bars representing 7 and 5 are joined together to create a bar that is 12 units long. The joining together models the operation of addition in a clear and efficient way. Similarly, subtraction of whole numbers such as 12 – 7 could be modeled well with a number line as in Figure 2.3.

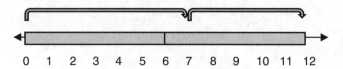

FIGURE 2.2. Number line model of 7 + 5 = 12.

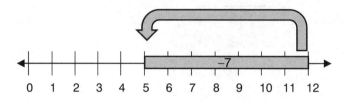

FIGURE 2.3. Number line model of 12 – 7 = 5.

The number line shows that subtraction of whole numbers is a "takeaway" model. That is, you begin with a quantity, in this case 12, and then remove 7 units to show that there are 5 remaining. The model is clear and represents the action of the computation well (SMP 7; NGA & CCSSO, 2010).

However, the number line model is less effective when integers are involved. For example, look at the model of a number line showing –8 – (–12) = 4 in Figure 2.4.

Notice that students must remember a process with specific rules for representing the subtraction on a number line. The process then becomes more like an algorithm where students have to remember or memorize a series of steps in order to get to the answer. As shown in Figure 2.4, the starting point at –8 seems reasonable, but the movement of 12 to the right of –8 is not as intuitive. The memorization of the process may hinder students' understanding, and rather than making sense of the model or representation, students with MLD and MD merely apply the steps with less understanding.

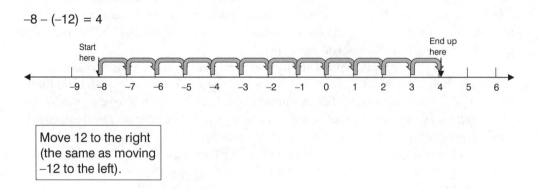

FIGURE 2.4. Number line model of –8 – (–12) = 4.

Therefore, it is important to include representations to model the mathematical ideas so that students with MLD and MD can make sense of the mathematics. However, it is equally important to consider how well the representation truly models the mathematics. If it requires students remembering multiple steps, and the final result is not clearly linked to the mathematics behind the model, then a different representation should be considered. By appropriately selecting a representation and combining it with other representations, students with MLD and MD can develop a better understanding that allows them to apply appropriate mathematical reasoning.

Tasks

Selecting appropriate tasks for students with MLD and MD is an important instructional decision. The tasks should provide different access points so that these students can engage in the mathematics, and they should be purposefully selected to focus on specific types of mathematical reasoning.

Stein, Smith, Henningsen, and Silver (2000) provided a matrix as shown in Figure 2.5 to help analyze tasks. As you look at the criteria for the four types of tasks, think about the types of thinking students with MLD and MD would use as they solved problems or tasks of each type and the challenges they may experience. It should be a goal of instruction for students with MLD and MD to promote reasoning and sense making and regularly include problems or tasks that align with the characteristics in the right column.

Some tasks and problems are given in Figure 2.6. Decide which type of task each of these represents as compared to the framework in Figure 2.5. You may want to try solving each of them as you determine the type of task it represents. As you solve them, also consider the challenges that students with MLD and MD might experience as they attempt the problem.

Notice that Task H is only a computational task that requires students to remember the process for converting a decimal to a fraction and to a percent. Although they look quite different, you might consider how Task D is similar to or different from Task H. What do the other tasks have in common? What are their differences? How would each task affect student thinking?

Specifically, Task D is situated in a real-life context that allows students with MLD and MD a way to connect with the problem. They can judge the reasonableness of answers because, based on their own experiences, when an item goes on sale, the price is reduced from the original cost. Thus, if students get an answer that is greater than $45 or is close to $45, they will know that it is not reasonable.

You may have also noticed that Task D asks students to explain how they found their answer. Students with MLD and MD may find this challenging; this is an opportunity to use worked examples where they can see ways in which other students might have solved it. By using worked examples, students with MLD and MD can identify a process that was similar to the one they used, and they can see ways in which a solution process can be explained (SMP 2 and 3; NGA & CCSSO, 2010).

Lower-Level Demands	Higher-Level Demands
• Memorization • involve either reproducing previously learned facts, rules, formulae, or definitions OR committing facts, rules, formulae, or definitions to memory. • cannot be solved using procedures because a procedure does not exist or because the time frame in which the task is being completed is too short to use a procedure. • are not ambiguous. Such tasks involve exact reproduction of previously seen material and what is to be reproduced is clearly and directly stated. • have no connection to the concepts or meanings that underlie the facts, rules, formulae, or definitions being learned or reproduced.	• Procedures with Connections • focus students' attention on the use of procedures for the purpose of developing deeper levels of understanding mathematical concepts and ideas. • suggest pathways to follow (explicitly or implicitly) that are broad general procedures that have close connections to underlying conceptual ideas as opposed to narrow algorithms that are opaque with respect to underlying concepts. • usually are represented in multiple ways (e.g., visual diagrams, manipulatives, symbols, problem situations). Making connections among multiple representations helps to develop meaning. • require some degree of cognitive effort. Although general procedures may be followed, they cannot be followed mindlessly. Students need to engage with the conceptual ideas that underlie the procedures in order to successfully complete the task and develop understanding.
• Procedures without Connections • are algorithmic. Use of the procedure is either specifically called for or its use is evident based on prior instruction, experience, or placement of the task. • require limited cognitive demand for successful completion. There is little ambiguity about what needs to be done and how to do it. • have no connection to the concepts or meanings that underlie the procedure being used. • are focused on producing correct answers rather than developing mathematical understanding. • require no explanations or explanations that focus solely on describing the procedure that was used.	• Doing Mathematics • require complex and nonalgorithmic thinking (i.e., there is not a predictable, well-rehearsed approach or pathway explicitly suggested by the task, task instructions, or a worked-out example). • require students to explore and understand the nature of mathematical concepts, processes, or relationships. • demand self-monitoring or self-regulation of one's own cognitive processes. • require students to access relevant knowledge and experiences and make appropriate use of them in working through the task. • require students to analyze the task and actively examine task constraints that may limit possible solution strategies and solutions. • require considerable cognitive effort and may involve some level of anxiety for the student due to the unpredictable nature of the solution process required.

FIGURE 2.5. Task analysis guide.

TASK A

Manipulatives/Tools: Counter

For homework, Mark's teacher asked him to look at the pattern below and draw the figure that should come next.

Mark does not know how to find the next figure.

A. Draw the next figure for Mark.

B. Write a description for Mark telling him how you knew which figure comes next.

(QUASAR Project—QUASAR Cognitive Assessment Instrument—Release Task)

TASK B

Manipulatives/Tools: None

Part A: After the first two games of the season, the best player on the girls' basketball team had made 12 out of 20 free throws. The best player on the boys' basketball team had made 14 out of 25 free throws. Which player had made the greater percentage of free throws?

Part B: The "better" player had to sit out the third game because of an injury. How many baskets, out of an additional 10 free-throw "tries," would the other player need to make to take the lead in terms of greatest percentage of free throws?

(Adapted from *Investigating Mathematics* [New York: Glencoe Macmillan/McGraw-Hill, 1994])

TASK C

Manipulatives/Tools: Calculator

Your school's science club has decided to do a special project on nature photography. They decided to take a few more than 300 outdoor photos in a variety of natural settings and in all different types of weather. They want to choose some of the best photographs and enter the state nature photography contest. The club was thinking of buying a 35 mm camera, but one member suggested that it might be better to buy disposable cameras instead. The regular camera with autofocus and automatic light meter would cost about $40.00, and film would cost $3.98

for 24 exposures and $5.95 for 36 exposures. The disposable cameras could be purchased in packs of three for $20.00, with two of the three taking 24 pictures and the third one taking 27 pictures. Single disposables could be purchased for $8.95. The club officers have to decide which would be the better option and justify their decisions to the club advisor. Do you think that they should purchase the regular camera or the disposable cameras? Write a justification that clearly explains your reasoning.

TASK D

Manipulatives/Tools: None

The cost of a sweater at a department store was $45. At the store's "day and night" sale, it was maked 30 percent off the original price. What was the price of the sweater during the sale? Explain the process you used to find the sale price.

TASK E

Manipulatives/Tools: Pattern blocks

½ of ⅓ means one of two equal parts of one-third.

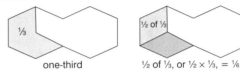

Find ⅓ of ¼. Use pattern blocks. Draw your answer.

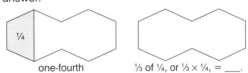

Find ¼ of ⅓. Use pattern blocks. Draw your answer.

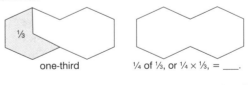

(continued)

FIGURE 2.6. Examples of tasks. From Smith and Stein (1998, p. 346).

TASK F

Manipulatives/Tools: Square pattern tiles

Using the side of a square pattern tile as a measure, find the perimeter of, or distance around, each train in the pattern block figure shown.

Train 1   Train 2   Train 3

TASK G

Manipulatives/Tools: Grid paper

The pairs of numbers in (a)–(d) represent the heights of stacks of cubes to be leveled off. On grid paper, sketch the front views of the columns of cubes with these heights before and after they are leveled off. Write a statement under the sketches that explains how your method of leveling off is related to finding the average of the two numbers.

9   5   7   7

(a) 14 and 8   (b) 16 and 7   (c) 7 and 12   (d) 13 and 15

By taking two blocks off the first stack and giving them to the second stack, I've made the two stacks the same. So the total number of cubes is now distributed into two columns of equal height. And that is what average means.

(Taken from Bennett and Fureman [1989/1991])

TASK H

Manipulatives/Tools: None

Give the fraction and percent for each decimal.

$0.20 = \underline{\hspace{1cm}} = \underline{\hspace{1cm}}.$

$0.25 = \underline{\hspace{1cm}} = \underline{\hspace{1cm}}.$

$0.33 = \underline{\hspace{1cm}} = \underline{\hspace{1cm}}.$

$0.50 = \underline{\hspace{1cm}} = \underline{\hspace{1cm}}.$

$0.66 = \underline{\hspace{1cm}} = \underline{\hspace{1cm}}.$

$0.75 = \underline{\hspace{1cm}} = \underline{\hspace{1cm}}.$

FIGURE 2.6. *(continued)*

As you compared the tasks, Tasks A and F ask students to use a pattern to solve a problem. Task F, however, is much more directive and stops short of having students describe the pattern or extend it. There is less rigor in this task than in Task A. Even though students with MLD and MD may be challenged by Task A, it is accessible because it first asks them to draw the next figure in the pattern. By drawing first, these students have a context that will help them create their description. A visual problem such as this one creates a scaffold to the more complex task of describing the thinking.

Keep in mind that even though the tasks appear to be quite different in the way in which a problem is solved or in the mathematics involved in the solution, each of the tasks represented in Figure 2.6 offers opportunities and challenges for students. In the case of the tasks that are computational, students have to recall processes from memory.

This may be a challenge for some and quite simple for others. Other tasks, such as Task C, require students to consider the relationships represented in the problem and then determine a solution path. For Task C, one possible solution pathway would be to find a cost for about 300 photos. When the costs for the two types of cameras are compared, students will find that the disposable cameras will be cheaper. However, they could make the argument that the regular camera has long-term capabilities. Thus, a problem like this gives students with MLD and MD opportunities to use creativity within a practical situation that helps to address the misconception that mathematics is a series of steps, rules, or algorithms (SMP 2; NGA & CCSSO, 2010).

It is important to provide a variety of tasks for students. They should not be given the same type of task (for example, straightforward skill computations) in large quantities every day. They should have a mixture of tasks that provide opportunities to think about the mathematics, look for structure or regularity modeled in the problems, and apply their skills (SMP 7; NGA & CCSSO, 2010). Even though students need to practice their skills to gain the automaticity that is efficient, they also need to engage in problems that require them to think creatively as they look for unique solution paths.

Questioning Techniques

Just as selecting an appropriate task is a major endeavor, so is deciding what questions to ask. Posing questions comprises a large portion of instructional time (Sahin & Kulm, 2008). They are used to begin a discussion or help students reflect on or analyze their thinking about a problem or idea. Sometimes, questions are used to engage students in a small-group or whole-class discussion. The types of questions you ask are closely related to the types of tasks you use in your classroom, and similarly, they can support the development of stronger mathematical reasoning. You will notice similarities as you go through this section.

There are different types of questions, some that focus on lower-level thinking and others that emphasize deeper thinking. Of the lower-level type, *factual questions* are most common, often comprising more than 64% of questions asked (Myhill & Dunkin, 2005). Factual questions are those questions that ask for a definition, a solution to a computation, a memorized fact or algorithm, or a formula.

A factual question often asks for:

1. A specific definition or fact
2. An answer to a problem or task (answer only with no explanation)
3. The next step in an algorithm or procedure
4. A yes/no or true/false response

You can see that the level of thinking required to answer a factual question is very low. Students generally rely on memorized responses or a skill-based process to respond. Students do need to develop fluent, automatic responses, but the majority of questions should not focus on memorized or recall responses.

Here is a typical factual question in fourth-grade mathematics:

What is the sum of ¼ + ½?

To solve the problem, students would typically apply an algorithm that would require them to get a common denominator, and then add the numerators to find the sum. This is considered a low-level question or task because students would recall the process and use it to find the answer, most often not considering if the answer they get is reasonable or why they use that process. Additionally, asking predominantly this type of question keeps all students from participating in the process because the student who remembers the process and can quickly apply it will often call out the answer while some students are just beginning to solve it. This may especially affect students with MLD and MD, as they often tend to work slower as they struggle to retrieve memorized facts or processes, especially when these may have been developed with no foundational understanding.

Working with students with MLD and MD requires that we explicitly focus their attention on structural aspects of the mathematics so they can make sense of and reason about the concept and skill (SMP 7 and 8; NGA & CCSSO, 2010). A questioning framework can be used to create questions that require students to think in different ways, to focus more on the mathematical ideas, and to form connections and generalizations about significant mathematics. One such framework uses reversibility, flexibility, and generalization questions (Dougherty, Bryant, Bryant, Darrough, & Pfannenstiel, 2015). (See Figure 2.7 for a comparison of these question types.) As the following examples are given, think about how student thinking changes when a question like this is posed.

In questions like the example at the top of this page, students follow a methodical, linear process to solve it, continuing to emphasize the misconceptions that *mathematics is linear and sequential* and *mathematics is a series of steps, rules, or algorithms*. If the question is slightly changed, it can force students to think more flexibly, using what they know to solve a slightly more complex problem. There are three types of questions that can promote this type of thinking: *reversibility, flexibility,* and *generalization questions.*

Reversibility questions are those that provide students with an answer and they create the problem. Students have to work backwards to find the solution. To change the previous example ("What is the sum of ¼ + ½?"), ask students to find two fractions with unlike denominators whose sum is ¾. There are an infinite number of solutions to this problem. In fact, you could ask students to find more than one example of two fractions that would work. This offers an advantage in the classroom because every student can share his or her solution; no student is left out. Because this type of question requires thinking time, students with MLD and MD who need time to think can still engage in the process and all students can enter into and engage in the problem at their own level. Reversibility questions offer multiple access points so that regardless of their level, students with MLD and MD can find an answer.

Because reversibility questions have multiple responses, you can use students' responses to find patterns and generalize their ideas. For example, given the question

	Computations	**Measurement**
Factual question	Multiply: ⅔ × ⅗	Find the area of a rectangle that measures 4 cm by 6 cm.
Reversibility question Thinking "backward." Given the answer, find the question or problem.	What are two fractions whose product is ⅔?	What are the measures of the sides of a rectangle that has an area of 24 sq cm?
Flexibility question 1. Identifying relationships between and across problems. 2. Solving a problem in multiple ways.	What is the product of 2⅔ × ½? What is another way to find the product? Write the fact team for this set of numbers: ⅔, 1, 1½.	What are two different methods you could use to find the area of a trapezoid?
Generalization question 1. Finding a pattern from multiple cases. 2. Identifying a specific case, given a generalization.	What are two fractions whose product is greater than 1? What are two fractions whose product is less than 1? What are two fractions whose product is equal to 1?	How is the area of a rectangle related to the area of a parallelogram? Explain using specific examples.

FIGURE 2.7. Comparison of the different types of questions (Dougherty, 2001).

"What are two fractions with unlike denominators that have a sum of ¾?," responses of students with MLD and MD can be used to focus on the magnitude of the fractions being added. Having students share their answers leads to asking them what they notice about the addends. Students with MLD and MD should note that both addends cannot be greater than ½. While this seems like a trivial generalization, it is an important one because it provides a means by which these students can assess the reasonableness of their answers to fraction addition problems and it allows them to predict the size of the sum (SMP 8; NGO & CCSSO, 2010).

There are two types of *flexibility questions*. The most common flexibility question is one that asks students to solve a problem in more than one way. In the first example, "What is the sum of ¼ + ½?," students would be given the problem as stated and then asked to find more than one way to solve it. In this example, students might use the addition algorithm by finding a common denominator for one method, but the other methods may vary. For example, some students might draw a picture or use physical materials. Others might reason the solution by describing a relationship between fourths and halves such as ¼ is the same as ½, and then use that relationship to find the sum. The multiple-solution approaches derived by asking a question in this way can offer other alternatives for students who were not sure where to begin or who could not think about the problem in a different way. The methods can be analyzed by asking students, How are the solution methods alike? How are they different? Whenever this type of flexibility question is asked, it should always be followed with having students analyze the similarities and differences of the various methods offered (SMP 7; NGA & CCSSO, 2010).

A second type of flexibility question is one that presents problems in a purposeful way to promote students using what they know about one problem to solve another problem. In the first problem posed, What is the sum of ¼ + ½?, the problem can be changed to a flexibility question by presenting it in this way:

Add: ¼ + ¼

¼ + ½

⅛ + ½

Most students would repeat the algorithm on each of the problems without thinking about how each problem is related. When a student is using flexible thinking, he or she would notice that the first problem results in a sum of ½, which can be used then to solve the second problem. The sum of that problem, in turn, informs the sum of the last problem. The sequence of these problems also provides a scaffold from a simpler problem to one that is more complex, and thus, it is important to ask students to explicitly describe how the problems are related. Note that it is sometimes preferable to have students with MLD and MD to explain in words how they solved the problem rather than to have them show the mathematical steps because the explanation helps to reinforce a deeper understanding than only performing an algorithm. If students with MLD and MD have difficulty describing their thinking, have them show their work and ask other students to describe what they think the process was. This gives the students with MLD and MD an opportunity to hear others talk mathematically and compare the description being given to what they thought the process they used was (SMP 3; NGA & CCSSO, 2010).

The third type of question is a *generalization question*. There are two types of generalization questions: one asks students to identify a pattern or make a *conjecture* (a pattern that was noticed but has not been proven to hold for all cases), and one asks students to give a specific example of a pattern. Using the original problem (What is the sum of ¼ + ½?), it can be changed to focus students on the reasonableness of their answers. Examples of generalization questions could include the following:

1. What do you notice about the sum when you add two fractions, both greater than 0 but less than ½?
2. What do you notice about the sum when you add one fraction greater than ½ but less than 1 to a fraction that is less than ½ but greater than 0?

One generalization that students with MLD and MD may note for question 1 is that the sum must be less than 1. Similarly, for question 2, students may share that the sum will be less than 1½. The responses to these questions can help these students develop a sense of judging reasonableness of their answers. When they confront other addition problems with fractions, they can first predict the size of the answer they should get, compute, and then check its reasonableness. The practice of first predicting before computing, and then checking reasonableness of an answer, is one that should be consistently used in the classroom (SMP 2; NGA & CCSSO, 2010).

To support students using the generalizations to predict and check for reasonableness, generalizations can be archived for reference with future topics. Figure 2.8 provides an example of some generalizations that were created by a third-grade class. The teacher put them on Google Docs and shared them with the class. Each student then had access to the generalizations, and the teacher could refer to them easily as students moved through topics.

Notice that the generalizations use mathematical language. Sometimes, as teachers, we use more informal language to describe the mathematical ideas, such as calling the commutative property the "ring-around-the-rosy" property. However, the informal language does not convey the same meaning as the mathematical language, and it will not be consistent from grade to grade or teacher to teacher. Using the mathematical language provides the consistency that students with MLD and MD need; it alleviates the need to relearn the mathematical language each year when they move to a new teacher.

Karp, Bush, and Dougherty (2014) discussed the impact of language on student learning. Using language that is not the academic language of mathematics can also lead to students developing misconceptions about mathematical ideas. Students can interpret the language in ways that are not mathematically appropriate. For example, when the fraction ¾ is read as "3 out of 4," students do not consider the fraction as a quantity but rather as two separate amounts, a 3 and a 4, two whole numbers that are only separated with a bar. When fractions are not viewed as a quantity, errors may appear in the application of algorithms. For example, ¼ + ½ can result in ⅖ because students considered the numerators and denominators to be whole numbers and used the addition algorithm for whole numbers to find the sum.

Figure 2.9 shows a table of mathematical language from Karp and colleagues (2014) that should be considered as you are planning and implementing your lessons. Look at the language presented in the table and think about the misconceptions that could result from using informal or less accurate language. (For additional examples for middle and high school grades, see Dougherty, Bush, & Karp, 2017; Karp, Bush, & Dougherty, 2015.)

You should also notice that the generalizations are not rules that fall apart as students progress through the grades and into more complex mathematics. "Rules that expire" (Dougherty et al., 2017; Karp et al., 2014, 2015) are not helpful for students. As

---

Our Third-Grade Big Ideas about Addition and Subtraction

1. When we add two three-digit numbers, our sum can only be three or four digits.
2. Addition means joining together two parts to make a whole.
3. The commutative property of addition means that I can add the parts in any order and still get the same sum.
4. The zero property of addition means that I can add 0 to any other addend and the sum will be that addend.
5. Adding 0 does not change the value of the other addend.

FIGURE 2.8. Example of generalizations made by a third-grade class.

Expired mathematical language and suggested alternatives	
What is stated	What should be stated
Using the words *borrowing* or *carrying* when subtracting or adding, respectively	Use *trading* or *regrouping* to indicate the actual action of trading or exchanging one place value unit for another unit.
Using the phrase ___ *out of* ___ to describe a fraction, for example, *one out of seven* to describe 1/7	Use the fraction and the attribute. For example, say *one-seventh of the length of the string.* The *out of* language often causes students to think a part is being subtracted from the whole amount (Philipp, Cabral, & Schappelle, 2005).
Using the phrase *reducing fractions*	Use *simplifying fractions.* The language of *reducing* gives students the incorrect impression that the fraction is getting smaller or being reduced in size.
Asking how shapes are *similar* when children are comparing a set of shapes	Ask, *How are these shapes the same? How are the shapes different?* Using the word *similar* in these situations can eventually confuse students about the mathematical meaning of *similar,* which will be introduced in middle school and relates to geometric figures.
Reading the equal sign as *makes,* for example, saying, *Two plus two makes four* for 2 + 2 = 4	Read the equation 2 + 2 = 4 as *Two plus two equals* or *is the same as four.* The language *makes* encourages the misconception that the equal sign is an action or an operation rather than representative of a relationship.
Indicating that a number *divides evenly* into another number	Say that a number *divides* another number *a whole number of times* or that it *divides without a remainder.*
Plugging a number into an expression or equation	Use *substitute values* for an unknown.
Using *top number* and *bottom number* to describe the numerator and denominator of a fraction, respectively	Students should see a fraction as one number, not two separate numbers. Use the words *numerator* and *denominator* when discussing the different parts of a fraction.

FIGURE 2.9. Examples of expired language and alternatives. From Karp, Bush, and Dougherty (2014, p. 23). Reprinted with permission from the National Council of Teachers of Mathematics.

Karp and colleagues (2014) noted, students with MLD and MD may overgeneralize rules and misapply them in inappropriate contexts. For example, the rule "You always subtract the smaller number from the larger number" creates difficulties for students when they are confronted with this problem: 725 – 268. When this is written in the vertical format, students may subtract inappropriately. See Figure 2.10 for a sample of third-grader Claire's work that shows how the student misapplied a rule that she had been given.

What are some other rules that you have heard or used? Compare your rules to those in Figure 2.11. Could these rules be rewritten or clarified so they do not "expire"? Why or why not? (You may also want to check Karp et al., 2015, and Dougherty et al., 2017, for other rules that are more specific to middle and high school grades.)

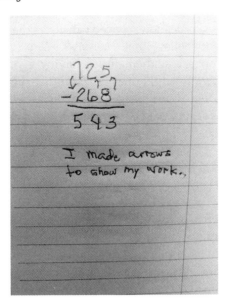

FIGURE 2.10. Claire's application of the rule "You always subtract the smaller number from the larger number."

1. When you multiply a number by ten, just add a zero to the end of the number.
2. Use keywords to solve word problems.
3. You cannot take a bigger number from a smaller number.
4. Addition and multiplication make numbers bigger.
5. Subtraction and division make numbers smaller.
6. You always divide the larger number by the smaller number.
7. Two negatives make a positive.
8. Multiply everything in the parentheses by the number outside the parentheses.
9. Improper fractions should always be written as a mixed number.
10. The number you say first in counting is always less than the number that comes next.
11. The longer the number, the larger the number.
12. Please Excuse My Dear Aunt Sally.
13. The equal sign means Find the answer or Write the answer.

FIGURE 2.11. Common rules found in elementary grades that expire (Karp, Bush, & Dougherty, 2014). Reprinted with permission from the National Council of Teachers of Mathematics.

Changing the way a task/question is posed can affect the way students think about mathematics. Many students believe that *mathematics is just a series of steps that have to be memorized* and they do not see mathematics as having many different ways of thinking. Changing questions from factual ones to those that require deeper thinking can provide opportunities to deepen understanding and the ability to reason mathematically in students with MLD and MD while developing a different perception about mathematics as a discipline.

Conclusion

Developing mathematical reasoning is an important aspect of learning mathematics. It is what helps students apply skills, interpret problems and relationships, and predict and assess the answers that they get. Mathematical reasoning can be developed by purposeful selection of multiple representations and tasks in conjunction with creating good questions. From these aspects, students with MLD and MD can identify and use generalizations in increasingly more powerful ways.

REFERENCES

Dougherty, B. J. (2001). Access to algebra: A process approach. In H. Chick, K. Stacey, J. Vincent, & J. Vincent (Eds.), *The future of the teaching and learning of algebra* (pp. 207–213). Melbourne, Victoria, Australia: University of Melbourne.

Dougherty, B. J. (2008). Measure up: A quantitative view of early algebra. In J. J. Kaput, D. W. Carraher, & M. L. Blanton (Eds.), *Algebra in the early grades* (pp. 389–412). Mahwah, NJ: Erlbaum.

Dougherty, B., Bryant, D. P., Bryant, B. R., Darrough, R. L., & Pfannenstiel, K. H. (2015). Developing concepts and generalizations to build algebraic thinking: The reversibility, flexibility, and generalization approach. *Intervention in School and Clinic, 50*(5), 273–281.

Dougherty, B. J., Bush, S. B., & Karp, K. S. (2017). Circumventing high school rules that expire. *Mathematics Teacher, 111*(2), 134–139.

Karp, K., Bush, S., & Dougherty, B. (2014). Avoiding 13 rules that expire. *Teaching Children Mathematics, 21*(1), 18–25.

Karp, K., Bush, S., & Dougherty, B. (2015). 12 math rules that expire in the middle grades. *Mathematics Teaching in the Middle School, 21*(4), 208–215.

Myhill, D., & Dunkin, F. (2005). Questioning learning. *Language and Education, 19*(5), 415–427.

National Council of Teachers of Mathematics. (2000). *Principles and standards for school mathematics*. Reston, VA: Author.

National Governors Association (NGA) Center for Best Practices & Council of Chief State School Officers (CCSSO). (2010). *Common Core State Standards for mathematics*. Washington, DC: Authors.

Piaget J. (1954). *The construction of reality in the child* (M. Cook, Trans.). New York: Basic Books.

Russell, S. J. (1999). Mathematical reasoning in the elementary grades. In L. V. Stiff (Ed.), *Developing mathematical reasoning in grades K–12, 1999 yearbook* (pp. 1–12). Reston, VA: National Council of Teachers of Mathematics.

Sahin, A., & Kulm, G. (2008). Sixth grade mathematics teachers' intentions and use of probing, guiding, and factual questions. *Journal of Mathematics Teacher Education, 11*(3), 221–241.

Smith, M., & Stein, M. K. (1998). Selecting and creating mathematical tasks: From research to practice. *Mathematics Teaching in the Middle School, 3*(5), 344–350.

Stein, M. K., Smith, M. S., Henningsen, M. A., & Silver, E. A. (2000). Implementing standards-based mathematics. New York: Teacher College Press.

Sternberg, R. J. (1999). The nature of mathematical reasoning. In L. V. Stiff (Ed.), *Developing mathematical reasoning in grades K–12, 1999 yearbook* (pp. 37–44). Reston, VA: National Council of Teachers of Mathematics.

CHAPTER 3

Data-Based Individualization

A Framework for Providing Intensive Intervention to Students with Mathematics Difficulties

PAMELA M. SEETHALER, LYNN S. FUCHS, and DOUGLAS FUCHS

LEARNING OUTCOMES

After studying this chapter, you will be able to answer the following questions:

1. How are students identified for intensive intervention?

2. How can data-based individualization be used to provide intensive intervention for Tier 3?

Research shows that early prevention activities in preschool (e.g., Clements & Sarama, 2007), kindergarten (e.g., Griffin, Case, & Siegler, 1994), and first grade (e.g., Fuchs, Fuchs, Yazdian, & Powell, 2002) can substantially improve the performance for students who otherwise will struggle with mathematics. For example, Fuchs and colleagues (2013) investigated the effects of a first-grade number knowledge intervention, centered on research-based understanding about mathematics development and instructional design for struggling students. This tutoring program, which may be conceptualized as a form of Tier 2 intervention within a multi-tiered system of supports, provided intensive instruction three times per week for 16 weeks to children identified as at risk for mathematics difficulty. In each 30-minute session, the major emphasis (25 minutes) was the conceptual and procedural bases for arithmetic, including a strong focus on number knowledge; the other 5 minutes involved practice in one of two forms. Nonspeeded practice reinforced relations and principles addressed in the number knowledge intervention. Speeded strategic practice promoted quick responding and use of efficient counting procedures to generate many correct responses to mathematics problems. The at-risk children who participated in this study were randomly assigned to remain in their school program without the research-based intervention ($n = 206$) or to participate in the research-based number knowledge intervention (195 in speeded practice; 190 in nonspeeded practice). *Random assignment* (i.e., assigning subjects to a treatment or control group using a chance procedure, such as flipping a coin or using a random number generator) ensures that each participant has an equal opportunity to be placed in any group and that differences between groups are not systematic at the start of the experiment.

Results of this study indicated that the number knowledge intervention with either form of practice produced stronger learning than occurred in the *control group condition* (i.e., the children who continued in their school program without research-based intervention). This was the case on all of the four mathematics outcomes assessed: arithmetic, two-digit calculations, number knowledge, and word problems. Also, speeded practice produced stronger learning than nonspeeded practice on arithmetic and two-digit calculations. The effects favoring both intervention conditions over the typical school program were generally large, suggesting strong practical value for moving these children onto a stronger course of mathematics learning.

Even so, as with all interventions, including interventions that are based on research and are implemented as intended, not all children responded. Let's consider responsiveness on this study's major outcome: arithmetic, which was strongly aligned with this intervention's content and on which effects were strong. If we define responsiveness in terms of amount of improvement (improving at least at the 25th percentile of not-at-risk classmates' improvement in the same *time frame,* i.e., over the 16 weeks in which intervention occurred), 88.6% of at-risk students responded to intervention (across the two conditions). This leaves 11.4% (or 44 of the 385 children) inadequately responsive and requiring something more intensive to address their needs.

As this illustrates, a need exists for intensive intervention, even when prevention services are strong and generally effective. So it is unfortunate that educators often have difficulty identifying how to intensify intervention (beyond available Tier 2 validated programs) for students who respond inadequately at Tier 2. Confusion about how to intensify limits the capacity of schools to analyze intervention options, and it dilutes the effectiveness of intensive intervention.

One signature feature of intensive intervention and special education is individualization (e.g., Fuchs, Fuchs, & Compton, 2012; McLaughlin, Shepard, & O'Day, 1995). A validated process for individualizing intervention is *data-based individualization* (DBI; Stecker, Fuchs, & Fuchs, 2005), a research-based process that integrates the systematic use of assessment data, validated interventions, and intensification strategies (National Center on Intensive Intervention [NCII], 2018). With DBI, the teacher (often a special educator) routinely (usually weekly) collects and graphs progress monitoring data from a target student. The purpose of this ongoing progress monitoring is to track the student's responsiveness to the "intensive intervention platform," a program the teacher identifies as providing a strong platform for potentially addressing the student's mathematics deficits.

However, in light of the student's history of inadequate response to standard intervention programs, the teacher does not assume this intensive intervention platform will produce strong learning for this student. Instead, the ongoing progress monitoring data inform a structured individualization process. The teacher applies validated DBI decision rules to the data he or she collects on a regular basis. When the data indicate the platform is not producing the rate of response necessary for the student to achieve his or her year-end goal, the teacher adjusts the intensive intervention platform.

This systematic teach–test–revise–test process continues throughout intensive intervention, and in this way, the teacher derives an intensive intervention program that is aligned with the student's individual needs and accelerates the student's learning trajectory. Randomized control trials demonstrate that this DBI process improves the mathematics outcomes of intensive intervention students (Stecker et al., 2005). The website of the NCII (*www.intensiveintervention.org*) provides resources for selecting progress monitoring tools and for implementing DBI. (NCII resources are made available at no cost with support from the Office of Special Education Programs, within the U.S. Department of Education.)

In this chapter, we explain the intensive intervention DBI process by providing a case study in which a special educator, Ms. Kubek, used DBI with a kindergarten child named "Giselle" (a hypothetical student). It may seem unusual to select a kindergarten child to illustrate DBI's intensive intervention framework. For this reason, we begin by explaining how Giselle was identified for intensive intervention. Then we provide a detailed case study showing how Ms. Kubek set up her progress monitoring system and used the resulting data to individually tailor Giselle's intensive intervention.

How the Student Was Identified for Intensive Intervention

Giselle entered kindergarten with severe mathematics delays. This included a failure to achieve understanding of the *cardinality principle* (i.e., when counting a set of items, the last numeral stated in the counting sequence represents the number of items in the set [Gelman & Gallistel, 1978]), despite having attended the school district's preschool program. As Geary and colleagues (2017; Geary & van Marle, 2018) recently demonstrated, children who do not achieve understanding of cardinality by the start of kindergarten are at increased risk for mathematics disability. With the cardinality principle, children appreciate that the last number reached when counting items in a set represents the entire set, understand how many items are in a set, and begin to differentiate sets of at least four items. Geary and colleagues found that failure to achieve this understanding during the preschool years is an indicator of severe risk for poor mathematics learning in school.

Misconceptions regarding cardinality may stem from poor understanding of one or more essential implicit counting principles, as described by Gelman and Gallistel (1978). These essential counting principles include *one-to-one correspondence* (i.e., assigning one and only one number name to each item in a group when counting); *stable order* (i.e., consistently referring to the same order of word tags when assigning number names); *cardinality*; *abstraction* (i.e., any array or collection of physical or nonphysical entities may be counted); and *order irrelevance* (i.e., the order in which any items may be tagged, or counted, is irrelevant; items do not need to be counted in adjacent fashion). Studies suggest that young students who are at risk for developing mathematics difficulty often make counting errors indicative of poor understanding of abstraction and order-irrelevance principles (Geary, 1994; Geary, Bow-Thomas, & Yao, 1992), even as other counting principles seem intact.

Failure to achieve the cardinality principle in some children may occur for two additional reasons. First, some children have experienced inadequate opportunities to learn prior to school entry. Second, some children have limitations in the cognitive processes associated with mathematics competence, for example, poor working memory or oral language comprehension (Fuchs et al., 2006; Swanson & Beebe-Frankenberger, 2004). Such vulnerabilities make these children less responsive to the instructional opportunities that were available to them prior to kindergarten entry and make them inadequately responsive to the classroom instruction they receive in school. Further complicating the picture is that, as Geary and colleagues (2017) demonstrated, children's learning of the relations among symbolic numbers (number words and Arabic numerals) begins only after they understand cardinality. Thus, children who achieve this insight at a delayed age have less time to elaborate their number system knowledge than do children who achieve this insight at a younger age.

Thus, an important idea that emerges from Geary and colleagues' (2017) line of preschool work is that lack of understanding of the cardinality principle during the preschool years can serve as an indicator of severe risk for poor mathematics outcome, which signals the need for intensive intervention (not just the early prevention services available with standard Tier 2 programs). In the case of Giselle, failure to achieve understanding of cardinality is only one red flag that intensive intervention is required. The second rationale for intensive intervention is her inadequate response to the classroom teacher's validated Tier 1 classroom adaptation, Peer-Assisted Learning Strategies (PALS).

In each PALS session (which occurs twice weekly), the classroom teacher does a brief lesson in which she or he previews the day's mathematics idea skills, as well as the day's activities and game board. Then the children in the class break into pairs, where they take turns being the "coach" and "player" using the game board in a highly structured manner to practice critical mathematics ideas and skills. As children work together, with the coach providing corrective feedback in a structured way, the teacher circulates to observe pairs working together and infuse instructional support as needed. PALS is a validated classroom practice for improving children's mathematics achievement and reducing the number of children who require more intensive intervention (Fuchs, Fuchs, & Karns, 2001).

However, after 6 weeks of PALS, it was clear to the classroom teacher that Giselle was not responding adequately. The classroom teacher referred Giselle to the school's study team, where an additional evaluation corroborated the need for intensive intervention. Ms. Kubek's approach to intensive intervention relied on DBI. What follows is a description of the progress monitoring system Ms. Kubek employed and how she used the resulting data to individualize Giselle's mathematics intervention.

How DBI Was Used to Provide Intensive Intervention at Tier 3: Giselle's Case Study

Ms. Kubek carefully examined the results of the school's study team evaluation of Giselle's strengths and weaknesses in early numeracy understanding. The team noted that Giselle recognized numbers to 5 and counted by *rote* to 10 (i.e., recited the sequence of the numbers in order from 1 to 10) when prompted, along with her kindergarten peers. However, Giselle was not commensurate with her peers in terms of conceptual and procedural early mathematical knowledge. For example, the study team noted Giselle did not consistently and correctly state the number names for numbers greater than 5 and did not understand the concept of *one-to-one correspondence* or the *principle of cardinality* (i.e., understanding the last number stated when counting items in a set represents the entire amount of set items). This was evident by interactions with her classroom teacher and during PALS sessions. Furthermore, Giselle seemed to lack even a rudimentary understanding of *addition* (i.e., combining two or more sets to make a larger set) and *subtraction* (i.e., removing a portion of a set to make a smaller set). Therefore, the intervention Ms. Kubek planned to individualize for Giselle targeted number recognition, counting, cardinality, and basic addition and subtraction.

Selecting an Appropriate Progress Monitoring System

Before Ms. Kubek met with Giselle, she selected a *curriculum-based measurement* (CBM; Deno, 1985) progress monitoring system that aligned closely with the intervention focus. CBM refers to a measurement system that is composed of alternate, equivalent forms, brief to administer, technically adequate, and sensitive to growth in specific academic content areas. Careful monitoring of a student's response to intervention, with respect to both *level* (i.e., static, or one-time, information regarding a student's overall competence at a given point in time) and *slope* (i.e., growth on the measure over time), is an essential component of DBI. The teach–test–revise–test process requires a valid and reliable indicator of the student's response to instruction, to alert the instructor when an adjustment to the intervention is required. Toward this end, an alternate CBM form is administered before intervention begins and then consistently throughout the intervention period. To gauge Giselle's reaction to instruction at this level, Ms. Kubek planned to administer an alternate CBM form at the end of each week. The progress monitoring system she selects is Vanderbilt Kindergarten Mathematics CBM (KM-CBM; Seethaler & Fuchs, 2011).

Developed at Vanderbilt University for use with kindergarten students to measure beginning mathematics growth, KM-CBM is a 5-minute timed assessment of counting, addition, and subtraction fluency (Seethaler & Fuchs, 2011). Twenty alternate KM-CBM forms (i.e., identical in format and level of difficulty but differing on actual items) are used to monitor student behavior on a weekly (or biweekly) basis across the academic year. Each form (see Figure 3.1 for an example) includes 25 items (five items each of five problem types) presented in random order on one side of an 8.5" by 11" piece of paper. The five types of problems are counting stars in a single set (counting stars), counting

Name: _____   Teacher: _____

0 + 1 = ____	* ____	Cross out 1 *. ★ ★ ★ ★ ★ ★ ____	★★★★ + ★★ = ____	5 – 3 = ____
★ + ★★★★★★★★ = ____	4 – 2 = ____	0 + 2 = ____	★ ★ ★ ★ ★ ★ ★ ★ ____	Cross out 0 *. ★ ★ ★ ____
Cross out 4 *. ★ ★ ★ ★ ★ ★ ★ ★ ____	2 + 1 = ____	★ ★ ★ ★ ____	★★ + ★★★★★★ = ____	5 – 0 = ____
3 + 0 = ____	★ + ★ = ____	Cross out 2 *. ★ ★ ★ ★ ★ ★ ★ ____	1 – 1 = ____	★ ★ ★ ____
3 – 1 = ____	Cross out 3 *. ★ ★ ★ ★ ★ ____	★★★★★ + ★★★ = ____	★ ★ ★ ★ ★ ★ ____	2 + 2 = ____

Form 2   Date: _____

FIGURE 3.1. Example of Vanderbilt KM-CBM form. From Seethaler and Fuchs (2011). Reprinted with permission from Sage Publications.

two sets of stars (adding stars), subtracting crossed-out stars from a single set (subtracting stars), addition facts with numerals (presented without star icons and with sums up to 5; addition facts), and subtraction facts with numerals (presented without star icons and with minuends up to 5; subtraction facts). Students are instructed to answer as many items as they can before the timer beeps and to skip the ones they don't know how to answer. Performance is scored as number of correct items in the given time. Each item on each KM-CBM form is coded for type of *skill* (i.e., counting stars, adding sets of stars, subtracting sets of stars, addition facts, and subtraction facts). The percentage correct on type of skill is available for each form.

Ms. Kubek selected KM-CBM as the progress monitoring system to use in conjunction with Giselle's mathematics instruction for several reasons. First, the test developers evaluated the system scientifically with kindergarten students and found it to be a reliable and valid measure of kindergarteners' skill level and growth in early mathematics. Since Ms. Kubek planned to rely on the resultant CBM data to monitor and adjust Giselle's ongoing intervention experience, a technically sound progress monitoring system was essential. Second, because the DBI process could take several weeks for Giselle, the progress monitoring system Ms. Kubek chose must have multiple alternate forms that would tap the same numeracy skills each week but differ with respect to the actual items to prevent an increase in score due to a simple practice effect. KM-CBM has 20 alternate forms of documented equivalency with respect to skill type and difficulty; these 20 forms could be used to monitor Giselle's progress weekly for as long as the intervention period lasted.

Third, Ms. Kubek needed to select a progress monitoring system with legitimate and reasonable benchmarks, or indicators of risk, for various points of time across the academic school year. The developers of KM-CBM provide a table that allows teachers to identify students who may be at risk for developing more pervasive mathematics difficulty, given certain (low) scores at the fall, winter, and spring of the kindergarten year, as well as an expected level of performance at the end of the school year. Based on this table, Ms. Kubek learned the average score for students in the spring of kindergarten is 18 problems correct (i.e., of 25); she used this as Giselle's end-of-year goal. The final reason Ms. Kubek selected KM-CBM to use with Giselle is the system's skills analysis feature. Although the overall score Giselle earned each week will be used to monitor her rate of response to the intervention, the skills analysis feature, which highlights the proportion correct of each type of problem, will help guide Ms. Kubek's instructional adaptations to address specific areas of weakness.

After selecting the progress monitoring system to use with Giselle's mathematics development, Ms. Kubek set up the graph she used to plot Giselle's weekly data and interpret its meaning (see the top half of Figure 3.2). Across the x-axis (i.e., bottom row) of the graph, Ms. Kubek marked one notch for each week of instruction. Along the y-axis (i.e., left-hand side) of the graph, Ms. Kubek labeled the range of possible scores Giselle could earn on each weekly form (i.e., 0 to 25). Before beginning intervention, Ms. Kubek administered a weekly form to Giselle; Giselle's score was 0, and Ms. Kubek plotted it accordingly on the graph.

Then she drew a dashed line, the "goal line," to connect Giselle's current level of functioning (0) with the end-of-year goal (18). This goal line played an important role during the DBI process in that each time four consecutive data points fell below the goal line, indicating a rate of response to instruction that would not allow for Giselle to meet the year-end goal, Ms. Kubek adjusted Giselle's intervention in an effort to increase the slope. As a special educator, Ms. Kubek was well versed in her understanding and interpretation of data as it is used to guide instruction. However, had she required guidance on how to interpret Giselle's data trend, she could have accessed the NCII online module "Using Academic Progress Monitoring for Individualized Instructional Planning" (*https://intensiveintervention.org/resource/using-academic-progress-monitoring-individualized-instructional-planning-dbi-training*) to determine if the instructional plan was working or if a change was needed.

Individualizing Giselle's Mathematics Intervention

Applying the Taxonomy of Intervention Intensity to Select a Platform

At this point, Ms. Kubek was ready to monitor Giselle's growth in counting, cardinality, addition, and subtraction skills. The next step was to select an appropriate intervention platform and to build an intensive intervention platform to address Giselle's conceptual

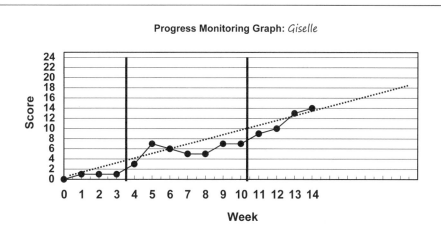

Progress Monitoring Graph: *Giselle*

Weekly Progress Monitoring by Problem Type: *Giselle*

	Score: /25	% Correct: Count Stars	% Correct: Add Stars	% Correct: Subtr Stars	% Correct: Add Facts	% Correct: Subtr Facts
Week 1	1	20%	0%	0%	0%	0%
Week 2	1	20%	0%	0%	0%	0%
Week 3	1	20%	0%	0%	0%	0%
Week 4	3	40%	20%	0%	0%	0%
Week 5	7	100%	40%	0%	0%	0%
Week 6	6	80%	40%	0%	0%	0%
Week 7	5	60%	40%	0%	0%	0%
Week 8	5	60%	40%	0%	0%	0%
Week 9	7	80%	20%	20%	20%	0%
Week 10	7	100%	20%	20%	0%	0%
Week 11	9	100%	40%	20%	20%	0%
Week 12	10	100%	60%	20%	20%	0%
Week 13	13	100%	80%	40%	20%	20%
Week 14	13	100%	80%	20%	40%	20%

FIGURE 3.2. KM-CBM progress monitoring graph for Giselle, showing total score correct (0–25) for each week. The skills profile (relating to the five problems types) is below the graph. Each row shows the total number of items correct (of 25) on weekly KM-CBM along with the proportion correct of each of the five problem types (counting stars, adding stars, subtracting stars, addition facts, and subtraction facts). Each KM-CBM has five items of each type, so 20% represents one correct problem for that type and 80% represents four correct problems for that type.

and procedural deficits. To select an appropriate platform, Ms. Kubek relied on the *taxonomy of intervention intensity* (Fuchs, Fuchs, & Malone, 2017), which describes seven principles for selecting, evaluating, and building intervention intensity. Her goals were to select an intervention platform, individualize the intensity of the intervention, and efficiently address Giselle's unique learning needs. The taxonomy's seven dimensions of intensity are strength, dosage, alignment, attention to transfer, complexity, behavioral support, and individualization. See Table 3.1 for definitions.

The taxonomy's first dimension for selecting the intensive intervention platform is the *strength* of the intervention. Strength indicates how well the program works specifically for students with intensive intervention needs and is expressed in terms of *effect sizes*. Ms. Kubek knew that if a given program was strong for this group of learners, then the program was more likely to support Giselle's learning as well and would be less likely to need program adjustments to suit Giselle's unique needs.

TABLE 3.1. The Taxonomy of Intervention Intensity

Intensity Dimension	Definition
Strength	How well the program works for students with intensive intervention needs, expressed in terms of effect sizes
Dosage	The number of opportunities a student has to respond and receive corrective feedback
Alignment	How well the program (1) addresses the target student's full set of academic skill deficits; (2) does *not* address skills the target student has already mastered (extraneous skills for that student); and (3) incorporates a meaningful focus on grade-appropriate curricular standards
Attention to transfer	The extent to which an intervention is designed to help students (1) transfer the skills they learn to other formats and contexts and (2) realize connections between mastered and related skills
Complexity	The number of explicit instruction principles the intervention incorporates (e.g., providing explanations in simple, direct language; modeling efficient solution strategies instead of expecting students to discover strategies on their own; ensuring students have the necessary background knowledge and skills to succeed with those strategies; gradually fading support for students' correct execution of those strategies; providing practice so students use the strategies to generate many correct responses; and incorporating systematic cumulative review)
Behavioral support	The extent to which interventions incorporate (1) self-regulation and executive function components and (2) behavioral principles to minimize nonproductive behavior
Individualization	A validated, data-based process for individualizing intervention, with which the special educator systematically adjusts an intensive intervention platform over time to address the student's complex learning needs

Intervention effects are quantified in terms of effect sizes, which indicate how much higher intervention students score at posttest compared to students who did not receive that intervention. Let's say the intervention developers report an effect size of 1.0 standard deviation on an achievement test with a mean of 100 and standard deviation of 15. Let's also say this effect size is specifically for students who start intervention with academic performance at or below the 20th percentile (as is often the case for intensive intervention students). This means that if the average posttest score for students who did *not* receive intervention is 85, then the mean posttest score for students who did receive the intervention is 100. An effect size of 1.0 standard deviation is large. Generally, effect sizes of 0.25 standard deviation indicate an intervention has value in improving outcomes. Effect sizes of 0.35–0.40 are moderate; effect sizes of 0.50–0.70 are strong.

Ms. Kubek used the NCII Tools Chart to search for a validated program for Giselle's intensive intervention platform and to note the effect size reported with her choice (*https://charts.intensiveintervention.org/aintervention*). Based on the Tools Chart, Ms. Kubek noticed that the average effect size for the kindergarten-level mathematics intervention ROOTS (Whole Number Foundations Level K; Clarke et al., 2015), disaggregated for students who began the intervention below the 20th percentile in mathematics, was 0.34, suggesting this intervention has value in improving mathematics outcomes for kindergarten students with academic difficulty.

Ms. Kubek decided to look closer at ROOTS. She read the information describing ROOTS on the NCII website carefully and contacted the developers of the intervention to obtain more information, including a curriculum sample and materials list. She also read about the scientific evaluation the authors conducted to develop the intervention, as published in a peer-reviewed journal. Based on her information, Ms. Kubek learned that ROOTS is a 50-lesson kindergarten intervention program designed to develop conceptual understanding and procedural fluency with whole-number concepts and vocabulary across approximately 20 weeks. She discovered that the manual for the intervention includes scripted lessons using an explicit and systematic approach to provide instruction. Specific areas of instruction include counting and cardinality, number operations of addition and subtraction, and place value; Ms. Kubek realized these targeted foci of instruction aligned well with Giselle's areas of deficit. ROOTS is supplemental to core classroom instruction, is meant to be delivered in small groups of five students, lasts approximately 20 minutes per session, and does not demand prerequisite skills prior to the start of intervention. Armed with this information, Ms. Kubek began to note her findings on the Taxonomy of Intensive Intervention Form (see Figure 3.3). She awarded ROOTS a score of 2 for Strength, given the reported average effect size of 0.34 (each dimension is scored from 0 to 3, to reflect how well the intervention addresses each dimension).

Ms. Kubek still had six dimensions to consider. The taxonomy's second dimension for selecting the intensive intervention platform is the *dosage* of the intervention, or the number of opportunities a student has to respond and receive corrective feedback. This is influenced in various ways: the size of the instructional group, the number of minutes each session lasts, or the number of sessions per week the intervention is delivered,

TAXONOMY OF INTENSIVE INTERVENTION FORM

Student Name: _Giselle_

Intensive Intervention Platform: _ROOTS (Whole Number Foundations Level K)_

Taxonomy Dimension	IIP	ADJ 1	ADJ 2	Notes
1. Strength	2	■	■	Notes:
2. Dosage	3	NC	NC	Notes: IIP: before intensive intervention, increased dosage to 1:1 (ROOTS is intended to be 5:1)
3. Alignment	2			Notes:
4. Attention to Transfer	3	+	NC	Notes: Adj 1 (Wk 4): added 5 min of counting objects in class; making small marks when counting objects on paper; Adj 2 (Wk 10): added 5 min of word problem practice
5. Complexity	3	NC	NC	Notes:
6. Behavioral Support	2	+		Notes: Adj 1 (Wk 4): introduced a star chart to earn points for increasing verbal responses; Adj 2 (Wk 10): altered behavior chart to earn points for generating story problems
7. Individualization	■			Notes: Adj 1 (Wk 4): struggling with 1:1 correspondence, hesitant to speak out loud; Adj 2 (Wk 10): difficulty understanding concepts of add/subtract

LEGEND

Rating Schedule:

IIP — Teacher analyzes potentially suitable interventions *before* implementation.

ADJ 1 — Instructional Adjustment 1: Teacher reanalyzes intervention because student is making inadequate progress and requires individualization.

ADJ 2 — Instructional Adjustment 2: Teacher reanalyzes intervention because student is making inadequate progress and requires individualization.

Coding Scale for Dimensions 1–6:

0 Fails to address standards

1 Addresses standards minimally

2 Addresses standards moderately

3 Addresses standards well

FIGURE 3.3. Completed Taxonomy of Intensive Intervention Form for Giselle using ROOTS (Clarke et al., 2015) as the intensive intervention platform (IIP). ADJ 1 is Ms. Kubek's first adjustment to the platform; ADJ 2 is her second adjustment. Note that strength is based on studies conducted on groups of children. It does not consider Giselle specifically. Therefore, this dimension is relevant only prior to the beginning of intervention implementation. Plus signs denote that a dimension of the taxonomy was adjusted at that time. NC denotes no change.

for example. Ms. Kubek had two sample lessons of the curriculum obtained from the website, one from a lesson near the beginning of instruction and one from a lesson near the end. To determine an estimate of the dosage Giselle would receive, Ms. Kubek read carefully through the two scripts and counted how many opportunities a single student (not all students) has to respond and receive corrective feedback during the course of a lesson.

Ms. Kubek found that there are more than 50 opportunities for students to respond in a sample 20-minute session; however, since ROOTS is meant to be delivered in a small group of up to five students, that reduces greatly the number of opportunities a single student would have to respond. Since Ms. Kubek planned to deliver the instruction individually to Giselle, that is, one-on-one, the response opportunities increase accordingly and she rated this dimension a score of 3 on the taxonomy form. She noted her intention to increase dosage from the standard 5:1 (i.e., an instructional grouping ratio of five students to one teacher) to an intensive 1:1 in the "Notes" section and indicated with a plus mark (+) on the dosage row in the first column that the platform was adjusted to reflect this increase prior to implementation.

The third dimension of intervention intensity is *alignment*. This reflects the extent to which the intervention (1) addresses the student's full set of academic deficits, (2) does not address skills the target student has already mastered (except while engaged in cumulative and meaningful review), and (3) focuses on grade-appropriate curricular standards. Ms. Kubek understood that alignment is a vital factor to consider. Selecting an intervention platform that aligns well with a student's specific learning needs serves to maximize the likelihood of remediating deficits while minimizing the need to make multiple adjustments to the intensive intervention platform.

To grade ROOTS on alignment, Ms. Kubek referred to the school's study team evaluation (describing Giselle's mathematics deficits as including number recognition, one-to-one correspondence, cardinality, and basic operations) and examined information from the program developer to note how closely the two intersected and how well the program addressed the kindergarten mathematics Common Core State Standards for Mathematics (CCSSM; National Governors Association [NGA] Center for Best Practices & Council of Chief State School Officers [CCSSO], 2010). Because the program developers include a chart detailing the scope and sequence of the lessons and noting which specific CCSSM are included in each lesson, it was clear to Ms. Kubek that this program aligned tightly with both Giselle's demonstrated need and the school's grade-level mathematics standards. Notably, the intervention platform seems to be influenced strongly by standards from the CCSSM domains of Counting and Cardinality and Operations and Algebraic Thinking, two major areas of developmental need for Giselle. Ms. Kubek awarded Alignment a score of 2 and continued to the next taxonomy dimension.

Attention to transfer is the fourth dimension of intervention intensity. This refers to the extent to which an intervention is systematically designed to help students transfer the skills they learn to other formats and contexts. It also refers to the extent to which an intervention helps students make connections between known and novel (but related) skills, which are required to produce meaningful transfer. Ms. Kubek judged ROOTS to provide a moderate (not strong) focus on explicitly teaching for transfer; based on the sample lessons she has obtained from the program developer, it was not clear how the skills taught during intervention (e.g., using number lines and connecting cubes to work on counting and cardinality) would be explicitly taught to apply to other settings in everyday life or to transfer to related but untaught skills. Ms. Kubek noted this may be an area in which she might intensify the intervention on Giselle's behalf.

Ms. Kubek moves to the fifth dimension of intervention intensity: *complexity*. Complexity reflects the number of explicit instruction principles the intervention incorporates. Strong evidence suggests that explicit instruction provides better response among intensive intervention students (for syntheses in mathematics and reading, see Gersten et al., 2009; Vaughn, Gersten, & Chard, 2000). Explicit instructional principles include the following: (1) providing explanations in simple, direct language; (2) modeling efficient strategies; (3) ensuring students have the necessary background knowledge and skills to succeed with these strategies; (4) gradually fading support for students' correct execution of strategies; (5) providing practice so students have multiple opportunities to generate many correct responses; and (6) incorporating systematic cumulative review.

Ms. Kubek carefully read the sample lessons provided by the program developer and identified each occasion where ROOTS incorporates these explicit instructional principles. For example, she made a mark in the margin of the lesson script for every teacher-led explanation that is simple and direct (rather than complex or indirect), and she marked every occasion where strategies students are expected to learn are clear and provide efficient routes to a correct solution (rather than inefficient or ambiguous strategies). She found that ROOTS relies exclusively on principles of explicit instruction and awarded complexity a score of 3 on the taxonomy form.

The sixth dimension of intervention intensity is *behavioral support*. Many students with significant academic difficulty struggle with attention, motivation, and self-regulation of on-task behavior, which further impedes their academic progress (e.g., Montague, 2007; Schunk & Zimmerman, 2011). Interventions that incorporate *executive function* components (i.e., neurologically based skills that involve and integrate mental control and self-regulation) are more intensive than programs that do not incorporate such components. The goal for special educators is to encourage students to work hard and persevere through difficult academic tasks, to self-reflect, and to question if something does not make sense. Many students with academic difficulty require systematic encouragement and support for learning this type of noncognitive academic mindset. Thus, the behavioral support dimension of intervention intensity reflects the extent to which interventions incorporate this focus and systematically support students' skill with this mindset.

At the same time, some intervention students exhibit noncompliant behaviors that impede learning. This may include, for example, refusing to respond (or speaking too softly to be heard), disrupting intervention sessions (by constantly speaking off-topic or refusing to sit still), or distracting other students. Therefore, the behavioral support dimension also reflects the extent to which the intervention platform incorporates principles to minimize or diminish nonproductive behaviors, even as it encourages productive ones. Ms. Kubek awarded a score of 2 for ROOTS with respect to behavioral support. From what she could tell from her perusal of the materials, executive function and behavior management components are included. She was concerned, however, that these supports might not be sufficient to address Giselle's needs and notes that this dimension (along with attention to transfer) may require an adjustment.

Ms. Kubek acknowledged that with respect to these first six dimensions, most standard intervention programs score higher on some than other dimensions. In this situation, for example, she judged ROOTS to score higher in complexity and alignment than attention to transfer and behavioral support. Understanding the program's strengths and weaknesses according to the taxonomy's dimensions, along with the target student's skills and deficits, helped Ms. Kubek judge this intervention for its utility as an intensive intervention platform for Giselle. Based on her analysis of the taxonomy's first six dimensions, Ms. Kubek selected ROOTS as Giselle's intensive intervention platform. Her school district purchased a site license and manual directly from the program developer, using the link found on the NCII website, and the full program was immediately available for download to her school's computer server.

Ms. Kubek had already initiated consideration of the seventh dimension, *individualization,* when she identified the progress monitoring system (KM-CBM) to use to track Giselle's response to the platform. Once Ms. Kubek began implementing ROOTS with Giselle, she routinely collected progress monitoring data with KM-CBM and applied validated DBI decision rules on a regular basis to determine if the intervention was producing adequate response for Giselle. Whenever the data indicated (via 4 consecutive data points below the goal line on the graph) that Giselle was not on track to meet her year-end goal, Ms. Kubek adjusted the program in ways that extended or altered the intensive intervention platform.

The Implementation Stage

At this point, Ms. Kubek was ready to begin implementing Giselle's intervention. She continued to use the taxonomy and revisited the first six dimensions whenever Giselle's CBM data indicated that her response to instruction was not adequate. Each time Ms. Kubek made an adjustment to the intensive intervention platform, she altered the taxonomy form to indicate what the adjustment addressed and what week it occurred. Prior to implementation, Ms. Kubek planned two changes to intensify the instructional design and delivery of intervention: (1) increase dosage from the standard 5:1 to 1:1 instruction and (2) collect progress monitoring data on a weekly basis instead of every 2 weeks.

She then used the DBI process, in conjunction with the taxonomy, to individualize Giselle's program. Ms. Kubek administered the first CBM immediately prior to conducting ROOTS sessions and continued to administer an alternate from, graphing the resultant data, each Friday (see Figure 3.2). After Week 3, Ms. Kubek applied decision rules to the graphed data, which indicated Giselle's progress was not satisfactory. At this point, Giselle had 4 data points below the goal line, warranting a need for instructional change. As shown in Figure 3.2, during the first weeks of ROOTS tutoring, Giselle's performance increased from only 0 points to 1 point correct, clearly not mastering any of the problem types (the bottom half of Figure 3.2 shows the skills profile, documenting

Giselle's mastery of counting stars, adding stars, subtracting stars, addition facts, and subtraction facts). Ms. Kubek indicated proportion of mastery for the five problem types for each week below the graph; since each problem type has five items on a form, 20% indicates one item correct (of five), 40% indicates two problems correct, and so on.

After careful analysis of Giselle's performance during tutoring, and of her CBM graph and skills analysis, and given her initial concerns about the ROOTS platform (see Figure 3.3, IIP column), Ms. Kubek decided that the taxonomy dimensions appropriate for adjustment and individualization were attention to transfer and behavioral support. In the Adjustment 1 (ADJ 1) column, Ms. Kubek made a plus mark (+) to indicate further intensification for those two dimensions; she wrote NC for *no change* for the remaining dimensions. In the Individualization row, she briefly summarized Giselle's difficulties, and in the Notes boxes she indicated the changes she made.

In terms of attention to transfer, Ms. Kubek judged that Giselle lacked one-to-one correspondence when counting. She often double-counted objects when counting a group of items or skipped an item altogether; this happened when counting physical objects (such as linking cubes) and abstract symbols on worksheets. Ms. Kubek also noted that Giselle was erroneous in her belief that only like objects could be grouped together and counted; the emphasis in ROOTS sessions on practicing counting exclusively using linking cubes may have contributed to this misunderstanding. She therefore added 5 minutes of transfer counting practice to each session. Ms. Kubek had Giselle gather small items from the classroom (e.g., pencils, dry-erase markers, plastic linking chains), assemble them in a group of mixed objects, and count each one. She had Giselle physically touch and move an item from its original position on the table to remind her which objects have and have not been counted. Likewise, when counting symbols on a worksheet (pictures of houses or dogs), she had Giselle use her pencil to make a small mark next to each item, once it had been counted.

In terms of behavioral support, Ms. Kubek noted that Giselle needs encouragement to speak out loud. Although Giselle knows and is able to use English, it is not the language spoken in her home, and she often prefers to communicate nonverbally (i.e., with gestures), rather than verbally. This made it difficult for Ms. Kubek to know when Giselle did not understand a lesson component, or to pinpoint Giselle's counting errors. Therefore, Ms. Kubek created a star chart and awarded Giselle stickers to place on her chart when she responded verbally to Ms. Kubek's instructions to do so. To mark the point in the program that these adjustments were made, Ms. Kubek drew a strong dark vertical mark on Giselle's graph after Week 3 (see Figure 3.2).

As shown in the graph, Giselle's overall CBM score level increased over the next several weeks in response to this adjustment to the platform, and her skills profile indicated an improvement with counting and cardinality. However, the rate of Giselle's developmental trajectory was not adequate to reach her end-of-year goal, as evidenced by another 4 consecutive data points below the line (i.e., Weeks 7, 8, 9, and 10). Ms. Kubek returned to her taxonomy form, examined Giselle's CBM data and skills profile, and considered Giselle's performance in ROOTS tutoring sessions.

Again, Ms. Kubek judged that the intervention platform was not providing sufficient opportunity for Giselle to transfer her burgeoning addition and subtraction skills to real-life events. Although Giselle's number recognition, counting, and cardinality skills had improved with the explicit instruction afforded by the carefully sequenced lessons and activities, showing an increase in procedural skills of rote and rational counting, Giselle continued to struggle with conceptual understanding of addition and subtraction, particularly when presented in short word problems. Ms. Kubek therefore introduced a second adjustment to the intensive intervention platform (see ADJ 2 on Figure 3.3), again with respect to the dimensions of attention to transfer and behavioral support.

With this second adjustment, Ms. Kubek added 5 minutes to each lesson in order to allow Giselle opportunities to create and role-play simple addition and subtraction word problems, using concrete objects. Because of Giselle's reluctance to speak, Ms. Kubek altered the star chart to award points for increased student discourse. That is, Giselle earned points on her chart for verbalizing word problems that she generated on her own. With this second adjustment to the platform, Giselle's slope of improvement became steeper and her skills profile indicated continued progress toward mastery of all five problem types. (See Figure 3.4 for a reproducible Taxonomy of Intensive Intervention Form.)

Conclusion

Giselle's case study illustrates how a special educator uses the DBI process, in conjunction with the taxonomy of intervention intensity, to individualize and intensify instruction for a student with academic difficulty. Thoughtful evaluation and deliberation when selecting an intensive intervention platform and an appropriate progress monitoring system; adhering to high fidelity of implementation of the platform as well as the progress monitoring system; and continuing to reflect, react, and revise while administering the intervention ensures the best outcome for the student.

ACKNOWLEDGMENTS

Research described in this chapter was supported in part by Grant No. R324D130003 from the Institute of Education Sciences in the U.S. Department of Education to Vanderbilt University. The content is solely the responsibility of the authors and does not necessarily represent the official views of the Institute of Education Sciences and the U.S. Department of Education.

REFERENCES

Clarke, B., Doabler, C., Smolkowski, K., Kurtz Nelson, E., Fien, H., & Baker, S. K. (2015). Testing the immediate and long-term efficacy of a Tier 2 kindergarten mathematics intervention. *Journal of Research on Educational Effectiveness, 9*, 607–634.

Clements, D. H., & Sarama, J. (2007). Effects of a preschool mathematics curriculum: Summative research on the Building Blocks Project. *Journal for Research in Mathematics Education, 38*, 136.

TAXONOMY OF INTENSIVE INTERVENTION FORM

Student Name: _____

Intensive Intervention Platform: _____

Taxonomy Dimension	IIP	ADJ 1	ADJ 2	
1. Strength		■	■	Notes:
2. Dosage				Notes:
3. Alignment				Notes:
4. Attention to Transfer				Notes:
5. Complexity				Notes:
6. Behavioral Support				Notes:
7. Individualization	■			Notes:

LEGEND

Rating Schedule:

IIP — Teacher analyzes potentially suitable interventions *before* implementation.

ADJ 1 — Instructional Adjustment 1: Teacher reanalyzes intervention because student is making inadequate progress and requires individualization.

ADJ 2 — Instructional Adjustment 2: Teacher reanalyzes intervention because student is making inadequate progress and requires individualization.

Coding Scale for Dimensions 1–6:

0 — Fails to address standards

1 — Addresses standards minimally

2 — Addresses standards moderately

3 — Addresses standards well

FIGURE 3.4. Blank Taxonomy of Intensive Intervention Form.

Deno, S. L. (1985). Curriculum-based measurement: The emerging alternative. *Exceptional Children, 52,* 199–204.

Fuchs, D., Fuchs, L. S., & Compton, D. L. (2012). Smart RTI: A next-generation approach to multi-level prevention. *Exceptional Children, 78,* 263–279.

Fuchs, L. S., Fuchs, D., Compton, D. L., Powell, S. R., Seethaler, P. M., Capizzi, A. M., . . . Fletcher, J. M. (2006). The cognitive correlates of third-grade skill in arithmetic, algorithmic computation, and arithmetic word problems. *Journal of Educational Psychology, 98,* 29–43.

Fuchs, L. S., Fuchs, D., & Karns, K. (2001). Enhancing kindergarten children's mathematical development: Effects of peer-assisted learning strategies. *Elementary School Journal, 101,* 495–510.

Fuchs, L. S., Fuchs, D., & Malone, A. S. (2017). The taxonomy of intervention intensity. *TEACHING Exceptional Children, 50,* 35–43.

Fuchs, L. S., Fuchs, D., Yazdian, L., & Powell, S. R. (2002). Enhancing first-grade children's mathematical development with peer-assisted learning strategies. *School Psychology Review, 31,* 569–584.

Fuchs, L. S., Geary, D. C., Compton, D. L., Fuchs, D., Schatschneider, C., Hamlett, C. L., . . . Changas, P. (2013). Effects of first-grade number knowledge tutoring with contrasting forms of practice. *Journal of Educational Psychology, 105,* 58–77.

Geary, D. C. (1994). *Children's mathematical development: Research and practical applications.* Washington, DC: American Psychological Association.

Geary, D. C., Bow-Thomas, C. C., & Yao, Y. (1992). Counting knowledge and skill in cognitive addition: A comparison of normal and mathematically disabled children. *Journal of Experimental Child Psychology, 54,* 372–391.

Geary, D., & van Marle, K. (2018). Growth of symbolic number knowledge accelerates after children understand cardinality. *Cognition, 177,* 69–78.

Geary, D., van Marle, K., Chu, F., Rouder, J., Hoard, M., & Nugent, L. (2017). Early conceptual understanding of cardinality predicts superior school-entry system knowledge. *Psychological Science, 29,* 191–205.

Gelman, R., & Gallistel, C. (1978). *The child's understanding of number.* New York: Springer-Verlag.

Gersten, R., Chard, D. J., Jayanthi, M., Baker, S. K., Morphy, P., & Flojo, J. (2009). Mathematics instruction for students with learning disabilities: A meta-analysis of instructional components. *Review of Educational Research, 79,* 1202–1242.

Griffin, S. A., Case, R., & Siegler, R. S. (1994). Rightstart: Providing the central conceptual prerequisite for first formal learning of arithmetic to students at risk for school failure. In K. McGilly (Ed.), *Classroom lessons: Integrating cognitive theory and classroom practice* (pp. 25–50). Cambridge, MA: MIT Press.

McLaughlin, M. W., Shepard, L. A., & O'Day, J. A. (1995). *Improving education through standards-based reform.* Report by the National Academy of Education Panel on Standards-Based Education Reform. Washington, DC: National Academy of Education.

Montague, M. (2007). Self-regulation and mathematics instruction. *Learning Disabilities Research and Practice, 22,* 75–83.

National Center on Intensive Intervention (NCII). (2018). NCII's approach to intensive intervention is data-based individualization or DBI. Retrieved from *https://intensiveintervention.org/intensive-intervention.*

National Governors Association (NGA) Center for Best Practices & Council of Chief State School Officers (CCSSO). (2010). *Common Core State Standards for mathematics.* Washington, DC: Authors. Retrieved from *www.corestandards.org/the-standards/mathematics.*

Schunk, D. H., & Zimmerman, B. (Eds.). (2011). *Handbook of self-regulation of learning and performance*. New York: Routledge.

Seethaler, P. M., & Fuchs, L. S. (2011). Using curriculum-based measurement to monitor kindergarteners' mathematics development. *Assessment for Effective Intervention, 16,* 210–219.

Stecker, P. M., Fuchs, L. S., & Fuchs, D. (2005). Using curriculum-based measurement to improve student achievement: Review of research. *Psychology in the Schools, 42,* 795–820.

Swanson, H. L., & Beebe-Frankenberger, M. (2004). The relationship between working memory and mathematical problem solving in children at risk and not at risk for serious mathematics difficulties. *Journal of Educational Psychology, 96,* 471–491.

Vaughn, S., Gersten, R., & Chard, D. (2000). The underlying message in LD intervention research: Findings from research syntheses. *Exceptional Children, 67,* 99–114.

CHAPTER 4

Intensifying Early Numeracy Interventions

BENJAMIN S. CLARKE, CHRISTIAN T. DOABLER, MARAH SUTHERLAND,
MARISSA P. SUHR, and ELISHEBA W. KIRU

LEARNING OUTCOMES

After studying this chapter, you will be able to answer the following questions:

1. What are the critical concepts of early numeracy?
2. What is a recommended way to teach mathematics?

Developing a strong foundation in early mathematics is widely understood to be a critical goal of the beginning grades (Frye et al., 2013). Despite the de facto recognition of the importance of a successful start in early mathematics, schools are faced with challenges from the start of formal schooling. First, early childhood educators face the difficult task of teaching students entering the classroom with widely disparate levels of mathematical knowledge and skill. Children from low socioeconomic status (SES) households enter kindergarten with less mathematical readiness and knowledge compared to their peers from middle- and high-SES backgrounds (e.g., Ehrlich & Levine, 2007; Klibanoff, Levine, Huttenlocher, Vasilyeva, & Hedges, 2006), and mathematics knowledge at school entry strongly predicts mathematics achievement in the later grades (Duncan et al., 2007). Thus, students who are disadvantaged upon entering kindergarten and do not receive high-quality mathematics instruction and support may continue to experience lower mathematics achievement throughout their early education. The result of exiting kindergarten and first grade at risk leads to a mathematics opportunity gap that continues to manifest in the later elementary grades as large numbers of students, including those from disadvantaged backgrounds, students with disabilities, and English language learners, fail to achieve at desired or even basic levels (National Assessment of Educational Progress, 2015).

The second challenge facing schools is that they are often structured to support student achievement in reading (Clarke et al., 2014) through mandated instructional time blocks, an array of intervention programs and assessments, and staffing (e.g., reading coaches). Whether due to the amount of finite resources available or other reasons, the same level of support is not found in mathematics (La Paro et al., 2009). Considering that students who struggle in mathematics often have comorbid difficulties in reading and other areas (Landerl & Moll, 2010), schools and teachers face a tyranny of time and potentially limited resources in deciding how best to develop mathematical understanding within multi-tiered systems of support (MTSS) where students are provided an intensifying degree of support at each successive tier of instruction. Despite these challenges, the field has made significant advances that can guide efforts to improve early mathematics achievement (Gersten et al., 2009; National Mathematics Advisory Panel, 2008). Through the remainder of this chapter, we focus on three key areas that should form the foundation of efforts to ensure that all children have a successful start in early mathematics. Collectively these areas of focus will aid in deciding what content to teach, how to teach that content, and how to use assessment to aid in instructional decision making.

Critical Concepts of Early Numeracy

Mathematics curriculum in the United States has commonly been criticized for being "a mile wide and an inch deep" (Schmidt & Houang, 2007). In other words, teachers are asked to cover a vast number of topics, without going into depth and developing concrete understanding of mathematical ideas for learners. This leaves students—particularly those entering kindergarten with less mathematical knowledge—at risk for not receiving sufficient exposure and fully developing an understanding of the most critical concepts of number, including a strong understanding of relations among numbers and ability to manipulate numbers to solve mathematical problems. Often loosely termed "number sense" (Gersten & Chard, 1999), instruction in the early elementary grades should be targeted toward developing a deep understanding of numbers. Consequently, teachers must be knowledgeable about the critical concepts of early numeracy to ensure that fundamental skills are taught early on to help struggling learners succeed. In the following section, we detail the critical big ideas of early numeracy that should form the cornerstone of intervention support and programs.

Counting and Cardinality

One of the earliest and most critical mathematical objectives taught in kindergarten is understanding of counting and cardinality. Hudson and Miller (2006) describe counting as "one of the most important components of developing number sense" (p. 171). Counting is the first formal introduction to number and sets the foundation for many of the mathematical skills that children must master in grades K–2. For example, children use counting and their understanding of cardinality to solve simple addition and subtraction problems (e.g., in solving 4 + 3, a student may start with four and count up three more to reach an answer of 7). Understanding of counting and cardinality also sets the stage for other operations such as mastering multiplication and division in the later grades.

Because of the connections between counting and cardinality and mastery of later skills, the importance of developing strong skills in counting and cardinality cannot be understated. Fortunately, young children can use counting to answer interesting questions that are relevant to their worlds, such as how many cookies they get after dinner or how many fingers and toes they have. Teachers should capitalize on this natural curiosity and excitement about number and emphasize the usefulness of counting by using multiple real-world examples when introducing concepts in their classrooms (Hudson & Miller, 2006).

The first major milestone toward counting and cardinality is learning the number list from 1 to 10. Often students entering kindergarten are already able to list numbers from 1 to 10, as children typically begin to develop this skill around the age of 2–3 (Clements & Sarama, 2004). Knowledge of the counting numbers depends greatly on early child environment, however, and teachers must remember that children enter the classroom with varying amounts of exposure to the number list. Teachers can support development of learning the initial number list from 1 to 10 in a number of ways. Students learn to recite the numbers 1–10 by memorizing and reciting the numbers in order—similar to the way the alphabet is first memorized in early childhood. Because students are reciting a string of words, teachers should emphasize that each number word represents a single number. This can be taught by clapping with each number or touching written numerals as students recite the number list to develop understanding that each number word represents a single number (Clements & Sarama, 2004).

These early skills form the basis for *rote counting*, where students recite the number list aloud from memory. As children begin to rote count, they may or may not be aware of certain rules about the counting numbers. For example, children must learn that there is a set order to the number list (e.g., 3 always comes before 4, and 5 always comes after it). In early counting, teachers can detect understanding of the stable order of the number list even if students recite an inaccurate number list, as long as it is consistent (Gelman & Gallistel, 1978). Helping students learn the accurate number list and emphasizing each number's unique placement in the list will help students begin to form a mental number line as they internalize the order of the counting numbers. Having a mental number line helps students later when they are asked to do more advanced tasks such as comparing numbers (e.g., greater than/less than), or performing simple addition and subtraction problems. Learning the number list has payoff in the short term too because it leads into the skill of counting objects. Teachers should ensure that students are fluent rote counters before moving them on to counting objects, as students need to be able to allocate attention not only to saying the counting numbers but also to touching or moving objects as they count (Cross, Woods, & Schweingruber, 2009).

To count objects, students must understand the concept of *one-to-one correspondence*, where each number in the number list is matched to a single, counted object. Here, having emphasized each individual number when teaching the number list (e.g., by clapping or touching each number as students count) will allow students to make the connection more clearly between distinct numbers in the number list and individual objects. Although as adults and teachers we view counting objects as a simple task for a student entering kindergarten, without prior exposure to counting, learning these principles can be difficult. Teachers will need to closely monitor student counting and provide models and corrective feedback as students apply beginning counting principles. Common errors when learning one-to-one correspondence that teachers should watch for include double-counting an object, skipping over an object, or failing to stop counting on the last object (Cross et al., 2009).

The most critical connection students must make when learning to count objects is that the last number counted represents the total number of items in the group (Clements & Sarama, 2004). Making this connection leads to understanding the transition from counting numbers to *cardinal numbers,* which are used to represent the quantity in a collection of items. Students who have not mastered this concept may believe the answer to a question such as "How many tokens are there?" is the physical act of counting the tokens (e.g., "1, 2, 3, 4, 5") instead of saying the cardinal number representing the total number of tokens (e.g., "5"; Wynn, 1990). Making the connection between counting and cardinality is a powerful step for the student as it converts the counting numbers, which are inherently abstract, into meaningful entities that provide information about the amount in a group (e.g., 6 could stand for 6 toy cars, or represent 6 marshmallows). Teachers should ensure students master this concept in kindergarten (K.CC.4; Common Core State Standards for Mathematics [CCSSM]; National Governors Association [NGA] Center for Best Practices & Council of Chief State School Officers [CCSSO], 2010).

Once students have learned to connect the number list and cardinality, patterns residing within the counting numbers should be made explicit for students. Teachers can support student development by intentionally linking their understanding of counting to more advanced work, including beginning to solve simple addition and subtraction problems (Cross et al., 2009). For example, students learn that each successive counting number represents the quantity that is one more than the number just counted (e.g., 6 is one more than 5, 7 is one more than 6). Teachers should explicitly teach this pattern to students, as it will help them when they begin to solve simple addition problems such as +1 facts (e.g., 5 + 1). These patterns should also be emphasized for subtraction problems. For example, when counting, the number said previously is one less than the number just counted, leading into eventual solving of –1 facts (e.g., 3 – 1, 9 – 1). Placing special focus on these patterns provides a "double whammy" effect for students, as it not only helps solidify the number list and where numbers fall on their mental number line but also equips students with the knowledge of how to solve several basic facts when they are first introduced in the classroom (e.g., 2 + 1, 3 – 1).

Along with using existing patterns in the number list to solve simple addition and subtraction problems, teachers should support students in using increasingly advanced counting strategies to solve other addition and subtraction problems. In kindergarten, teachers should have students use their counting skills to solve problems such as 5 + 2 by counting out a group of five objects and a group of two objects, and then combining the groups and counting the total number of objects all together (K.OA; NGA & CCSSO, 2010). This strategy is referred to as "counting all." Having students initially use manipulatives to represent and solve mathematical problems creates a deeper understanding of what is happening mathematically when given addition and subtraction problems. Eventually, teachers should fade these tools out, but only after conceptual understanding of addition as "adding together," and subtraction as "taking away," has been developed.

Once students have mastered "counting all" and demonstrated concrete understanding of addition and subtraction, teachers can introduce the more efficient strategy of "counting on." This skill is typically introduced in grade 1 (1.OA; NGA & CCSSO, 2010). Here, instead of counting out each addend individually and then counting the group as a whole, students are taught to count starting on the first number and then counting up to the value of the second number to reach their answer. For example, given the problem "5 + 2," students learn to start their count on five and count up two more (e.g., a student would count "five, six, seven!"). Teachers should encourage the use of fingers or other counting tools to help students keep track of the second addend.

Depending on exposure to counting strategies at home, some students may easily pick up on these types of advanced counting strategies, while other students will need targeted support to master this strategy. Additionally, students with mathematics learning disabilities often rely on simpler, less efficient strategies to solve addition and subtraction problems instead of progressing to more advanced strategies such as counting on (Geary, 1990). These students will need additional teacher modeling and guided practice on how to perform these procedures. Encouraging transition strategies, such as having students quickly and quietly count up to the first addend (e.g., given 5 + 2, saying "one-two-three-four-five, six, seven!") can help ease the shift from counting all to counting on (Cross et al., 2009). Teachers should also provide additional practice with rote counting starting from numbers other than 1 (e.g., having students count up to 8, starting with 3) so that counting starting from a given number becomes more fluid for students (Hudson & Miller, 2006). Teachers should support student use of counting up to solve subtraction problems as well, which results in fewer errors than counting backward.

Once students become proficient with counting on, they can be taught additional strategies to increase efficiency. For example, teachers should show students that two numbers may be added in any order to produce the same answer, also known as the *commutative property of addition*. Students can use this rule to rearrange addends in a problem for more efficient problem solving. For example, when counting on, teachers should encourage students to start with the larger addend (whether it is the first or second addend in the problem) and count on from there for greater efficiency. In the problem 2 + 8, instead of starting with 2 and counting 8 more, teachers should encourage students to use the commutative property of addition to switch the numbers around—starting with 8 and counting two more. Using these strategies may not be initially obvious to students. Teachers should explicitly introduce them to students, provide teacher modeling, and then provide guided practice until students are able to use the strategies independently.

Manipulating numbers to make problems easier to solve, such as switching around the addends to solve an addition fact more easily, is a complex skill for students to learn and necessitates a deep conceptual understanding of number. Successful use of such strategies indicates continued development of number sense. Counting and cardinality forms the foundation for making these types of number manipulations; however, deeper understanding of number is realized with base-ten understanding. We describe this in the next section.

Base-Ten Understanding

Understanding our number system—known as the base-ten numeration system—adds significantly to the development of number sense and should be emphasized in core instruction and early intervention programs. In combination with counting and cardinality, base-ten understanding gives students new ways to think about number and leads to more advanced mathematics such as working with multidigit numbers. Building concrete understanding of the base-ten system for students presents a difficult task for teachers. In the following section, we describe the base-ten system and provide suggestions for how teachers can facilitate base-ten understanding for their students and help students use this knowledge to progress in their mathematical skill.

The base-ten system provides a way for people to represent an infinite amount of numbers by stringing together only 10 digits: 0, 1, 2, 3, 4, 5, 6, 7, 8, and 9. The 10 digits we use to represent values 0–9 are completely arbitrary—we could represent these values using different words or symbols and still operate using the same base-ten system (Cross et al., 2009). The heart of the base-ten system relies upon "repeated bundling by ten," using the 10 digits identified earlier (K.NBT 5; Common Core Standards Writing Team [CCSWT], 2015, p. 2). For example, 10 ones make a group known as a "ten," 10 "ten" groups make a group called a "hundred," 10 "hundred" groups make a new group known as a "thousand," and so on. This results in predictable relationships between numbers (K.NBT 5; CCSWT, 2015).

Base-ten understanding is critical for students to master so that they are aware of the structure of our number system. In teaching base-ten understanding, teachers should first help students to learn that numbers can be decomposed into smaller numbers and smaller numbers can be put together to make new numbers (i.e., compose). Manipulating numbers in this way is a key skill for establishing number sense and, as described in Chapter 9, leads to the development of algebraic reasoning. Teachers should introduce this skill in kindergarten by first teaching the number partners that add to five (e.g., 2 + 3), and then to ten (1 + 9, 2 + 8, etc.; K.NBT 5; CCSWT, 2015). By emphasizing how a single number has different number partners, teachers can help students understand the different ways in which numbers can be composed and decomposed. Teachers can build this skill by having students find the number partners of a given number using manipulatives and sorting them into different groups (e.g., having students divide a group of 5 objects into various groups, such as 1 and 4, 2 and 3).

Once students are familiar with the number partners up to 10, teachers should provide additional practice by having students decompose 10 into number combinations.

Students should be asked to provide the addend that makes 10 when given a single-digit number (e.g., "6 and what number equal 10?"). Learning to make a 10 is essential because it helps students transform unknown mathematical problems into more solvable ones, using strategies such as the make-a-ten strategy (National Research Council [NRC], 2001). This strategy relies upon students decomposing and recomposing numbers in a problem to form a 10, leading to forming an easier addition or subtraction problem. For example, if students are given the problem 7 + 5, they might pull from their knowledge of forming a 10 that 7 and three more make 10. They would decompose the 5 into 3 and 2, add the 3 to the 7 to make 10, and then add the remaining 2 to 10 to make 12. This type of mathematical thinking takes time and practice. Teachers should model various ways to think about solving problems and encourage students to talk aloud about strategies they use to promote flexible problem solving.

The next step toward developing base-ten understanding is teaching *place value*, which refers to the numerical value that a digit has because of its position in a number. The beginning of place value understanding comes with having students learn to count collections making groups of tens and then groups of tens with some ones left over. This is a critical skill addressed in the CCSSM and should be introduced in kindergarten (K.NBT; CCSWT, 2015). Initially, students must learn that two-digit numbers are composed of a ten and some amount of ones. Teachers can use a variety of tools to help solidify these concepts for students, such as place value cards, number families of 10 numbers containing 10, and five and ten frames (see Figures 4.1 and 4.2; K.NBT; CCSWT, 2015). Eventually, as students learn other two-digit numbers, teachers should have students practice representing these numbers as tens and ones (e.g., 47 = four tens and seven ones). As students learn to master this skill, teachers should ensure that students have practice writing and aligning single- and two-digit numbers in their respective place value columns to set them up for success when multidigit addition and subtraction are introduced (Hudson & Miller, 2006).

Practice with forming groups of "10" and working with place value should ultimately allow students to see 10 ones as comprising a group of "10" and that a group of "10" is equal to 10 ones. This flexibility on forming and breaking apart groups of 10 lays the foundation for later understanding that 10 "10" groups equals 100, introduced in grade 2 (NGA & CCSSO, 2010), and so on. Teachers can facilitate this understanding by having students use manipulatives, such as base-ten models, to compose and decompose numbers into groups of 10. Flexibility with forming a 10 and breaking it apart into 10 ones sets the foundation for solving multidigit addition and subtraction problems in grades 1 and 2.

As students move into working with three- and four-digit numbers, further understanding of the base-ten system comes from learning that numbers can be expressed as the number of ones, tens, hundreds, and thousands they possess. Thus, the number 2,491 can be expressed as 2 thousands, 4 hundreds, 9 tens, and 1 one. Teachers can support student learning of the base-ten form using place value charts and base-ten models. Teachers should also emphasize the relations between the place and value of numbers within the base-ten system. That is, place values to the left of the decimal point increase by powers of 10 (NGA & CCSSO, 2010).

Knowledge of the base-ten system provides students with a toolkit of strategies to solve more advanced addition and subtraction problems. Understanding relations between number decades (e.g., each successive number decade is 10 more than the last) allows students to solve problems such as "What is 10 more than 24?" or "Tell me the number that is 10 less than 55." With a strong understanding of the relations between numbers, students can learn to answer these types of questions using mathematical reasoning instead of counting (NGA & CCSSO, 2010). Base-ten instruction may also be used to teach students how to compute within decades, and solve problems such as 50 + 20, or 60 – 30. Place value understanding allows students to compare two-digit numbers by first comparing the digit in the tens place and then (if necessary) the digit in the ones place to determine which quantity is greater (NGA & CCSSO, 2010). Accordingly, a solid grasp of the base-ten system contributes to more advanced understanding of number and sets students up for success as they encounter increasingly difficult problems.

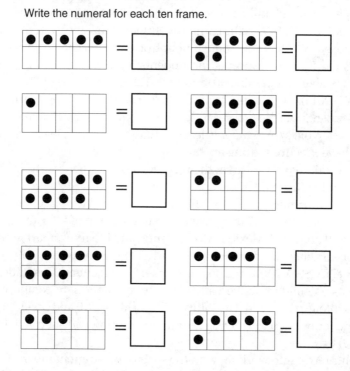

FIGURE 4.1. Practice with ten frames can support student learning of base-ten understanding in making a 5 or making a 10. Reprinted with permission from Whole Number Foundations Level K, University of Oregon Center on Teaching and Learning.

Count the models in each box starting with 10 for the ten-stick. Write the numeral for each model in the space below.

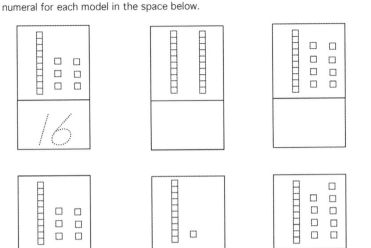

Trace and write the numerals from 15-20.

FIGURE 4.2. Having students work with representational models, such as pictures of base-ten blocks and unit cubes, can help develop understanding of place value and composing and decomposing numbers into tens and ones. Reprinted with permission from Whole Number Foundations Level K, University of Oregon Center on Teaching and Learning.

Operations and Algebraic Thinking

As described throughout this chapter, counting and cardinality and base-ten understanding are foundational areas, or domains, in the CCSSM that are critical for students to master. The final key early numeracy domain area in the CCSSM is *operations and algebraic thinking*, which includes initially the operations of addition and subtraction and later the operations of multiplication and division. Because of the generalization of procedures within the basic operations to more advanced mathematics, developing a strong foundation for problem solving with basic operations early on is key (NGA & CCSSO, 2010). This domain also includes applications of mathematical operations to word-problem solving. Word problems allow children to make meaningful connections between mathematics and real-world scenarios (NRC, 2001). Chapter 6, on whole-number operations, and Chapter 8, on word-problem-solving strategies, detail the developmental process by which students develop these skills and ways that teachers can support learners.

How to Teach: Explicit Mathematics Instruction

Although the content of mathematics interventions (i.e., what to teach) is critical, prioritizing concepts and skills of early numeracy alone is insufficient. Equally important for supporting mathematical proficiency among students with or at risk for mathematics difficulties (MD) is how mathematical content is delivered during instruction (i.e., how to teach). Within MTSS in mathematics, the *how to teach* can be used as a way in which to obtain an optimal level of instructional intensity. For example, in a three-tiered model, if a student does not adequately respond to Tier 1 instruction, the goal of Tier 2 is to deliver instruction at a more systematic, intensive level. A similar increase in intensity is conceptualized in moving from Tier 2 to Tier 3.

One instructional approach found important for intensifying mathematics instruction in MTSS is *explicit mathematics instruction*. A growing evidence base suggests the beneficial effects of explicit mathematics instruction for increasing mathematical learning for students with or at risk for MD. Over the past several decades, mathematics intervention studies have consistently demonstrated that students with or at risk for MD demonstrate greater gains in classrooms that provide explicit instruction compared to other instructional approaches. One recent meta-analysis has summarized much of this work.

In 2016, Dennis and colleagues conducted a meta-analysis of experimental and quasi-experimental studies on interventions for students with or at risk for mathematics learning disabilities (MLD) conducted between 2000 and 2014. A total of 25 interventions studies were analyzed based on five instructional approaches: (1) providing data and feedback on students' mathematics performance to teachers, (2) peer-assisted learning, (3) providing students with data and feedback on their mathematics performance, (4) explicit or contextualized teacher-facilitated instruction, and (5) computer-assisted instruction. Results suggested a large effect for interventions that employed an explicit instructional approach.

Although the operational definition of explicit mathematics instruction varies, there is consensus among experts that explicit mathematics instruction is a systematic methodology for effectively and efficiently teaching critical mathematical concepts and skills to mastery (Archer & Hughes, 2011; Gersten et al., 2009; Hughes, Morris, Therrien, & Benson, 2017). Moreover, there is agreement that explicit mathematics instruction comprises recurring instructional sequences that begin with the teacher demonstrating a learning objective centered on a critical mathematics concept or skill. Students then practice that objective through guided support from the teacher. As students gain initial proficiency with the objective, support is systematically withdrawn to increase opportunities for students to independently demonstrate what they have learned. When students make errors during independent practice, the teacher provides feedback to correct errors immediately and then resumes the instructional sequence, making sure to provide additional practice on the types of items that prove difficult for students.

The Instructional Design of Explicit Mathematics Interventions

The manner in which Tier 2 and Tier 3 mathematics interventions are engineered is integral for facilitating important instructional sequences on critical mathematics concepts and skills. When interventions are systematically designed, they offer *scaffolds* or instructional supports that help teachers break down complex tasks into more manageable chunks for struggling learners. The purpose of these supports is to help students obtain a high success rate with targeted mathematics content (Allsopp, Lovin, & van Ingen, 2017; Rosenshine, 2012).

To provide some context for how instructional scaffolding unfolds during explicit mathematics instruction, imagine an activity drawn from a first-grade Tier 2 mathematics intervention focused on teaching students how to decompose two-digit numbers into tens and ones. Because place value has important implications for understanding more complex mathematics (NGA & CCSSO, 2010), it is imperative that students develop a deep and lasting understanding of this foundational construct. However, research suggests that students with or at risk for MD often struggle with place value (Cawley, Parmar, Lucas-Fusco, Kilian, & Foley, 2007). Therefore, instructional scaffolding is necessary to promote mathematical proficiency. At a glance, this scaffolding would entail the following instructional sequence.

1. The teacher would begin instruction by explaining to the students that they are going to decompose two-digit numbers into tens and ones.
2. The teacher would then model for students several different two-digit numbers. For each two-digit number, the teacher would explicitly show and state how many tens and ones (e.g., "19 has 1 ten, and 9 ones").
3. The teacher would incorporate base-ten models in the demonstrations to build students' conceptual understanding and include different two-digit numbers to teach students how to recognize place value differences among a range of numbers.
4. Next, the teacher would have the students (group and individuals) verbally identify the place value of two-digit numbers.
5. For incorrect responses, the teacher would provide immediate corrective feedback to address the errors.

In the next sections, we provide a brief overview of three essential components of explicit instruction. These components include teacher modeling, student practice opportunities, and teacher-provided academic feedback.

Teacher Modeling

A hallmark of explicit instruction is teacher modeling. Teacher models entail teachers clearly explaining the purpose of mathematics activities and overtly demonstrating what students are expected to do during such activities. The purpose of explicit teacher modeling is to make new and complex mathematics content conspicuous to students (Archer & Hughes, 2011; Hughes et al., 2017). For instance, when decomposing numbers, a teacher can provide a student with an overt example for how to decompose 34 into tens and ones (i.e., 30 + 4).

Student Practice Opportunities

Another key component of explicit instruction is student practice opportunities. Research has found that student practice opportunities are essential for improving important mathematics outcomes (Doabler et al., 2015; Gersten et al., 2009). One important form of student practice opportunities focuses on developing students' automaticity of mathematical skills, such as solving number combinations or mathematical facts. When students develop automaticity or procedural fluency with mathematical skills, it allows them to free up working memory for solving complex problems and using efficient strategies (Rosenshine, 2012). Teachers can help students build procedural fluency with number combinations by incorporating activities such as flashcard practice and worksheet practice.

Another important form of practice opportunities involves students manipulating visual representations of mathematical ideas, such as number lines and base-ten blocks, through a concrete–representational–abstract (CRA) sequence of instruction. For instance, when learning how to decompose 34, a teacher will begin the lesson by using base-ten blocks (concrete). In this case, the teacher models decomposing using three tens and four cubes as one way to decompose the number concretely. Instruction then transitions to decomposing 34 using pictures (representation or semiconcrete) and eventually numerical symbols (abstract or symbolic). As noted in Chapter 1, this sequence is well researched in the field of special education. Another way to think about "concrete," "representational," and "abstract" is to consider these terms as multiple representations that can be used to model mathematics problems.

Student mathematics verbalizations represent another critical form of student practice. It is imperative for students to engage in mathematics discourse or "math talk" during instruction as this provides them with active learning opportunities to showcase their mathematical thinking and processing. Student mathematics verbalizations also facilitate opportunities for students to use mathematically precise language and vocabulary (Powell & Driver, 2015). Additionally, mathematics verbalizations allow teachers to identify student errors or underdeveloped mathematical ideas.

Using explicit instruction, teachers can prompt students to verbally respond as a group or individually. Individual response opportunities permit teachers to monitor an individual student's mathematical understanding and learning. Group responses provide multiple students the opportunity to simultaneously verbalize their mathematical thinking and allow the teacher to check for general understanding within the classroom. For instance, in small groups, teachers can incorporate cooperative learning strategies such as "turn and talk" to your partner activities. In these activities students engage in a brief mathematical conversation with their partner, sharing answers and discussing solution methods. Teachers can then have partner groups share their answers with the group at large.

Teacher-Provided Academic Feedback

Explicit instruction includes providing students with meaningful and timely feedback (Halpern et al., 2007). Similar to student mathematics verbalizations, feedback allows teachers to extend students' learning opportunities and help students circumnavigate known pitfalls or errors. For example, when working with two-digit numbers, a teacher may have a student compose 57 with base-ten blocks. Unfortunately, the student composes 57 using 7 tens and 5 ones. As the teacher listens to the student explain his reasoning, the teacher identifies the student's error and provides explanatory feedback on how to correctly compose 57. The teacher then has the student correctly repeat the task.

Additional Factors for Intensifying Mathematics Instruction

There are two factors for intensifying mathematics instruction. These factors include group size and instructional time.

Group Size

In addition to attending to the elements described earlier related to delivery of instruction, teachers can also intensify instruction through group size or the instructional format in which interventions are provided. In early literacy, researchers have begun to accumulate a strong body of evidence in favor of reducing group size to improve student reading achievement (Elbaum, Vaughn, Hughes, & Moody, 2000). Although research on instructional formats in the area of mathematics lags behind what has been established in early literacy, recent research has begun to shed light on the important role group size has in intensifying the teaching of critical mathematics concepts and skills.

For example, in a recent study involving nearly 600 kindergarten students with MD, Clarke and colleagues (2017) found two interesting findings about group size in the context of a Tier 2 kindergarten mathematics intervention. First, students who were randomly assigned to receive the intervention in groups with 5:1 student–teacher ratios performed commensurate to their at-risk peers who received the intervention in groups with 2:1 student–teacher ratios. In other words, the intervention's impact was essentially the same regardless of whether students participated in the 2:1 or 5:1 groups. A second interesting finding was that the number of practice opportunities that students received differed by group size. Students in the 2:1 intervention groups received more opportunities to practice on their own, and students in 5:1 intervention groups participated in more practice opportunities with their peers. Meanwhile, other studies have shown promise for increasing student outcomes by decreasing group size (Bryant, Bryant, Roberts, & Fall, 2016).

Instructional Time

Instructional time is another key factor in intensifying mathematics instruction. Over the years, special education researchers have focused on ways to intensify instruction by increasing factors of instructional time, such as the amount of time spent in each session and the number of days taught per week (Gersten et al., 2009). For example, Bryant and colleagues (2011) systematically increased the amount of instructional time across a series of mathematics intervention studies. In their most recent study, Bryant and colleagues found that increased intervention time was a decisive factor in improving the mathematics achievement of at-risk learners.

Although a growing body of research suggests that increased instructional time improves student mathematics achievement, important questions remain over how schools and teachers can capitalize on this extra time. Take, for example, a school that decides to increase Tier 2 mathematics instruction from 30 to 45 minutes. The school must decide on the type of content to teach during the additional 15 minutes. For example, should teachers use the extra time to introduce new concepts and skills? In this way, the 15 minutes would allow teachers to expand the breadth of content that students are exposed to in a given intervention time period. Another important question is whether teachers should use the 15 minutes to provide additional opportunities for students to independently practice with previously learned mathematical topics. Accumulating research indicates that distributed practice benefits long-term retention of academic content (Dunlosky, Rawson, Marsh, Nathan, & Willingham, 2013). In light of the various ways teachers can use extra instructional time and arrange small-group instruction, we suggest that future research is needed.

Assessment to Improve Instructional Decision Making

Effective mathematics content (i.e., what to teach) and instruction (i.e., how to teach) should be paired with appropriate mathematics assessment (i.e., how knowledge acquisition is measured). Use of an appropriate assessment framework in conjunction with explicit and systematic mathematics instruction may help to improve the mathematics achievement of students with or at risk for MD above and beyond the use of effective instruction alone (Gersten et al., 2009). As with an explicit mathematics instructional framework, the intensity of the assessment approach taken must match the intensity of academic need. In other words, assessment dosage, content, and target population (e.g., school vs. classroom vs. individual student) should vary based on the unique needs of a given situation. MTSS in mathematics can help to determine how knowledge acquisition is measured in different contexts. MTSS helps schools to make thoughtful decisions about the intensity of assessment that should be used based on the type of assessment data needed to effectively problem-solve at each tier. In this section, we describe how mathematics assessments can be implemented within a three-tiered system to improve the mathematics outcomes of students with, or at risk of, MD.

Tier 1

At Tier 1, schools can use mathematics assessments as preventative tools for (1) gauging students' overall mathematics performance and (2) identifying students who may be at risk for developing mathematics difficulties. *Universal screeners* are brief assessment measures designed to accomplish these tasks. Traditionally administered three times per year, they paint a broad picture of the general mathematics proficiency of all students across time. These measures emphasize breadth over depth, and at the K–1 level, they typically assess student performance in one or more key indicators of early number sense, including counting, numeral identification, magnitude comparison (e.g., identifying which number is greatest), and strategic counting (e.g., counting efficiently). Student performance on these foundational skills provides an indicator of risk for mathematics difficulties, with early struggles often indicative of challenges mastering critical mathematics domains in later grades (Fuchs et al., 2007; Gersten et al., 2012).

Universal screeners are intended to accomplish two key purposes: (1) to assess whether current mathematics instruction is adequately meeting student need by examining data at the classroom and school levels and (2) to "catch" students who may be in danger of falling behind academically by comparing individual student performance data to their peers (Clarke et al., 2014). To assess the appropriateness of current mathematics instruction, teachers can work with their school psychologist and grade-level teams to use universal screening data to determine whether mathematics instruction is generally effective for all students in the school, and to make resource allocation decisions. For example, screening data may suggest that a large percentage of grade 1 students are struggling with number sense development as measured on a magnitude comparison assessment. In this case, schools might decide to allocate instructional resources to schoolwide supports, for example, through Tier 1 supplemental instruction to improve general student performance in mathematics.

To identify students who may be at risk for falling behind academically, teachers can compare individual student screening data to data from grade-level peers. For example, when examining classroom performance data on a strategic counting screener, a teacher may notice that a few students have scored much lower than the rest of the class. This discrepancy may be indicative of a need to provide these students with more intensive Tier 2 or 3 interventions. Thus, at the individual student level, screening data indicates that most students are on track, enabling schools to spend their limited resources on the relatively few students who may need more intensive instructional supports through Tier 2 or 3 interventions.

Tiers 2 and 3

For Tiers 2 and 3, schools can use mathematics assessments to monitor the effectiveness of interventions for students struggling with mathematics. At the heart of effective Tier 2 and 3 assessment–instruction pairing is a process called *formative assessment*. Within a formative assessment framework, student performance data is collected in an ongoing manner and is directly used to inform instructional decisions. Research shows that when teachers use formative assessment data to design and adjust their instruction, student performance improves (Gersten et al., 2009). It should be noted that schools may vary their specific approach to supporting students in Tiers 2 and 3. However, as with mathematics instructional approaches, similar assessment tools are typically effective for students in both tiers, with intensity of need determining the specific assessments provided for students at Tier 2 versus Tier 3. Thus, matching the intensity of the assessment to the intensity of student need will be especially vital at this level of instructional decision making.

In Tiers 2 and 3, intervention effectiveness should be comprehensively monitored through frequent "check-ins" on student mathematics progress using progress monitoring tools. *Progress monitoring* is a formative assessment type that relies on routinely administered, brief measures to monitor student academic progress. To keep tabs on the mathematics development of students in Tiers 2 and 3, it is beneficial to use two types of progress monitoring measures in tandem, *curriculum-based measures* (CBMs) and *curriculum-embedded mastery assessments* (Gersten et al., 2009).

CBMs are brief, timed measures that broadly sample key mathematics concepts that are believed to be indicative of overall mathematics proficiency. These assessments should be administered at least once a month for students in Tier 2 and as frequently as once per week for students in Tier 3, to monitor whether students are making adequate mathematics progress. Because CBM measures sample a wide range of skills, they can shed light on whether student performance with the discrete mathematics skills taught in class generalizes to a broader understanding of important mathematics concepts. Another benefit of CBM measures is that they are often the same as universal screening measures, and so the same assessment can be used for both universal screening and progress monitoring. Within this integrated approach, CBM progress monitoring tools provide individual student data that can be seamlessly compared to classroom (or school) mathematics performance, thus facilitating schoolwide instructional decision making within and across tiers.

Curriculum-embedded mastery assessments target mastery of skills directly taught within the curriculum. These assessments may be administered as frequently as daily, embedded within or following the completion of individual instructional lessons. The frequency of assessment administration and explicit link to curriculum help interventionists to make day-to-day adjustments to instruction based on student performance. For example, an interventionist who administers a curriculum-embedded mastery assessment following the completion of a lesson on comparison of two-digit numbers may notice that several of her students have failed to grasp that they must begin by comparing the tens column. Based on this data, the interventionist may choose to revisit this strategy in greater depth in the following lesson. Many core and supplemental curricula have built-in curriculum-embedded mastery assessments that teachers can administer as a part of their daily instruction. Alternately, teachers can create their own mastery assessments by drawing from material within their lessons.

For Tiers 2 and 3, interventionists can jointly use CBMs and curriculum-embedded mastery assessments to develop an in-depth understanding of student progress within an intervention program and toward general mathematics proficiency. Combined use of these measures provides interventionists with the appropriate tools to determine the types of instructional adjustments that are necessary for a specific student or subgroup of students. If a discrepancy exists between student performance on CBMs and curriculum-embedded mastery assessments such that the student is mastering in-program assessment content but failing to show growth on the CBM, the interventionist should consider examining what is or isn't working with the intervention program. In this case or in cases where neither assessment indicates desired growth, interventionists may opt to consult with their school psychologist about whether diagnostic testing may be an effective approach to adapting their student's instruction.

Diagnostic testing is an additional resource interventionists can use to support students who persistently struggle to make adequate mathematics progress. Diagnostic testing takes mastery assessments a step further and may involve an in-depth analysis of a student's progress monitoring data and/or additional assessments that target specific mathematics concepts. The goal of diagnostic testing is to develop a hypothesis regarding the student's unique instructional needs that can be used to create an individualized intervention plan for the student, along with consistent progress monitoring to assess the efficacy of the intervention (e.g., Data-Based Individualization; Capizzi & Fuchs, 2005). Because of the high intensity of this level of problem solving, diagnostic testing should be reserved for students with the highest level of instructional need. Thus, teachers should consult with their school psychologist about the use of diagnostic testing only after students have shown persistent mathematics difficulties with increasingly intensive instruction for Tiers 1 and 2, usually documented through a continued lack of expected growth on progress monitoring measures at the Tier 2 level of instruction.

Conclusion

Effective support in mathematics for students with mathematics difficulties requires consideration of multiple factors. Teachers and schools can surmount the challenges in teaching early mathematics by investing their time and talents to developing a targeted approach to teaching the critical concepts of early numeracy, working to ensure that instructional approaches are systematic and explicit in delivering that content and creating an iterative approach linking assessment to instructional decision making. Collectively these steps will allow all students to reach their full potential in learning mathematics.

REFERENCES

Allsopp, D., Lovin, L. H., & van Ingen, S. (2017). Supporting mathematical proficiency. *Teaching Exceptional Children, 49,* 273–283.

Archer, A. L., & Hughes, C. A. (2011). *Explicit instruction: Effective and efficient teaching.* New York: Guilford Press.

Bryant, B. R., Bryant, D. P., Roberts, G., & Fall, A-M. (2016). Effects of an early numeracy intervention on struggling kindergarteners' mathematics performance. *International Journal for Research in Learning Disabilities, 3*(1), 29–45.

Bryant, D. P., Bryant, B., Roberts, G., Vaughn, S., Pfannenstiel, K. H., Porterfield, J., & Gersten, R. M. (2011). Early numeracy intervention program for first-grade students with mathematics difficulties. *Exceptional Children, 78,* 7–23.

Capizzi, A. M., & Fuchs, L. S. (2005). Effects of curriculum-based measurement with and without diagnostic feedback on teacher planning. *Remedial and Special Education, 26*(3), 159–174.

Cawley, J. F., Parmar, R. S., Lucas-Fusco, L. M., Kilian, J. D., & Foley, T. E. (2007). Place value and mathematics for students with mild disabilities: Data and suggested practices. *Learning Disabilities—A Contemporary Journal, 5*(1), 21–39.

Clarke, B., Doabler, C. T., Kosty, D., Kurtz Nelson, E., Smolkowski, K., Fien, H., & Turtura, J. (2017). Testing the efficacy of a kindergarten mathematics intervention by small group size. *AERA Open, 3*(2), 1–16.

Clarke, B., Doabler, C. T., Smolkowski, K., Baker, S. K., Fien, H., & Strand Cary, M. (2014). Examining the efficacy of a Tier 2 kindergarten mathematics intervention. *Journal of Learning Disabilities, 49,* 152–165.

Clements, D. H., & Sarama, J. (2004). Mathematics everywhere, every time. *The Arithmetic Teacher, 10*(8), 421–426.

Common Core Standards Writing Team (CCSWT). (2015). *Progressions for the Common Core State Standards in mathematics: Number and operations in base ten, K–5.* Tucson: Institute for Mathematics and Education, University of Arizona. Retrieved from *https://achievethecore.org/content/upload/ccss_progression_nbp_k5_2015_03_16.pdf.*

Cross, C. T., Woods, T. A., & Schweingruber, H. (2009). *Mathematics learning in early childhood.* Washington, DC: National Academies Press.

Dennis, M. S., Sharp, E., Chovanes, J., Thomas, A., Burns, R. M., Custer, B., & Park, J. (2016). A meta-analysis of empirical research on teaching students with mathematics learning difficulties. *Learning Disabilities Research and Practice, 31,* 156–168.

Doabler, C. T., Baker, S. K., Kosty, D. B., Smolkowski, K., Clarke, B., Miller, S. J., & Fien, H. (2015). Examining the association between explicit mathematics instruction and student mathematics achievement. *Elementary School Journal, 115,* 303–333.

Duncan, G. J., Dowsett, C. J., Claessens, A., Magnuson, K., Huston, A. C., Klebanov, P., . . . Japel, C. (2007). School readiness and later achievement. *Developmental Psychology, 43,* 1428–1446.

Dunlosky, J., Rawson, K. A., Marsh, E. J., Nathan, M. J., & Willingham, D. T. (2013). Improving students' learning with effective learning techniques: Promising directions from cognitive and educational psychology. *Psychological Science in the Public Interest, 14,* 4–58.

Ehrlich, S. B., & Levine, S. C. (2007, March–April). *What low-SES children do know about number: A comparison of Head Start and tuition-based preschool children's number knowledge.* Paper presented at the biennial meeting of the Society for Research on Child Development, Boston, MA.

Elbaum, B., Vaughn, S., Hughes, M. T., & Moody, S. W. (2000). How effective are one-to-one tutoring programs in reading for elementary students at risk for reading failure?: A meta-analysis of the intervention research. *Journal of Educational Psychology, 92,* 605–619.

Frye, D., Baroody, A. J., Burchinal, M., Carver, S. M., Jordan, N. C., & McDowell, J. (2013). *Teaching math to young children: A practice guide* (Practice Guide No. NCEE 2014-4005). Washington, DC: National Center for Education and Regional Assistance (NCEE), Institute of Education Sciences, U.S. Department of Education. Retrieved from *https://ies.ed.gov/ncee/wwc/Docs/PracticeGuide/early_math_pg_111313.pdf.*

Fuchs, L. S., Fuchs, D., Compton, D. L., Bryant, J. D., Hamlett, C. L., & Seethaler, P. M. (2007). Mathematics screening and progress monitoring at first grade: Implications for responsiveness to intervention. *Exceptional Children, 73,* 311–330.

Geary, D. C. (1990). A componential analysis of an early learning deficit in mathematics. *Journal of Experimental Child Psychology, 49,* 363–383.

Gelman, R., & Gallistel, C. R. (1978). *The child's understanding of number.* Cambridge, MA: Harvard University Press.

Gersten, R. M., Beckmann, S., Clarke, B., Foegen, A., March, L., Star, J. R., & Witzel, B. (2009). *Assisting students struggling with mathematics: Response to intervention (RTI) for elementary and middle schools* (Practice Guide Report No. NCEE 2009-4060). Washington, DC: National Center for Education Evaluation and Regional Assistance, Institute of Education Sciences, U.S. Department of Education. Retrieved from *https://ies.ed.gov/ncee/wwc/Docs/PracticeGuide/rti_math_pg_042109.pdf.*

Gersten, R. M., & Chard, D. J. (1999). Number sense: Rethinking arithmetic instruction for students with mathematical disabilities. *Journal of Special Education, 33,* 18–28.

Gersten, R. M., Clarke, B., Jordan, N., Newman-Gonchar, R., Haymond, K., & Wilkins, C. (2012). Universal screening in mathematics for the primary grades: Beginnings of a research base. *Exceptional Children, 78,* 423–445.

Halpern, D. F., Aronson, J., Reimer, N., Simpkins, S., Star, J. R., & Wentzel, K. (2007). *Encouraging girls in math and science* (IES Practice Guide No. NCER 2007-2003). Washington, DC: National Center for Education Research. Retrieved from *https://ies.ed.gov/ncee/wwc/Docs/PracticeGuide/20072003.pdf.*

Hudson, P., & Miller, S. P. (2006). *Designing and implementing mathematics instruction for students with diverse learning needs.* Boston: Pearson Education.

Hughes, C. A., Morris, J. R., Therrien, W. J., & Benson, S. K. (2017). Explicit instruction: Historical and contemporary contexts. *Learning Disabilities Research and Practice, 32*(3), 140–148.

Klibanoff, R. S., Levine, S. C., Huttenlocher, J., Vasilyeva, M., & Hedges, L. V. (2006). Preschool children's mathematical knowledge: The effect of teacher "math talk." *Developmental Psychology, 42,* 59–69.

La Paro, K. M., Hamre, B. K., Locasale-Crouch, J., Pianta, R. C., Bryant, D., Early, D., . . . Burchinal, M. (2009). Quality in kindergarten classrooms: Observational evidence for the need to increase children's learning opportunities in early education classrooms. *Early Education and Development, 20,* 657–692.

Landerl, K., & Moll, K. (2010). Comorbidity of learning disorders: Prevalence and familial transmission. *Journal of Child Psychology and Psychiatry, 51,* 287–294.

National Assessment of Educational Progress. (2015). *The nation's record card: Mathematics 2015: National Assessment of Educational Progress at grades 4 and 8.* Washington, DC: National Center for Education Statistics, Institute of Education Sciences, U.S. Department of Education. Retrieved from *www.nationsreportcard.gov/reading_math_2015/#?grade=4.*

National Governors Association (NGA) Center for Best Practices & Council of Chief State School

Officers (CCSSO). (2010). *Common Core State Standards for mathematics.* Washington, DC: Authors. Retrieved from *www.corestandards.org/the-standards/mathematics.*

National Mathematics Advisory Panel. (2008). *Foundations for success: The final report of the National Mathematics Advisory Panel.* Washington, DC: U.S. Department of Education.

National Research Council (NRC). (2001). *Adding it up: Helping children learn mathematics.* Washington, DC: Mathematics Learning Study Committee.

Powell, S. R., & Driver, M. K. (2015). The influence of mathematics vocabulary instruction embedded within addition tutoring for first-grade students with mathematics difficulty. *Learning Disability Quarterly, 38,* 221–233.

Rosenshine, B. V. (2012). Principles of instruction: Research-based strategies that all teachers should know. *American Educator, 36*(1), 12–19, 39.

Schmidt, W. H., & Houang, R. T. (2007). Lack of focus in the mathematics curriculum: Symptom or cause? In T. O. M. Loveless (Series Ed.), *Lessons learned: What international assessments tell us about math achievement* (pp. 65–84). Washington, DC: Brookings Institution Press.

Wynn, K. (1990). Children's understanding of counting. *Cognition, 36*(2), 155–193.

CHAPTER 5

Time and Money Measurement

DIANE PEDROTTY BRYANT, MARYAM NOZARI, and BRIAN R. BRYANT

LEARNING OUTCOMES

After studying this chapter, you will be able to answer the following questions:

1. What are the critical concepts and skills for time and money?
2. What are specific guidelines for teaching time and money?
3. How can interventions be intensified for Tier 2 and Tier 3?

Consider the importance of understanding and accurately using time and money measurement every day. How often over the course of a day do you check the current time or estimate the amount of time it will take to do a task? How often do you make a time line for getting things done, whether they involve tasks at home, at work, or in school? How often do you use your knowledge and understanding of money for examining records of income, expenses, and balances in your online banking account; developing a budget for a month's activities; ensuring that you have enough money in your checking account to make a purchase; or determining when using cash whether you were given the correct change from a cashier? It is safe to say that proficiency with time and money measurement is an essential life skill, and students must be able to apply these concepts and skills whether in school settings, at home, or in the community.

Measurement is "the process of describing a continuous quantity with a numerical value" (Van de Walle, Karp, & Bay-Williams, 2016) and involves the act of measuring attributes, such as length, volume and capacity, and area, of designated items or objects. Measurement is based on (1) determining the unit to use for measuring an item or object, and (2) measuring that item or object through multiple iterations of the unit

(National Council of Teachers of Mathematics [NCTM], 2000). Measurement is one of the domains from two very important sets of standards that have influenced school districts' mathematics curriculum leaders in their development or selection of programs for their mathematics intervention teachers. The NCTM Principles and Standards for School Mathematics (2000) is one set of important standards including measurement with time and money. The Common Core State Standards for Mathematics (CCSSM; National Governors Association [NGA] Center for Best Practices & Council of Chief State School Officers [CCSSO], 2010) is another important set of standards in which time and money measurement fall under the Measurement and Data domain. Time and money are more heavily emphasized in the early grades, presumably with the assumption that children will be sufficiently adept with time and money concepts and skills in the earlier grades.

Time is a type of measurement that relates to the duration of events from start to finish and the intervals between units of time (e.g., minute, hour). A time interval is the length of time between two events. For instance, one event is at 8:45 and the other event is at 8:55; the time interval is 10 minutes. Clocks show time intervals in seconds, minutes, and hours.

Money is "something generally accepted as a medium of exchange, a measure of value, or a means of payment" (*Merriam-Webster Dictionary*, 2019). Unfortunately, time and money receive less instructional time and textbook emphasis than the other types of measurement (i.e., length, volume/capacity, area, weight). Time, in particular, is challenging to teach because it cannot be seen or touched and because the concepts, unit of time, duration of events, and time interval are abstract for students in the early grades when time and money concepts are mostly taught (Van de Walle et al., 2016). Money has its own set of challenges related to the necessary prerequisite skills, such as counting by 5's, but also because of the need to be able to switch denominations easily when counting and making change.

Teaching time and money measurement concepts and skills to students with mathematics difficulties (MD) and mathematics learning disabilities (MLD) is challenging. Teachers and researchers have noted that even though time and money are ubiquitous, students with MD and MLD face problems learning the concepts and skills for these two areas for several reasons. First, these students lack the necessary prerequisite skills associated with the grade-level skills and concepts. Consider, for example, the two following problems, which illustrate the *application* of time and money concepts and skills. Besides the ability to read the words in the problems and know solution strategies, think about the prerequisite time and money concepts and skills that are included in these word problems. Think back to Chapter 1 where the ADAPT framework was introduced. In our example that follows, what prerequisites, or the "D" of the framework ("Determines the prerequisite skills of the task"), can you identify?

Time:

What time does Mikayla have to leave her house to be at her friend's house by a quarter past 4:00 in the afternoon if the trip takes 60 minutes?

Money:

Pablo wants to buy a notepad. The notepad costs 48¢. Pablo has quarters, dimes, nickels, and pennies. What combination of these coins should Pablo give the store clerk to buy the notepad if he receives no change back?

For time, if you indicated the need to understand the concepts "quarter past" and "60 minutes," then you would likely be able to identify the correct answer. For money, if you identified that Pablo needs to be able to count by coin quantities and switch coin denominations, you would be right again.

Second, students have difficulties with learning and applying the vocabulary associated with time and money. This issue becomes even more problematic as symbols are used to denote meaning that cannot be determined from the context in which the symbols occur. For instance, a problem is given where students must leave the house at 5:20 P.M. in order to arrive at the play at 5:45. Students must interpret the meaning of symbols associated with time, such as the colon in 5:20 where the colon is used to separate hours from minutes with no space before or after the colon. The student must infer that 20 minutes after 5:00 is when it is time to go. Money also has symbols that students must understand such as the $ and ¢, thus $0.15 is read as "0 dollars and 15 cents" and 15¢ is read as "15 cents." As noted many years ago and remains true today, Wiig and Semel (1984) referred to mathematics as "conceptually dense," which means that students must understand the meaning of each mathematics symbol and word because context clues, such as in reading, are limited or nonexistent.

Third, students may have misconceptions that could interfere with understanding; these misconceptions must be recognized and remediated. According to SanGiovanni (2017), a *misconception* is an erroneous understanding of a mathematical idea, such as telling time or working with money. For instance, misconceptions about the hands on an analog clock can create serious difficulties for telling time accurately. In their study with typically achieving 8-year-olds, Ryan and Williams (2007) found that 31% of the students misread the hands of a clock, confusing the hour and minute hand. Misconceptions with money can be identified with children who do not discriminate among the values of coins (Bamberger, Oberdorf, & Schultz-Ferrell, 2010). Early on students are taught to distinguish the differences between coins and understand that the size of the coin does not indicate its value; for students who become confused as these concepts are taught, they will likely face delays in their ability to count money and make change. Another issue related to learning money is problems with skip counting by 5's and 10's and adding and subtracting quantities. Students who have misconceptions about how to use skip counting to count change must understand that the change should be counted in relation to the value of the coins rather than as a group of coins each with a value of 1 (Bamberger et al., 2010). Misconceptions with either of these issues can impede the ability to compute an amount of money accurately, whether it is determining if they have enough cash to pay for purchases or making sure the change they receive is correct. These misconceptions will affect the ability to solve word problems that require counting money and making change (Bley & Thornton, 2001).

For students with MD and MLD, we must ensure that they have the knowledge to help them succeed with mastering time and money measurement concepts and skills as they are taught, and as they are applied to more advanced problems in middle and high school grades (Jones & Arbaugh, 2004). Thus, the purpose of this chapter is to discuss the critical concepts and skills for time and money, to provide guidelines for teaching time and money, and to give examples of how time and money interventions can be intensified for Tier 2 and Tier 3. Furthermore, we delve into the CCSSM, explain how students with MD and MLD struggle with learning and applying time and money concepts and skills oftentimes because of misconceptions, and identify examples of important vocabulary for time and money instruction.

Time and Money Concepts and Skills

Learning about time and money concepts and skills has its roots in informal experiences before children start their formal education in kindergarten. For instance, as part of informal experiences, children become familiar with the language associated with time and money as they hear adults talk about these topics. Young children learn about the concept of time and begin to develop a sense of time when they hear adults say, "It's almost time to clean up for lunch," "It's time to go," "It's snack time," and "Time for bed." Young children may hear references to someone not having enough time to do something or a task that took a long time to complete. Thus, the notion of time is pervasive in a young child's surroundings.

For money, children begin to learn about this topic through experiences in grocery and department stores as family members make purchases using cash or debit or credit cards. Children might be given a coin to put in a candy machine for a gumball or in a piggy bank for saving, for example. Through these two examples, young children begin to understand that it takes a coin (money) to get something they want or, for a pricier item, that saving one's pennies will have to suffice. Oftentimes, young children recognize a few coins, such as a penny, nickel, and dime, and perhaps their values before entering school and receiving more formal education in money. Although young children may not accurately say the name of a coin and its value, they do begin to understand that coins have names and values (Bley & Thornton, 2001). Thus, informally young children begin to develop an understanding of time and money that becomes increasingly developed across the grades as a crucial life skill throughout adulthood.

When children enter school, formal schooling begins where students learn more specific information about critical time and money concepts and skills, which fall under the Measurement and Data domain in the CCSSM (NGA & CCSSO, 2010). These standards focus primarily on grades 1 through 4 for time and grades 1, 2, and 4 for money. In first grade, we see the standard "tell and write time in hours and half-hours using analog and digital clocks" (1.MD; NGA & CCSSO, 2010), and in second grade, the standard is "work with time and money from analog and digital clocks to the nearest five minutes, using a.m. and p.m. [and] to solve word problems involving dollar bills, quarters, dimes, nickels, and pennies, using $ and ¢ symbols" (2.MD; NGA & CCSSO, 2010). In third grade, time intervals are emphasized including "solve problems involving measurement and estimation of intervals of time . . . [to] tell and write time to the nearest minute and measure time intervals in minutes [and] solve word problems involving addition and subtraction of time intervals in minutes (3.MD; NGA & CCSSO, 2010). In fourth grade, students are expected to use money and intervals of time within the context of applying knowledge of these concepts and skills to word-problem solving (4.MD; NGA & CCSSO, 2010).

When teaching the standards, the mechanism for telling time and working with money must be considered. One might think that in this digital age, telling time using an *analog clock* (a clock that has the hours, half-hours, and minutes displayed with moving hands on a clock "face") or watch, or making change using dollar bills and coins for a purchase are less important now that we are immersed in a society of digital time and electronic banking. However, students must understand what 8:45 A.M. means if they have to be in class before the bell rings at 8:50 A.M. Also, students must know that when purchasing lunch items, if there is only 85¢ left on the meal card, this amount will not be enough to buy lunch items such as a main meal that costs $1.25 plus a cookie at 25¢. Understanding time and monetary concepts is critical, regardless of the actual materials for telling time (different types of clocks) and working with money (different coin values and dollar denominations). We now focus on more specific content for time and money concepts and skills with connections to the CCSSM (NGA & CCSSO, 2010). We discuss misconceptions associated with learning time and money and the difficulties students with MD and MLD exhibit.

Time

Time can be thought of as the duration of an event from the beginning to the end. Telling time is about identifying or labeling specific moments in the continuum of time, such as reading a scale (e.g., digital display) or examining clocks, calendars, or timetables. It is important to note that telling time is really a dial-reading task, where the scale of interest might be a dial, a digital display, or a grid such as calendar (Gidwitz, 2001). In fact, standard units such as seconds, minutes, and hours, which are used to express the time of day, are rooted in measurement (Kamii & Long, 2003).

In this section, we discuss three important aspects of time: telling time, passage of time, and vocabulary of time. Teachers must be aware of common misconceptions that hinder understandings about time. We begin this section by identifying a few misconception examples for telling time. For example, telling students that the hour hand of a clock always points to the number representing that hour may be true sometimes, but as minutes are introduced it becomes evident that the hour hand moves slightly toward the next hour as the minute hand approaches the next hour. Students who believe that the hour hand always points directly to the hour will encounter problems when the teacher introduces the minute hand because of the misconception that the hour hand points directly to the number for that hour. On a different but related note, sometimes students make careless errors, and when asked, they quickly correct their mistakes or errors. Although these error patterns may not be misconceptions per se, these types of mistakes or errors can cause confusion and must be corrected with students as soon as possible so they do not continue making these same error patterns.

Telling Time

Although the concepts and skills for teaching time fall under the Measurement and Data domain (NGA & CCSSO, 2010), the focus for time is on teaching students how to tell time usually beginning with the analog clock or "dial-type of instrument" (Van de Walle et al., 2016). Beginning with the analog clock helps students to see hours and minutes and the rotation of the hands in a clockwise fashion depicted on the clock's dial. The digital dial can be introduced to complement the times shown on the analog clock.

Telling time involves two primary approaches in everyday life, including using a clock and reading the calendar. Telling time with the clock dial requires *units of time* (i.e., established quantity that is a standard measurement) or *time periods* (i.e., established beginning and ending) that must be specified. A clock records the time for a day and night using the units of time, including seconds, minutes, and hours. Interestingly, the second is considered to be the base unit for time, according to the International System of Units, from which other units result. Other units or time periods include days, weeks, months, and years ("Exactly What Is Time?," 2019).

In grade 1, as students with MD and MLD are taught about time using clocks, some may have difficulty telling and writing time using an analog clock. Student difficulties stem from challenges discriminating the hour (shorter) and minute (longer) hands and recalling which hand represents hours or minutes. Relatedly, telling time on an analog clock face is another challenge because students must be able to say the actual time— "It is 6 o'clock"—and write this time as 6:00 or 6 o'clock. On the other hand, a *digital clock,* which displays time in numerical form rather than by hands on a dial, shows the exact time and may be easier to read, but time concepts such as "quarter past," "half past," and "quarter to" can be difficult to infer when only numbers are displayed. For instance, the part–whole association of minute and hour units is not evident because the student cannot see the movement of the minute hand from 9:00 to 9:30, and the hour hand approaching 10 from 9; thus, the concept of measuring time cannot necessarily be comprehended.

Reading the numerals on an analog and a digital clock implies that students are able to correctly name numerals such as 57, 15 (not 51), and 35. Students must know the magnitude of quantity (e.g., 45 is greater than 35) displayed in time to determine, for example, that 45 minutes have passed a certain hour, and thus, telling time is closer to the next hour. Students must also be able to count sequentially from 1 to 60 and count by 5's to at least 60. However, number recognition, magnitude of quantity, and counting may pose problems, especially for young, struggling students who have not yet mastered these skills.

In grade 2, teaching time focuses on telling and writing time, now to the nearest 5 minutes, with "A.M." and "P.M." Thus, students must be able to distinguish A.M., which refers to the time period between midnight (12:00 A.M.) and noon (12:00 P.M.), and P.M., which means the hours between noon and midnight, and remember what these abbreviations mean. The notion of A.M. and P.M. is quite abstract, so struggling students must have ample opportunities with concrete experiences. For instance, a possible scenario for talking about A.M. and P.M. can reside with the school day's activities, such as "Class, it is 9:00 A.M. It is time to take out your clocks for us to practice telling time." The teacher then elaborates on this activity, asking, "Do we work with our clocks in the morning before lunch or in the afternoon? If I say 9:00 A.M., does this mean we are in the morning or afternoon?" In this example, the teacher is connecting a class event or activity to the time of day and is expecting that students will be able to say that the event is occurring in the morning, thus 9:00 A.M. is in the morning.

In grade 3, the focus is on telling time and computing time intervals in minutes using addition and subtraction word-problem situations. There are concepts and skills inherent in this standard that are difficult for students with MD and MLD. For example, students must come to understand that reading the time, such as 4:46, on an analog or a digital clock, means that "4" represents a unit—hour—and 46 is a different unit—minutes. The minutes and hours are multiplicatively associated. This association means that when considering minutes and hours, 60 minutes equals 1 hour, 120 minutes equals 2 hours, and so forth. This multiplicative association could be a major problem for computing time intervals involving word problems where hours and minutes must be decomposed or composed to solve passage of time or duration problems (Earnest, 2017; Kamii & Russell, 2012).

The calendar is another approach to teaching telling time. A calendar is used for noting longer periods of time to represent units such as a week and a month. The calendar is widely used in the early grades, especially kindergarten and grade 1, as a mechanism for teaching the units of time, including month, weeks, days, and year, and the date. "Calendar time" is popular with younger children because typically they enjoy changing the date and putting up the next numeral for the day on the calendar chart. Children learn gradually the units of time and begin to understand that 1 year equals 12 months or 52 weeks, a month has 4–5 weeks, a week has 7 days, and a day and night each have 12 hours. However, for students with MD and MLD, numeral recognition such as saying the numerals can be challenging, especially the teen numbers. Students may struggle with reading the name of the month and the day of the week. The terms *month, week,* and *year* are abstract and thus could cause confusion regarding the meaning of the unit of time (Van de Walle et al., 2016).

Passage of Time

Passage of time is about measuring the time interval (i.e., length of time, elapsed time) that transpires between the beginning and ending of an event, daily routines, seasons, and a class activity, to name a few. An often-overlooked concept, "passage of time" may be difficult for some students to grasp because they have not sufficiently developed the idea of how long something takes to do. To address this issue, students will require many opportunities to talk about events and routines that are familiar to them, such as getting ready for school and eating breakfast (Horn, Schuster, & Collins, 2006).

In grade 4, application of time concepts is emphasized within the context of word-problem solving involving the four operations. In this grade, the assumption is that students have learned (1) how to tell time to the minute, (2) what various time units mean, and (3) how to compute time intervals. Yet, as already discussed, students with MD and MLD struggle with aspects of time. They have difficulties with adding and subtracting, especially when regrouping is involved, and have low performance on solving word problems because of reading and language comprehension difficulties (see Chapter 8 for more information about word-problem solving).

Vocabulary of Time

Related to telling time and passage of time, there are concepts that tap difficulties associated with vocabulary knowledge. For instance, think about the abstract nature of concepts such as the seasons; references to time periods including *today, yesterday, tomorrow, past, present, future, earlier,* and *later*; sentences with time-related adverbs such as *now* and *soon*; references to common prepositions when measuring time, such as *until, before,* and *after*; and calendar vocabulary such as *months* and *weeks*. What difficulties can you anticipate? Issues, particularly related to temporal (i.e., relating to time) words, can contribute to the misuse of a term such as *yesterday* when students are referring to something earlier in the day, or limited understanding of the cyclic nature of the seasons and time of year when they occur, or confusion with calendar activities. Haycock and Cockburn (1997) point out that the abundance of words connected to time contribute significantly to children's problem learning to tell time and to understand the passage of time. Vocabulary words should be taught explicitly with opportunities to practice. The words would make a great Word Wall for the classroom. The words can be placed on index cards for games such as Pick a Card and Define the Word. Words can include additional cards with definitions for a game of Concentration with the words and definitions. Now, we turn our attention to money.

Money

Money is typically thought of as a medium of exchange, including coins and paper money, which is currency or money in paper form. Working with money entails recognizing coins and coin values, recognizing and counting dollar bills, counting groups of coins, making change, and writing money amounts. Take, for example, the following scenario: Maria is given a jar with coins to count, including 3 dimes, 2 nickels, and 6 pennies. Maria sorts the coins into a dime group, a nickel group, and a pennies group. Maria is able to say that a dime = 10¢, a nickel = 5¢, and a penny = 1¢, and she is able to skip-count to count the 10's and 5's. She is asked to count the money. Maria starts with the largest amount, the dime, and skip-counts to be able to say that she has 30¢. Next, Maria moves to the smallest amount, the penny, saying that pennies are easy to count because each penny = 1¢. She starts with 30¢ and proceeds to count on the pennies touching each penny as she counts: "30¢, 31¢, 32¢, 33¢, 34¢, 35¢. Finally, she starts with 35¢ and skip-counts by 5 to reach 40¢ and then 45¢. Her teacher counts the change out loud and arrives at 46¢. On the other hand, José is not able to do skip counting quite yet; he knows the names but is not familiar with the values of the coins. He has 2 quarters, 2 dimes, 4 nickels, and 5 pennies. He sorts the coins into similar looking groups and labels the coins correctly: "This is a penny." When asked to count the money, he counts them by size of the coin with the quarter first, nickels next, pennies next, and dimes to finish the counting. He gives each coin a value of one and says he has 13¢.

Can you figure out Maria's and José's misconception about counting change? For Maria, the idea of how to count using a predetermined amount, 3 dimes, 2 nickels, and 6 pennies, finds her counting the largest valued coins (dimes) first and then continuing with lesser valued coins (pennies). She uses the *min strategy* to count, that is, she starts with the largest value and counts on from there. At issue is that Maria said, "30" for 3 dimes and then 31, 32, and so forth to arrive at 35¢; she proceeded to count the remaining coins arriving at an incorrect amount. What do you think are Maria's misconceptions about counting coins? Now, try to identify José's misconceptions about counting coin values.

In this section, we discuss important aspects of money, including recognizing coins and coin values, counting money amounts and making change, and understanding the vocabulary of money. Furthermore, teachers must be aware of common misconceptions that hinder understandings about money (see Bamberger et al., 2010 for common misconceptions at the elementary level related to mathematics understandings).

Recognizing Coins and Coin Values

In grade 2, students are expected to work with time and money. Relating to money, students are solving word problems with money amounts such as dollar bills, quarters, dimes, nickels, and pennies and use the $ and ¢ signs. Although the word problems are simple to solve, such as a simple join problem, students must be able to count the value of coins before they can add the quantities with a join problem. Consider this problem from the CCSSM (NGA & CCSSO, 2010): "If you have 2 dimes and 3 pennies, how many cents do you have?" What skills are involved in solving this problem? If you said counting by 10's or skip counting to equal 2 dimes (10, 20; 20¢) and counting on from 20, 20¢ + 1¢ + 1¢ + 1¢, to arrive at 23¢, then you are on track for understanding the necessary prerequisite skills that must be taught if students do not have this knowledge to solve a simple word problem. Now, write a simple word problem involving money incorporating money quantities and the "join" word-problem type. In your word problem, include quarters (2), dimes (4), nickels (2), and 1 penny. It is evident that skills related to coin recognition and their values, that is, knowing the attributes of coins, is important as students add quantities together.

It is clear that the value of coins is not proportional to the size of the coin. Yet students with MD and MLD will likely have trouble recognizing coins and their representative value. For instance, some students have the misconception that the larger-sized coins have greater values than smaller-sized coins, so a nickel has a greater value than a dime. Students may have the misconception that a smaller-sized coin such as a dime can't possibly be worth 10¢ and may struggle even further when asked, "How many

pennies equal a dime?" because they lack understanding of the meaning of coin values. Some students who are not adept with coin discrimination and coin values even
in grade 2 may question why 10 pennies are needed to equal 1 dime because the coins
are similar in coin size. This confusion can generalize to addition with regrouping and
place value, especially when students add the ones column (pennies) of an addition
problem and must regroup 10 pennies (ones) for 1 dime (ten) to the tens column in a
problem. Thus, understanding coin equivalencies (e.g., 10 pennies = 1 dime; 2 nickels
= 1 dime; 2 quarters = 1 50-cent piece) is important for related skills such as making
change. Once dollar bills are introduced, then more measurement equivalencies should
be discussed using real money. For example, 100 pennies = 1 dollar; 10 dimes = 1 dollar;
20 nickels = 1 dollar, and so forth. Finally, students must have ample opportunities to
read and write words for money amounts in preparation for the advanced skill of writing checks. In this case, reading money words and spelling and writing number words
can be incorporated into reading and spelling instruction.

Counting Money Amounts and Making Change

Students should become adept at making change, but before tackling this important
skill, students must be proficient with counting money amounts. Even today, many
people use only debit and credit cards to make purchases, but employees must still be
able to count money and make change. Instead of a debit or credit card, consider the
cashier at a store who totals the sale of a purchase; is given a large bill, such as $10.00;
and needs to count the change that remains from the $10.00 back to the customer. Even
though the computer shows how much change to give back to the customer, the cashier
still needs to be able to count this change, which may be in the form of coins and $1.00
bills, to complete the sale.

Counting amounts of coins first and then including dollar bills with quantities of
coins not only taps second-grade standards on money but also connects to fourth-grade
standards on money. In second grade, counting coins and dollar bills provides opportunities to apply an understanding of recognizing coins, stating coin values, and knowing dollar bill denominations to solving word problems. However, even for typically
achieving students, the skills of counting on and skip counting by 5's and 10's, for example, require much practice to master (Clements & Sarama, 2004). For students with MD
and MLD, the situation is direr because the amount of practice and time to master the
skills is much greater; however, this needed time may not be an option in classrooms
as teachers are held accountable for teaching the standards, which embrace other mathematics areas, for their grade level. In fourth grade, students are expected to express
a larger measurement unit, such as a nickel (larger monetary unit) as equivalent to 5
pennies (smaller monetary unit), $1.00 (larger monetary unit) as equivalent to 4 quar-
ters (1 quarter represents the smaller monetary unit), and $5.00 (larger monetary unit)
as equivalent to five $1.00 bills (smaller monetary unit). Additionally, in fourth grade,
students are expected to solve word problems containing monetary values, using the
four operations (addition, subtraction, multiplication, and division). The conversion of
units, larger to smaller, helps students compute amounts when adding and subtracting,

for instance, when regrouping a larger unit (a 100) to its equivalent smaller unit (ten 10's) is needed. Consider the problem $26.00 + $17.00; notice that the ones place requires regrouping of $13 to $10 (a ten) with $3 remaining; $20 + $10 becomes $20 + $10 + $10, equaling $40 or four groups of $10 with the grand total of $43.00.

Regarding making change, the prerequisite skills consist of recognizing coins, knowing coin values, counting on from a given amount to find the difference, and skip counting. For instance, counting or adding on is a preferred method to find the difference in a subtraction problem; thus, solving for x, 15¢ – 10¢ = x can be achieved by starting with 10¢ (smaller quantity) and counting on by pennies (ones) to 15¢ (larger quantity) to arrive at the solution of 5¢ (Van de Walle & Lovin, 2006). Thus, the challenges students with MD and MLD encounter with these prerequisite skills as previously noted continue as issues for making change (Clements & Sarama, 2004).

Vocabulary of Money

Much like the vocabulary for time, terms must be identified as possibly challenging for students to know and, thus, must be taught explicitly. Words such as the name of coins and symbols denoting money concepts (e.g., the cent and dollar signs) are examples of vocabulary that can be added to a Word Wall and used in games.

Instructional Guidelines for Teaching Time and Money

When teaching time and money concepts and skills, there are several factors to remember for designing instruction and interventions, which were previously discussed in this chapter. The first factor relates to connecting instruction to the CCSSM (NGA & CCSSO, 2010). When reviewing grades 4–5 CCSSM (NGA & CCSSO, 2010), it is evident that the majority of concepts and skills are taught in the elementary grades with application to solving word problems beginning in second grade. The second factor focuses on difficulties students with MD and MLD exhibit, which must be considered so that intervention development addresses these difficulties within the context of instruction. The third factor emphasizes using evidence-based guidelines that should be situated within specific concepts and skills. The fourth factor stresses the need to be aware of and plan for common misconceptions students possess about telling time and handling money. A few examples of these misconceptions were discussed in this chapter; teachers are advised to identify other potential misconceptions in their resources and to examine the resource cited in this chapter (e.g., SanGiovanni, 2017). Next, we discuss the guidelines for teaching students with MLD and MD concepts and skills for time and money.

Time

When preparing for teaching money concepts and skills in the elementary grades, there are guidelines for teachers to use when developing their intervention lessons for students who are struggling with mathematics. To begin, the *first guideline* is to ask children what they know about clocks, and time is a good place to start to provide teachers with a sense of what students understand about telling time. Teachers can show students a clock face and a digital clock and ask students to tell what they know about both time devices. Teachers can also ask students to point to or name places where they see or have seen the clock face and digital clock. This preliminary activity can help teachers to determine students' general awareness of and understanding about clocks and time.

The *second guideline* focuses on instructional materials that students can use as part of learning to tell time. First, have each student make their own clock; usually a paper plate with a brad can be constructed to hold the hour and minute hands. Provide a model of an analog clock with the numbers 1 through 12 already on the paper plate clock face. Second, have students make their clocks match your model. The paper plate clock is a good place to start with instructional materials. Then the paper plate clock can be replaced with a mechanical type of clock where the hands can be moved and the hours and minutes are already shown. The Judy Clock® is an example of one popular mechanical clock. The gears are visible and show accurate hour-hand and minute-hand relationships. *Time intervals* are shown in 5-minute intervals; time interval means the amount of *time* that passes from the beginning of an event to its end. Also, have a digital clock available as well for later instruction.

The *third guideline* relates to a sequence of instruction for teaching telling time. The sequence of instruction can vary somewhat depending on the source consulted or the needs of the students. Van de Walle and colleagues (2016) and Bley and Thornton (2001) offered guidelines for an instructional sequence:

1. Use a clock that has just the hour hand and the numerals 1–12 displayed initially to teach the hour. Have students chorally (together) count with you the numerals that represent each hour. Ask, "How many hours?" (12). Demonstrate how the hour hand can point to a number, the hour, on the clock. Model how to read the o'clock times and have students practice reading o'clock times such as 7 o'clock and 2 o'clock. Have students provide examples of activities that happen in school or at home beginning on the hour. For instance, if in school, lunch occurs at noon, then point the hour hand to 12:00. General agreement indicates that the hour is the first concept to teach. Students should be taught to read the o'clock times on both digital and analog clocks. It is important initially to ensure that the hour hand points directly to the number representing an hour on the analog clock. Of course, with the digital clock, the first number, for instance, 9:00, indicates the hour. If possible, on the digital clock, covering up the minutes can help to focus student attention on just the first number representing the hour.

2. Move the hour hand gradually to show "a little past 6 o'clock," "a little before 6 o'clock," "a little after 3 o'clock," and halfway between two numbers to show how the hour hand is gradually moving to the next number, or hour. Explain to students that the numeral closer to the hour hand represents the hour even though the hour hand is not directly pointing to the numeral. These examples illustrate the vocabulary of telling

time using "approximate language." For students who have difficulties discriminating position words such as *before, after, between,* and *near,* "approximate language" may be difficult to comprehend and thus makes it challenging for these students to accurately tell time. Thus, ample practice will be needed for students to master this potentially difficult skill to grasp.

3. Introduce the clock with both the hour and minute hands, using a mechanical clock. Begin by showing the minute hand pointing to the numeral 12 and the hour hand pointing to another number to illustrate 3 o'clock, 8 o'clock, and so forth. Model the minute hand pointing to 12 and the hour hand pointing to a number, saying, "It is 8 o'clock," "The time is 10 o'clock," and so forth. Show students how to write 8 o'clock and 8:00. Then, show different o'clock times and have students say and write the time. Next, say an o'clock time and have students turn the dial to show the time. Provide ample practice with this guideline. The use of a mechanical clock is recommended for the remaining activities.

4. Show students on the mechanical clock the marks that represent minutes. Begin by having students count by 5's orally without looking at the clock. Then, have students chorally (together) count with you the minutes beginning with 1 and ending with 60. Emphasize each 5-minute interval, pausing on the numerals (1–12) around the clock. For instance, count the minutes "one, two, three, four, <u>five</u>, six, seven, eight, nine, <u>ten</u>, 11, 12, 13, 14, <u>15</u>." Continue with this counting sequence to 60, saying that there are 60 minutes in one hour. Use a clock that has the minutes already labeled, including the number that represents the amount of minutes that have past. Next, ask, "How many minutes in an hour?" (60). Point to the numerals 1–12, asking if these numbers mean hours or minutes. Point to the minute marks, asking if these marks mean hours or minutes.

5. Point the hour hand to 10 and point the minute hand to 6. Ask students, "Which hour is the hour hand pointing to?" Then, have students chorally count by 5's stopping at the numeral 6. Ask students how many minutes they counted to reach the 6. Tell students the time is 10:30. Explain that the first number they say is the hour and the count-by-5's number is minutes. Set your clock to different examples for the hour and half hour, asking students to tell the time. Give different times such as 9:30 and have students show the times on their clocks. Students will need to practice this skill multiple times after you modeled it for them. Avoid using the language "half past" at this point.

6. Focus now on telling time to the minute using the mechanical clock. Begin by modeling telling time to the minute using intervals of 5 with times such as 8:10, 4:15, 9:45, and 2:35. Have students show the same times on their clocks, saying the time out loud. Once students have had many practice opportunities, then introduce telling time to the minute using the same procedure of modeling followed by student practice. Include telling time using "after," "before," and "almost." Continue to model showing and saying the times for students to show on their clocks. Include showing and saying a time and having students show the time on their clocks. Have students write the time. See Figure 5.1 for an example of an analog clock activity.

Directions: Give students the clock template. Have students put a dot in the middle of the face dial. Tell students to answer the questions in column A by drawing the hour and minute hands from the dot on the clock to show the times. Have students write the time in column B.

Column A	Column B
What time do I wake up?	
What time do I eat breakfast?	
What time do I go to school?	
What time do we have lunch at school?	
What time is afternoon recess?	
What time do we go to P.E.?	
What time is school over?	
What time do I need to be home for dinner?	
What time do I brush my teeth?	
What time do I go to bed?	

FIGURE 5.1. Time of day: analog clock activity.

From *Intensifying Mathematics Interventions for Struggling Students* edited by Diane Pedrotty Bryant. Copyright © 2021 The Guilford Press. Permission to photocopy this figure is granted to purchasers of this book for personal use or use with students (see copyright page for details). Purchasers can download enlarged versions of this figure (see the box at the end of the table of contents).

7. Introduce the digital clock with the analog clock. Set the time on the analog clock to match the time on the digital clock, saying and writing the time. Have students take turns setting their analog clocks to match the digital clock time and say the time.

8. Introduce A.M. and P.M. Discuss 12:00 A.M. and 12:00 P.M. Provide examples of times that occur in the A.M. and the P.M. during the school day and at home. During the school day, periodically ask students to pause during an activity, look at the clock, say the time, and tell whether their activity is occurring in the A.M. or the P.M.

9. Ask them to explain why they think it is a morning, A.M., or afternoon/evening activity, P.M.

10. Teach measuring time intervals in minutes to students in the third grade. Introduce the concept of time intervals by focusing on daily events, and their beginning and ending times. For instance, model how to write the beginning time such as 9:15 A.M. and ending time 9:37 A.M. Show students how to determine the time interval by counting by 5's and then by minutes. Have students locate 9:15 on their clocks and count by 5's to 9:35 and then by minutes to practice. Give students other examples of short time intervals to help them develop an understanding of the concept "time interval," which represents the passage of time. Present word problems involving addition and subtraction with situations that require computing the time interval.

11. Teach measurement equivalents of time units involving larger units in terms of smaller units. For example, teach 1 hour = 60 minutes. Introduce the idea that 1 minute = 60 seconds. Provide opportunities that require students to get a sense of how long a second is and how long a minute is. Then, teach measuring time intervals involving word problems and the four operations.

The *fourth guideline* refers to activities that focus on students learning about the calendar to help them see the sequence of the months of a year and the days of the week. One of the best ways for students to understand the calendar is to make "calendar time" part of the morning routine. Students can see the visual representation of not only the months, weeks, and days but also when important events and holidays occur, including each student's birthday. Teachers can use the vocabulary related to the calendar. For instance, the numbers of the day can be placed on small cards, and each day a student can be chosen to name the day of the week, tell the number for that day, and place the number card in that day's slot on the calendar. Teachers can use the calendar to ask such questions as (1) "What is the name of the month?"; (2) "What is the name of today's day?"; (3) "What number is today?"; (4) "How many weeks are in this month?"; (5) "How many days are in this month?"; (6) "If today is Tuesday, what day is tomorrow?"; (7) "If this month is February, what month comes next?"; (8) "How many weeks are in this month?"; (9) "Are there any holidays in this month?"; (10) "What day does the holiday fall on?"; (11) "How many months are in a year?"

Money

Much like when teaching about time, when preparing for teaching money concepts and skills in the elementary grades, there are guidelines for teachers to incorporate into the development of their intervention lessons for students who are struggling with mathematics. To begin, the *first guideline* refers to asking students what they already know about money to help teachers better understand what knowledge about money students bring to the instructional setting. Teachers can show various coins using both the "head" and "tail" of the coins to determine whether students can distinguish among the coins, asking, "What coin is this?" Teachers can also give students a few coins and ask them to count the money beginning with the greatest value (not the largest coin) and counting on the other coins by 1's, 5's, and 10's, if applicable. This task will illustrate not only how students count coins but also whether they understand that a nickel might be a larger-sized coin but the value is less than a smaller-sized coin, the dime. The teacher should listen for the use of counting by 5's and 10's, for instance, from the largest coin value. So, there is much to learn with a simple activity of giving students coins and asking them to count the value of their coins.

The *second guideline* relates to instructional materials for teachers to use when teaching money. Real coins or realistic versions (many commercial plastic coins are sufficiently authentic looking) should be used until students can name each coin and tell its value. Gradually, teachers can introduce less authentic looking "play or visually correct" money and then pictures of coins, pairing them with real coins to help students make the transition from real to "play" to pictures of coins. However, it should be noted that young children should have multiple opportunities when learning about money to use real money with cautions about how important it is not to lose the money and to take good care of it (Bley & Thornton, 2001). When students are ready, different denominations of bills should also be introduced. The transition from real coins to pictures of coins should be individualized depending on how quickly each student masters naming the coins and telling their values (Bley & Thornton, 2001).

The *third guideline* relates to an instructional sequence for teaching money concepts and skills. Much like learning time, the sequence of instruction can vary depending on the source consulted or the needs of the students. Van de Walle and colleagues (2016) and Bley and Thornton (2001) offer guidelines for an instructional sequence:

1. Teach the names of coins along with the values of the coins if students need this type of instruction. Teachers should be sure that both sides of the coins are taught in terms of coin recognition and value. By teaching the names of coins with the values of the coins together, students have opportunities with teacher guidance to see that the size of the coin does not translate to the value of the coin. Instruction should include showing the coins for students to discuss the attributes and values and showing amounts or values on index cards for students to indicate which coin equals that value.

2. Give students problems to fill in the blanks regarding coin value equivalences. For instance, a problem might be as follows: two nickels = ____ dimes; 5¢ = ____ nickels; five dimes = ____ ¢. Concrete objects such as real coins can be used initially to give students opportunities to recognize a coin and its value, such as a dime (10¢), and count out other coins, such as one nickel and five pennies to equal the dime. Next, pictures of coins and amounts can be created using a two-column format for students to draw a line from a coin in column A to a picture of other coins in column B that equals the value of the coin (or bill) in column A. Students will require multiple opportunities to practice these skills in preparation for more advanced money skills, such as counting money amounts and making change.

3. Teach students how to count money, which will prepare them for making change. Have students warm up with counting by 5's and 10's. Give students (individual or in pairs) groups of coins. Teach students how to start with the coin with the greatest value

and count on coins with smaller values to determine the amount of a designated group of coins. Begin with coins and then include dollar bills. Provide opportunities with a variety of different coins using initially real money and then pictures of coins and dollar bills.

4. Show pictures of everyday items that students would like, such as pencils, erasers, stickers, and food, and give the items price tags. Provide groups of coins with different amounts, and have students circle the coins that equal the value of the items.

5. Provide instruction on how to make change, beginning with smaller amounts of coins and very simple problems such as "Maria has $0.25 and wants to buy a pencil for 5¢ and a notepad for 15¢. How much change will Maria receive after paying with her quarter?" Notice that students will first need to add 5¢ + 15¢ = 20¢ and then count on from 20¢ to $0.25 resulting in the solution of 5¢. Maria will receive 5¢ in change. Students can draw a picture to illustrate their understanding of the actions in the problem to reach the final solution. Young students typically enjoy "playing store" to make purchases. Incorporate such an activity into a learning center or money instruction as a way to give practice opportunities that students will like.

6. Show pictures of everyday items with price tags. Indicate how much money is given to buy the item. Have pictures of coins with different amounts and have students

Directions: Provide students with a price for an item and the amount used to pay for it—for example: Item costs $3.86. Give $4.00. Determine change. Give students dollars and coins to work with on this activity. Have students work with a partner to fill out the following table for each item. Have students identify different coin combinations and dollars to find the change.

Price for Items	Amount Paid	Change
$0.26	$1	
$3.86	$4	
$2.25	$5	
$0.68	$1	
$2.50	$5	

FIGURE 5.2. Making change.

circle or underline the coins that represent the amount of change to receive. Figure 5.2 on the previous page can be used for students to practice making change.

7. Give money written in words. Have students read the words and practice writing the money words. Give hypothetical situations, such as Frank wants to purchase five stickers. Find the word that says "five," and spell the word and write the word. Eventually, ask students to spell and write money words from memory rather than from a model.

8. Play different card games to foster student engagement. Concentration is a good example, with money words on index cards and their corresponding values on different index cards. Play Go Fish, where money words are on some cards and their values on other cards. When students secure a match, have them name the money word and its value.

9. Teachers should spend part of the instructional time teaching the prerequisite skills for money that can be part of a warm-up or review for each lesson. Prerequisite skills should be taught or reviewed on an ongoing basis for money lessons. For instance, the concept "same and different," equivalence, and the skills for counting by units and counting by 5's or 10's (skip counting) are important prerequisites for the ability to discriminate among different coins and count change, respectively.

The *third guideline* concerns vocabulary. Teachers should teach the mathematics vocabulary associated with each money concept and skill. Vocabulary related to money can be explicitly taught and integrated into instruction on money lessons. For example, teachers should teach the concept *equal to* or *the same as*, and then present coins, the value of each type of coin, and which coins can be used to illustrate "equal to," such as "Five pennies equal one nickel," and "Five nickels are equal to one quarter, or two dimes and one nickel equal 25 cents." In addition to teaching the concept of equal as it relates to money, concepts such as "greater than," "less than," and "amount" should also be explicitly taught and integrated into lessons that require students to talk about the value of one coin or one group of coins in relation to another coin or group of coins.

The *fourth guideline* emphasizes students' use of multiple representations to respond to teacher questions and to justify their responses. *Multiple representations* include physical objects or manipulatives, drawings, pictures, tables, diagrams, symbols, and spoken and written language (Dougherty, Bryant, Bryant, & Shin, 2017). For example, the teacher could ask, "What is one way you can show how many dimes are needed to equal one dollar?" Students could respond by modeling 10 tens using rods or connecting cubes, or by drawing 10 tally marks or 10 circles as representations to depict money values. These multiple representations reflect flexible ways to answer teacher questions, taking into consideration that some students benefit from using manipulatives or physical object representations, while other students can draw pictures to answer questions. It is important to know that students must understand the meaning of representations, such as the use of tally marks or circles, in this case, represents the value of 10 rather than the quantity of one.

The *fifth guideline* relates to what is called *reversibility,* which can be emphasized to foster understanding by giving students solutions and having them identify ways to arrive at the solutions. Reversibility is a strategy to encourage students to generate possible problems depending on the solution and question presented to them. This approach allows students to develop different paths to a given solution (Dougherty, Bryant, Bryant, Darrough, & Pfannenstiel, 2015).

Let's look at an example of the reversibility strategy. Small groups of students can be given the solution of 60¢ and coins and asked to show the ways coins can be counted to equal 60¢. The teacher should have students count the coins to check that the amount equals 60¢. Students typically enjoy working with the reversibility strategy because of the ability to discuss options with their peers in small groups, for instance, and to be challenged to think in a different way, meaning the solution is given first and the possible ways to show equality for the solution (60¢ in this case) are identified.

The *sixth guideline* refers to a mastery score as a goal. Teachers should expect students to achieve 100% mastery with lessons that teach money and, for that matter, time. Less than this goal does not ensure that students really know the concepts and skills for money and, thus, daily living needs. However, teachers must also make allowances for careless mistakes, which is why 100% can be a goal, but 90% (assuming 10 problems, for example) or 95% (assuming 20 problems) accuracy with remediation on the missed items is acceptable.

Given the limited amount of textbook coverage on time and money in the general education elementary grades, students with MD and MLD will require additional help (e.g., interventions in Tier 2 or Tier 3 as part of a response-to-intervention [RTI] or multi-tiered system of supports [MTSS] program) to ensure that they master these important life skills. Taken together, time and money represent problematic areas for students with MD and MLD and thus must be the focus of intensifying interventions given that these are both important life skills.

Intensifying Interventions for Time and Money

In many schools today, universal screening for academic difficulties often occurs at the beginning or in the middle of the year in kindergarten and at the beginning, middle, and end of the year in grades 1 and 2. Students who score below the benchmark cut score (e.g., 25th or 35th percentile) on the mathematics screener are then eligible to receive Tier 2 supplemental or Tier 3 intensive interventions, in addition to continuing to receive core Tier 1 instruction, to ensure that they learn the critical concepts and skills associated with time and money measurement for school and everyday activities. In the following sections, we focus on the topic of money; however, the examples given can be easily developed for Tier 2 and Tier 3 interventions in time. We present an example of how instruction can look for students who are identified as in need of Tier 2. We also show how Tier 2 instruction can be adjusted for Tier 3 to address the more challenging needs of individual students.

Tier 2 Intervention Example

A mathematics intervention teacher can use adaptations to intensify instruction for students who are struggling with learning money concepts. For example, a lesson's objective might focus on teaching how to count given amounts of money to $1.00 and how to select coins to make a given quantity. An instructional delivery adaptation could be used by reducing the number of students in a group, such as reducing small-group, 6:1 instruction to smaller-group instruction of four to five students. A materials adaptation can be used with ten frames and instructional content limited to working with dime coins initially. The intervention should be delivered at least three times per week for 25–30 minutes until a predetermined mastery is achieved. The representation should be real coins and dollar bills or authentic-looking simulations.

For cumulative review during warm-up or preview, activities can be provided that have students say the names and values of coins, skip-count by 5's and 10's, and say the equivalence of coins, such as 5¢ = five pennies. The ¢ and $ symbols should be displayed on a Word Wall for students to reference as they say the name of the symbol and pair it with a number and the written words for the quantity. For instance, the ¢ is referenced, and students say the name of the symbol; a quantity card can be shown, such as 35¢, and students say the amount. Cards with the written money amount, such as five cents, can be added to this activity to extend the intervention to include written money words after the words have been taught explicitly as part of the intervention.

Interactive modeling can involve the teacher providing students with coins and modeling how to count groups of money beginning with the largest valued coin, 25¢, and ending at $1.00 or 100¢. Teachers should also state an amount and model how to make that amount using the least number of coins. Students are engaged by counting their groups of coins with the teacher and by answering teacher questions such as "Is 75¢ more than or less than 72¢? How do you know?"; "Why is it easier to start with the largest-valued coin and then count the rest of the coin values?"; "If I add a dime to this group, how much money is there now?"; "Why does 25¢ and 5¢ equal 30¢?"; "How much will be left in this group if I take away 10¢?"; "What coin do I need to add to this group to equal 65¢?"; "How can you make 50¢ using different coins?"; and "How can you make 85¢ using the fewest amount of coins?"

During *guided practice*, students can work with a partner to practice what was taught earlier by, for example, counting groups of coins aloud, including 25¢, 10¢, 5¢, and 1¢ to $1.00. Groups of coins should include multiple coins with the same values, such as two quarters, four dimes, three nickels, and five pennies. Other coin groups should include different combinations of coins equaling $1.00 or 100¢. Once students practice counting money amounts, they should be given an amount less than $1.00 and asked to make the amount using different coin values.

Progress monitoring, in the form of *independent practice,* could include opportunities orally or in writing to demonstrate they met the lesson's objective by, for instance, counting the amount of groups of coins and selecting coins to equal a designated amount. Mastery could be set at 100% accuracy for several days. For students who do not show improving scores over a period of time and continue to fall below benchmarks scores on district tests, Tier 3 may be a good next step.

Tier 3 Intervention Example

Mathematics intervention teachers can further adapt and intensify their lessons as a way to help students who fail to make adequate progress with Tier 2 supplemental instruction. In this case, the size of the group is reduced to a maximum of three students and the intervention delivery is increased to 5 days per week for 30–45 minutes each session. Real or realistic coins and dollar bills continue to be the representation, but the interventionist more frequently checks for understanding and provides error correction and feedback and, at the end of each week, plays a bingo type of game to increase opportunities to practice.

Cumulative review is adapted where students focus on skip counting by 10's and then 5's using a hundreds chart. Students use the chart to count by 10's starting with the easier count—10, 20, 30, and so forth—and then moving to other numbers—starting with 12 and then continuing with 22, 32, 42, and so forth. The same procedure is used for counting by 5's, moving from simpler to more complex skip counting, such as skip counting by 2's or 3's. Following several days of review, students count by 10's and 5's without the hundreds chart. Coin recognition and coin values are also reviewed. Review questions should be asked using explicit language, such as "This is a penny. What coin is this?"; "A penny is worth 1 cent. How much is a penny worth?" The teacher can then alternate between pointing to coins and having students name them and state their values and asking students for the coin that has a certain value.

During *interactive modeling,* teachers can engage students by providing them with a set of coins and bills and demonstrating how to use them to find their equivalents, such as "10¢ is the same as 2 nickels, which is the same as 1 nickel and 5 pennies, which is the same as 10 pennies." To further intensify instruction by providing more practice, teachers can make intentional mistakes and ask students how to correct the equivalence error. In subsequent lessons, teachers can state an amount, model how to make the amount using the fewest number of coins, and then have students perform the same task. Questioning and frequently checking for understanding remain important components of Tier 3 intervention. Students should move to the next activity only after demonstrating a predetermined competence during modeled practice.

During *guided practice,* rather than having a struggling student work with a partner, the teacher can work one-on-one as needed. Flash cards can be used to practice money recognition and values. Increased opportunities can be added for students to count amounts of money beginning with the largest coin and counting on by 1's, 5's, and 10's; increased teacher questioning, checking for understanding, and providing corrective feedback should also be included.

One day each week, Find the Money (bingo) can be played. Find the Money cards should have boxes with pictures of coins and dollar bills; coin and dollar bill values; and groups of money, such as one quarter, two dimes, and four pennies; set up in a bingo format. Teachers should have a set of the same cards and select a card randomly to call out for students to locate on their Find the Money cards—for example: "Find an amount that equals 72¢," "Find the dime," and so forth.

Finally, with *progress monitoring,* in the form of independent practice as an example, teachers can create sheets with two columns. One column shows pictures of coins and bills; the second column shows amounts of money. Students match items in the two columns. Students should be given the opportunity after matching to read their answers, such as "A quarter matches or is the same as 25¢."

Conclusion

Proficiency with time and money measurement is an essential life skill for students to be able to use whether in school settings, at home, or in the community. According to the CCSSM (NGA & CCSSO, 2010), time and money concepts and skills fall under the Measurement domain and are taught in the early grades. The assumption is that children will be sufficiently adept with them for application in the later grades. Unfortunately, time and money receive less instructional time and textbook emphasis than the other types of measurement (i.e., length, volume/capacity, area, weight).

Time is challenging to teach to students with MD and MLD because time cannot be seen or touched and because the concepts may be too abstract for students in the early grades when time and money concepts are mostly taught. Teaching money has its own set of difficulties because of the needed prerequisite skills, such as counting by 5's, and the need to be able to switch denominations easily when counting and making change. Therefore, students with MD and MLD require instruction that is characterized by adaptations to lessons, materials, and instructional delivery. These students benefit from Tier 2 and in some cases Tier 3 interventions to meet their individual needs. Success in these RTI tiers can help to ensure improved performance outcomes as the goal.

REFERENCES

Bamberger, H. J., Oberdorf, C., & Schultz-Ferrell, K. (2010). *Math misconceptions: PreK–grade 5.* Portsmouth, NH: Heinemann.

Bley, N., & Thornton, C. (2001). *Teaching mathematics to students with learning disabilities* (4th ed.). Austin, TX: PRO-ED.

Clements, D., & Sarama, J. (2004). Learning trajectories in mathematics education. *Mathematical Thinking and Learning, 6*(2), 81–89.

Dougherty, B., Bryant, D. P., Bryant, B. R., Darrough, R., & Pfannenstiel, K. (2015). Developing concepts and generalizations to build algebraic thinking: The reflectivity, flexibility, and generalization approach. *Intervention in School and Clinic, 50*(5), 273–281.

Dougherty, B., Bryant, D. P., Bryant, B. R., & Shin, M. (2017). Promoting understanding of ratios and proportional reasoning for middle school students with persistent mathematics difficulties. *Teaching Exceptional Children, 49*(2), 96–105.

Earnest, D. (2017). Clock work: How tools for time mediate problem solving and reveal understanding. *Journal of Research in Mathematics Education, 48*(2), 191–223.

Exactly what is time? (2019). Retrieved from *www.exactlywhatistime.com/measurement-of-time/units-of-measurement.*

Gidwitz, T. (2001). Telling time. *Archaeology,* 36–41.

Haycock, D., & Cockburn, A. D. (1997). *Understanding mathematics in the lower primary grades.* Thousand Oaks, CA: SAGE.

Horn, C., Schuster, J. W., & Collins, B. C. (2006). Use of response cards to teach telling time to students with moderate and severe disabilities. *Education and Training in Developmental Disabilities, 41*(4), 382–391.

Jones, D., & Arbaugh, F. (2004). What do students know about time? *Mathematics Teaching in the Middle School, 10*(2), 82–84.

Kamii, C., & Long, K. (2003). The measurement of time: Transitivity, unit iteration, and conservation of speed. In D. H. Clements & G. Bright (Eds.), *Learning and teaching measurement: 2003 NCTM yearbook* (pp. 169–180). Reston, VA: National Council of Teachers of Mathematics.

Kamii, C., & Russell, K. A. (2012). Elapsed time: Why is it so difficult to teach? *Journal for Research in Mathematics Education, 43*(3), 296–315.

National Council of Teachers of Mathematics (NCTM). (2000). *Principles and standards for school mathematics.* Reston, VA: Author.

National Governors Association (NGA) Center for Best Practices & Council of Chief State School Officers (CCSSO). (2010). *Common Core State Standards for mathematics.* Washington, DC: Author.

Ryan, J., & Williams, J. (2007). *Children's mathematics 4–15: Learning from errors and misconceptions.* Berkshire, UK: McGraw-Hill Education.

SanGiovanni, J. (2017). *Mine the gap for mathematical understanding.* Thousand Oaks, CA: SAGE.

Van de Walle, J. A., Karp, K. S., & Bay-Williams, J. M. (2016). *Elementary and middle school mathematics: Teaching developmentally* (9th ed.). Boston: Pearson.

Van de Walle, J. A., & Lovin, L.A. (2006). *Teaching student-centered mathematics.* Boston: Pearson.

Wiig, E. H., & Semel, E. M. (1984). *Language assessment and intervention for the learning disabled* (2nd ed.). New York: Macmillan.

CHAPTER 6

Improving Conceptual Understanding and Procedural Fluency with Number Combinations and Computation

SARAH R. POWELL, SUZANNE R. FORSYTH, and MELISSA K. DRIVER

LEARNING OUTCOMES

After studying this chapter, you will be able to answer the following questions:

1. What are the conceptual ways to explain addition, subtraction, multiplication, and division?
2. What are methods for increasing fluency with number combinations?
3. What are several alternate algorithms for addition, subtraction, multiplication, and division?

Students experiencing mathematics difficulty often show delays in conceptual understanding of early numeracy principles (Gersten & Chard, 1999) and demonstrate lower number combinations and computation performance than students without mathematics difficulty (Geary, 2004). In fact, difficulty with number combinations or computation can be considered a primary area of concern for students experiencing a mathematics learning difficulty (Fuchs et al., 2008), while poor conceptual understanding may delay growth in strategy use and reduce the likelihood that procedural errors will be recognized (Geary, 2004). Without targeted Tier 2 or 3 intervention, computation difficulties may persist across the elementary grades (Chong & Siegel, 2008) and into the secondary level (Calhoon, Emerson, Flores, & Houchins, 2007). With targeted intervention, however, outcomes can improve (e.g., Powell, Fuchs, Fuchs, Cirino, & Fletcher, 2009). The focus of this chapter is to describe ways to improve conceptual understanding and procedural fluency with both number combinations and computation.

In this chapter, we define *number combinations* as the set of 390 addition, subtraction, multiplication, and division facts. Addition number combinations include two single-digit addends added together for a single- or double-digit sum (e.g., 4 + 3, 8 + 6). Subtraction number combinations have a single- or double-digit minuend, a single-digit subtrahend, and a single-digit difference (e.g., 8 – 2, 17 – 9). Multiplication number combinations feature two single-digit factors multiplied for a single- or double-digit product (e.g., 3 × 5, 8 × 7). Division number combinations include a single- or double-digit dividend, a single-digit divisor, and a single-digit quotient (e.g., 9 ÷ 3, 48 ÷ 8). We define *computation* as addition, subtraction, multiplication, or division conducted in steps, most often with multidigit numbers (e.g., 104 + 29, 650 – 478, 23 × 42, 1900 ÷ 15). For computation, students may use an algorithm to work through the problem step-by-step.

Concepts of the Operations

Research suggests that students experiencing mathematics difficulty do not intuitively recognize the basic properties of whole-number operations and often require targeted instruction to develop conceptual understanding (Gersten & Chard, 1999). Yet, familiarity with the operations at a conceptual level is crucial to the flexible application of computation skills within problem-solving situations (Baroody, 2003). *One misconception that teachers may have is that there is only one meaning for each of the four operations. As you will read, each operation has multiple meanings, and teachers should emphasize the different meanings during instruction.* In this section, we describe strategies to build students' conceptual understanding of whole-number operations by using concrete representations within a framework of possible problem scenarios. We describe several options for extending problems to explicitly teach mathematics-reasoning skills and to encourage student verbalizations.

Addition

Addition is the combination of two or more quantities. The Common Core State Standards for Mathematics (CCSSM) address foundational addition concepts in kindergarten (K.OA) and first grade in two ways (1.OA): the first is "putting together," and the second is "adding to" (National Governors Association [NGA] Center for Best Practices & Council of Chief State School Officers [CCSSO], 2010). These approaches not only represent two ways of modeling and thinking about the application of addition but also offer differing routes to explore the commutative (i.e., when adding, the order of the addends does not matter) and associative properties (i.e., when adding three or more addends, it does not matter which two addends are added first) of addition.

When putting together, students join two or more subsets to make one larger set or combine two or more parts to make a whole. An example problem scenario for this view of addition is as follows: "André has five video games, Monique has four video games, and Zach has two video games. How many video games do the children have all together?" Using concrete items to represent the video games, students can model addition as putting together by having three separate groups of objects that are moved to a separate whole-group location, while counting (see Figure 6.1). Similarly, all the

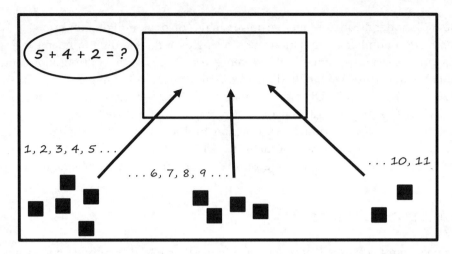

FIGURE 6.1. Concrete modeling for addition: putting together.

items may be simply pushed together and counted. The commutative and associative properties can be explored within the problem as students determine whether the total changes when groups are reordered (i.e., commutative), or when two sets are combined before the last group is joined (i.e., associative).

When adding to, or adding on, a student begins with a set and then joins more items, increasing the size of the set. A representative problem scenario is this: "Ashton had $3 and received $6 more for his birthday. How much money does Ashton have now?" Students can model this with concrete items by first creating groups to represent each quantity and then starting from the total number of items in the original set, counting up the number of items in the second set (i.e., 3: 4, 5, 6, 7, 8, 9; see Figure 6.2). During an exploration of the commutative property, the student can be explicitly taught

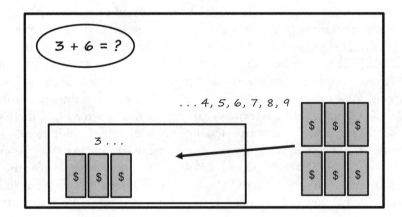

FIGURE 6.2. Concrete modeling for addition: adding to.

the min strategy (i.e., counting up from the larger addend), a skill that makes addition quicker for students struggling with fact retrieval but is unlikely to be inferred by a student with mathematics difficulty (Geary, 2004). The associative property can also be modeled by simply extending the story problem. For example, using the scenario from the previous page, "if Ashton received additional gifts throughout the day, does it matter whether gifts are grouped together as received, or will the total remain the same?"

Subtraction

Subtraction is the inverse of addition; it is the deduction, or taking away, of part of a whole set. Paralleling instruction in addition, the CCSSM addresses foundational subtraction concepts in kindergarten (K.OA) and first grade (1.OA). Students are expected to explore the concept of subtraction in three ways: "taking apart," "taking from," and "comparing." Students are also introduced to the inverse relationship of addition and subtraction as well as the associative property.

Taking apart models the inverse of putting together: while putting together joins subsets into a larger whole, taking apart breaks the whole into smaller subsets. A possible problem scenario is this: "If Emily has eight jelly beans and wants to eat three of them this morning, how many will she have left for a treat later this afternoon?" This may be modeled as a set of eight broken into two groups of three and five (see Figure 6.3). One enrichment activity for this view of subtraction is to rejoin the sets to reinforce understanding of the inverse relationship between subtraction and addition. Students who recognize this relationship display better conceptual understanding of subtraction and perform better on subtraction tasks than students who do not (Gilmore & Papadatou-Pastou, 2009). Additionally, experimenting with a given problem subtracting different amounts (e.g., in this scenario: "What if Emily only ate two jelly beans now?") reinforces the idea that there are many ways to break apart (and put back together) a specified quantity, while that initial quantity remains constant.

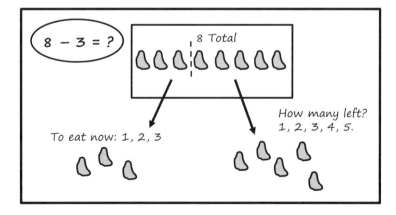

FIGURE 6.3. Concrete modeling for subtraction: taking apart.

In taking from (the inverse of adding to), the original set is broken and a subset is removed from the whole, leaving a portion of the original set. A representative problem is this: "Daniel had $5; then he spent $3 on a new yo-yo. How much money does he have left?" This view of subtraction is modeled by breaking the original set and removing the part subtracted (see Figure 6.4). To extend understanding of the noncommutative nature of subtraction, the student might be asked if it matters whether the equation is written as 5 – 3 = ? or 3 – 5 = ? (e.g., does the model change?). This foundational understanding that subtraction is not commutative affects a student's ability to comprehend why terms cannot be interchanged in subtraction computation.

The third way to model subtraction is comparing two sets. For example: "If Collin is 7 years old and Ariel is 5 years old, how much older is Collin than Ariel?" This can be easily modeled in two different manners: using snap-together cubes and comparing lengths, or by creating two sets, matching pairs from each set, and counting the remaining unmatched items (see Figure 6.5). Either model can be used to visualize and discuss why the result in subtraction is called the *difference*. This problem scenario can also be altered to create dialogue regarding the noncommutativity of subtraction as well as the inverse relationship between addition and subtraction (e.g., asking how much younger Ariel is than Collin results in the same equation because Collin's age is the minuend, or inversely, the sum of Ariel's age and the difference).

Multiplication

Multiplication determines the total for a specified number of equal groups. The CCSSM lays the groundwork for understanding multiplication by introducing repeated addition in the second grade (2.OA) and then focuses on developing a deeper conceptual knowledge of multiplication through the third (3.OA) and fourth grades (4.OA). In the Common Core, the operation of multiplication is explored conceptually as equal groups, arrays, and multiplicative comparisons, and students are expected to understand and apply the commutative, associative, and distributive properties.

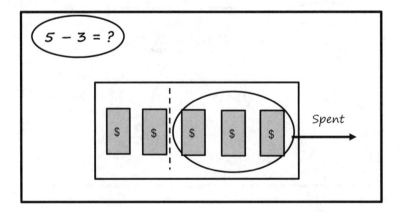

FIGURE 6.4. Concrete modeling for subtraction: taking from.

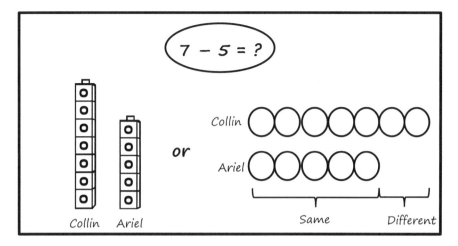

FIGURE 6.5. Concrete modeling for subtraction: comparing.

Modeling equal groups in multiplication reinforces the concept of multiplication as repeated addition. A potential problem scenario might be this: "Teddy bears are sold in packages of two. If Tristan buys three packages of candies, how many total teddy bear candies will he have?" A straightforward model can be created by using plates or trays to represent the packages, placing two items on each, and then joining them together (see Figure 6.6). Students can be encouraged to explore the properties of multiplication by altering the problem scenario: changing the number of packages bought requires students to add or remove entire groups, while altering the number of items in the packages allows the student to explore how the change must be distributed across all groups.

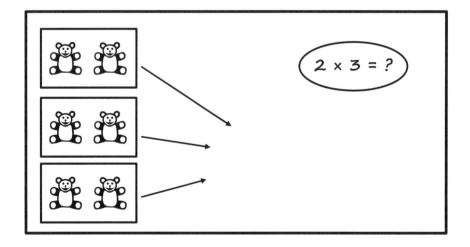

FIGURE 6.6. Concrete modeling for multiplication: equal groups.

Representing multiplication as a rectangular array allows students to see the two factors and how each affects the product. A potential problem might be this: "Aly, Damian, and Omar put their money together buy a birthday gift for their friend. If they each gave four dollars, how much money did they have to spend?" The array can be modeled with three sets of four cubes or tiles arranged in rows (see Figure 6.7). There are several ways to extend understanding of the properties of multiplication using this model. First, simply rotating the set 90 degrees to show four rows of three demonstrates the commutative property (i.e., $3 \times 4 = 12$ and $4 \times 3 = 12$). Altering the problem scenario by experimenting with the amount each person contributes can be used to illustrate the distributive property (e.g., if each contributes an extra \$2, does it matter whether that change is represented as $[(3 \times 4) + (3 \times 2) = ?]$ or $3 \times 6 = ?$). The associative property can be modeled by making another change to the problem scenario requiring additional multiplication. For example, what if a parent agreed to double the amount of money the students collected? Does the total amount of money depend on which factors are grouped first for multiplication? (i.e., $3 \times 4 = 12$, and then $12 \times 2 = 24$, is the same as $4 \times 2 = 8$, and then $8 \times 3 = 24$, which is the same as $3 \times 2 = 6$, and then $6 \times 4 = 24$).

By fourth grade, students are expected to model and explore multiplication as a comparison, and to contrast multiplicative comparison with additive comparison. Example problem: "Pedro made two goals at the soccer game, and Sharice made three times as many goals as Pedro. How many goals did Sharice make?" To model this problem, the student would make a group of two to represent Pedro's goals and then create iterations for Sharice's goals (see Figure 6.8). Given the parallel additive scenario ("Sharice made *three more goals than* Pedro . . ."), can the student model change to the scenario? Can the student verbally describe the differences between the two models?

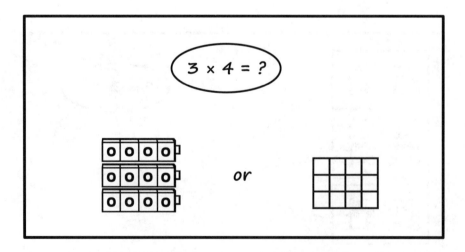

FIGURE 6.7. Concrete modeling for multiplication: arrays.

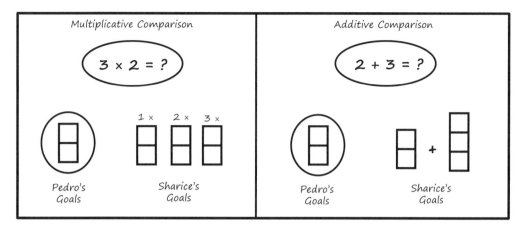

FIGURE 6.8. Concrete modeling for multiplication: multiplicative comparison versus additive comparison.

Division

Division is the inverse of multiplication: while multiplication combines equal groups into a greater whole, division separates the whole into lesser equal groups. In the CCSSM, division is expressed in the third-grade standards (3.OA) in two ways: partitive division or measurement division. Students are also expected to explore the inverse relationship between multiplication and division.

Partitive division is the separation of a whole into equal portions when the unknown quantity is how many items are in each group. This view of division is modeled as the reverse of equal groups in multiplication. An example problem: "Jessica, Saul, and Benji have a package of 18 candies to share. How many should each child receive if they all get the same amount?" For this model, students begin with 18 counters and place them, one at a time, into three different groups and then count how many counters are in each group (see Figure 6.9). To explore the characteristics of division more deeply, one might change how many people to divide among, pointing out that as the number of shares increases, the portions become smaller (an essential understanding for fractions), and that division may result in a remainder.

Measurement division is the separation of a whole into equal portions when the number of groups is unknown. It can be modeled by making a group the size of the divisor and then using that group to measure how many equal groups of that size can be formed from the dividend. Example problem: "Two eggs are needed to make a batch of cookies. Ian has six eggs. How many batches of cookies can he make?" For this problem, students would determine how many groups of two are in a total of six (see Figure 6.10). An extension activity is to discuss similarities and differences between division and subtraction, for example, they are both noncommutative because they both start with a given quantity and involve breaking the given set into parts.

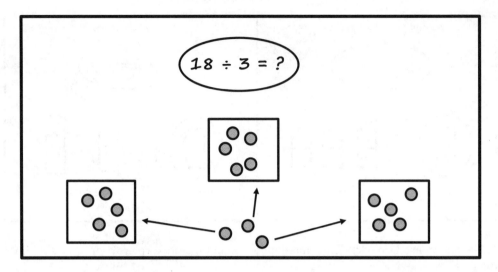

FIGURE 6.9. Concrete modeling for division: partitive model.

Building Fluency with Number Combinations

As students receive explicit instruction on the concepts of the operations, they need to simultaneously build fluency with number combinations through meaningful and frequent practice. Students experiencing mathematics difficulty often demonstrate lower fluency with number combinations than students without mathematics difficulty (Fuchs et al., 2005; Geary, Hamson, & Hoard, 2000). The CCSSM expectations are that students fluently add and subtract number combinations by the end of second grade (2.OA). Students should multiply and divide number combinations fluently by the end

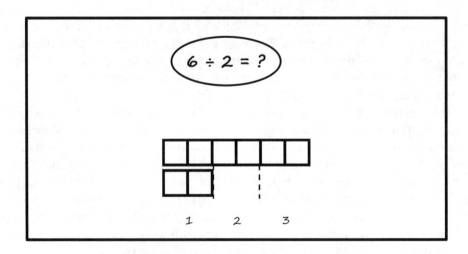

FIGURE 6.10. Concrete modeling for division: measurement model.

of fourth grade (4.OA). *A misconception that teachers may have is that fluency develops automatically. For some students, this may be true. But for other students, fluency practice has to be an intentional part of mathematics instruction.* In this section, we present several evidence-based instructional approaches that teachers can integrate into instruction for students experiencing mathematics difficulty. The goal of each fluency activity is to build automaticity in retrieving number combinations, freeing working memory resources for higher-level mathematics skills.

Explicit Instruction on Counting Strategies

Students experiencing mathematics difficulty commonly rely on inefficient counting strategies to solve number combinations (Shin & Bryant, 2015); therefore, it is often necessary to explicitly teach counting strategies. One evidence-based counting strategy is the *counting-up* approach, which can be used for both addition and subtraction (see Figure 6.11; Fuchs et al., 2009). For addition number combinations, students are taught to start with the greater addend (i.e., put the number in their fist) and then count up the lesser addend on their fingers, and the sum is the last number counted. For example, 3 + 6 is "6 (place 6 in closed fist): 7 (hold up one finger), 8 (hold up a second finger), 9 (hold up a third finger). 3 + 6 = 9." Beginning with the greater addend deepens student understanding of the commutative property of addition (i.e., 2 + 6 = 6 + 2; Garnett, 1992) and encourages flexible problem-solving skills.

Students experiencing mathematics difficulty often struggle with counting backward, and counting up is an efficient and easy-to-remember strategy to solve subtraction number combinations accurately. When subtracting (see Figure 6.11), students are taught to start with the subtrahend, count up on fingers to the minuend, and the difference is the number of counts (i.e., fingers up).

COUNTING UP Addition	COUNTING UP Subtraction
1. Put the greater addend in your fist and say it.	1. Put the subtrahend in your fist and say it.
2. Count up the other addend on your fingers.	2. Count up your fingers to the minuend.
3. The sum is the last number you say.	3. The difference is the number of fingers you have up.

FIGURE 6.11. Counting-up strategies for addition and subtraction.

Similar to counting up for addition and subtraction, students can count up using *skip counting* to arrive at products or quotients for multiplication and division number combinations, respectively (i.e., to solve 5×7, count up by 5's across seven fingers (5, 10, 15, 20, 25, 30, 35), and the product is the last number said; to solve $15 \div 3$, count up across fingers by 3's to 15 (3, 6, 9, 12, 15), and the quotient is the number of fingers held up). To facilitate skip counting, teachers could model the strategy using a multiplication table and give students ample practice opportunities to use such a table. To extend conceptual understanding, teachers should emphasize the commutative property within multiplication (i.e., if 7×6 is 42, then 6×7 is 42), explicitly teach the inverse relationship between multiplication and division, and demonstrate how this inverse relationship is displayed within a multiplication table.

Activities to Build Fluency

Understanding which strategies students use, and do not use, is helpful to inform instructional decision making for how to best support and build fluency with number combinations (Garnett, 1992). As students learn to use efficient counting strategies, teachers can continue to build fluency by reinforcing automatic retrieval of number combinations through several evidence-based approaches: cover–copy–compare, taped problems, flash cards, and incremental rehearsal.

Cover–Copy–Compare

The cover–copy–compare method is an instructional approach designed to facilitate independent fluency practice, and the method has been validated with both spelling patterns and number combinations (Konrad & Joseph, 2014). With this method, students are taught to view and study a worked example (i.e., a number combination with the correct answer) on the left side of their paper (see Figure 6.12). Then students *cover* the worked example with a card or a hand. Next, students *copy* the entire problem (see handwritten $13 - 4 = 9$) from memory into the space to the right of the solved problem. Last, students uncover the worked example to *compare* their work to the model. Students move on to the next number combination after correctly copying the number combination.

This evidence-based approach incorporates several aspects of effective instruction for students experiencing mathematics difficulty, including modeling, guided practice, corrective feedback, and opportunities to learn self-regulation (Cook & Schirmer, 2003; Gersten et al., 2009). A variation of the cover–copy–compare method is known as *model cover–copy–compare*, in which students first copy the worked example before covering and attempting to reproduce from memory (Grafman & Cates, 2010). Students could also use the *write–say* method where students repeat the worked example in both oral and written forms (Kearney & Drabman, 1993). A review of existing research on variations of the cover–copy–compare method suggests this intervention shows promise for students with and without disabilities, especially when paired with other effective instructional components (Joseph et al., 2012).

13 − 4 9	13 − 4 9	14 − 8 6	
12 − 8 4		16 − 7 9	
16 − 8 8		18 − 9 9	
16 − 9 7		12 − 6 6	
17 − 8 9		14 − 9 5	

FIGURE 6.12. Cover–copy–compare.

Taped Problems

A similar approach incorporating worked examples is the use of taped problems. In a comparison study with the cover–copy–compare method, researchers found that while both cover–copy–compare and taped problem interventions increased students' accuracy and fluency with number combinations, the taped-problems approach took less time to implement (Poncy, Skinner, & Jaspers, 2007). Using taped problems to build fluency in mathematics involves students listening to audio-recorded number combinations that include a brief pause after each problem (i.e., 1–5 seconds) and then providing the correct answer (McCallum, Skinner, & Hutchins, 2004; McCallum, Skinner,

Turner, & Saecker, 2006). For example, students are presented with a set of number combinations (see Figure 6.13). The recording would say, "6 times 5 equals . . . (pause 5 seconds) . . . 30." Students are prompted to "beat the recording" by writing down the correct response before the audio recording states the answer. With a taped-problems intervention, the duration of the pause varies: to begin with, the pause is brief; then it's longer to provide students more time to solve the problem, and then again it's shortened to promote rapid and automatic response (Bliss et al., 2010). This approach can be used to build fluency across a variety of academic content.

6 × 5 30	8 × 6 48	7 × 9	6 × 9
9 × 8	8 × 5	7 × 8	6 × 6
7 × 7	6 × 9	5 × 9	8 × 4
9 × 4	6 × 9	9 × 5	8 × 7
6 × 7	8 × 8	4 × 8	5 × 7

FIGURE 6.13. Taped problems.

Flash Cards

Incorporating brief practice using flash cards is another effective instructional approach to build fluency across content areas. Flash card activities are a common component of mathematics intervention programs that activate student knowledge and provide fluency-building practice to support students experiencing mathematics difficulty as they engage in complex problem solving, including word problems (e.g., Fuchs et al., 2009, 2010; Jitendra et al., 2013).

Flash card practice involves presenting individual cards with number combinations without the correct answer. Students quickly solve the combination using automatic retrieval or an efficient counting strategy. During practice, flash cards can be sorted into correct and incorrect piles to quickly allow both students and teachers to determine needed areas of support and additional practice. Spacing, or distributing, flash card practice across time is more effective than large consolidated practice sessions (i.e., cramming; Kornell, 2009), and distributed practice using explicit timed trials (i.e., "How many can you answer in 1 minute?") is especially effective for building fluency in number combinations (Schutte et al., 2015).

With flash card practice, students should receive immediate feedback affirming correct responses and brief corrective instruction for incorrect responses. When paired with explicit counting strategy instruction, such as counting up, feedback is effective and efficient, quickly reinforcing the strategy students can use if the answer is not immediately known. Alternatively, flash cards can include the correct answer on the back, to allow students to practice independently and still receive corrective feedback. As students develop stronger metacognition skills, determining for themselves which facts they know automatically, those they almost know, and those they find most difficult, the ability to use flash cards independently increases (Kornell & Bjork, 2008).

Flash card activities can be practiced individually or in small groups. In addition to building fluency, flash cards can also be used to encourage student progress and to increase intrinsic motivation. Timed practice drills can be recorded and graphed, allowing students to visually see progress in mastering a set of targeted number combinations. See Figure 6.14 for an example of a flash card graph.

Incremental Rehearsal

Number combination flash cards can be used to strategically target and build fluency using a process called *incremental rehearsal*. Incremental rehearsal is an evidence-based approach to improve accuracy and fluency with number combinations, and research indicates that gains are maintained over time and generalized to similar tasks (Codding, Archer, & Connell, 2010). Incremental rehearsal involves drills that include practicing a skill in isolation, allowing frequent opportunities to practice, and pairing known and unknown items during practice to appropriately challenge students experiencing mathematics difficulty (Burns, 2005).

40																	40
39																	39
38																	38
37																	37
36																	36
35																	35
34																	34
33																	33
32																	32
31																	31
30																	30
29																	29
28																	28
27																	27
26																	26
25																	25
24																	24
23																	23
22																	22
21																	21
20																	20
19																	19
18																	18
17																	17
16																	16
15																	15
14																	14
13																	13
12																	12
11																	11
10																	10
9																	9
8																	8
7																	7
6																	6
5																	5
4																	4
3																	3
2																	2
1																	1
Day																	

FIGURE 6.14. Flash card graph.

Burns's (2005) research on incremental rehearsal provides a detailed guide for implementing this approach. For example: A student is presented with 20 flash cards of number combinations (i.e., 5×7; 8×9) at the start of an intervention session. The flash cards are sorted into known (i.e., correct responses within 2 seconds) and unknown (i.e., incorrect responses, no answer, or correct answer after 2 seconds) number combinations. The student is then presented with the first unknown combination and the correct answer. The student restates (i.e., rehearses) the unknown combination with the correct answer. As unknown combinations become "known," previously identified known combinations are taken out of the flash card set and replaced with a new unknown number combination.

A variety of fluency-building strategies can be used to introduce and reinforce number combinations. Students experiencing mathematics difficulty should continue to practice after they have reached mastery to maintain and further strengthen their automaticity with number combinations. Building fluency with number combinations supports students' ability to perform computations accurately and efficiently and engage in more complex problem solving.

Building Efficiency with Computation

Beyond number combinations, students must develop efficiency with computation. This is another area in which students experiencing mathematics difficulty often demonstrate challenges (Chong & Siegel, 2008; Fuchs et al., 2008). The CCSSM states that students should fluently add and subtract within 1,000 by the end of third grade (3.NBT) with multiplication in fourth grade (4.NBT) and division in fifth grade (5.NBT). Strong understanding of the operations and fluency with number combinations assists students in improved efficiency with computation. *Similar to the concepts of the operations, some teachers may have the misconception that there is only one algorithm for each of the operations. In reality, there are multiple algorithms, and teachers need to help students find the algorithm that is most efficient for the individual student.* In this section, we describe different algorithms for solving addition, subtraction, multiplication, and division computation problems, and we highlight several practices for teaching computation supported by research. Compared to typical performers, students experiencing mathematics difficulty may have difficulty with computation by committing various errors, such as adding all digits in the numbers, using the incorrect operation, and making regrouping errors (Nelson & Powell, 2018).

Addition

For addition, the two most prevalent computation strategies include the traditional algorithm and partial sums. Look at the problem 129 + 43 (see Figure 6.15). With the *traditional algorithm for addition,* a student starts the problem in the ones column and regroups from right to left. With the *partial-sums algorithm,* a student starts in the problem in the greatest place value column and works to the ones column. The student

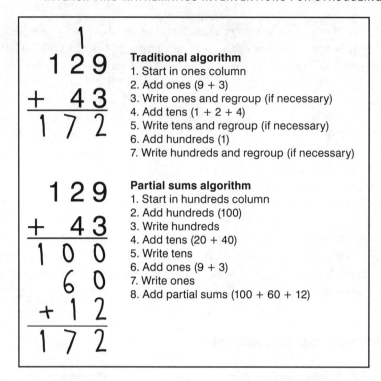

FIGURE 6.15. Computation algorithms: addition.

interprets the digit in each column by its place value (e.g., the 2 in the tens place is interpreted as 20). After calculating all the partial sums, the student adds the partial sums together for the sum.

Subtraction

For subtraction, some of the more popular computation strategies include the traditional algorithm, partial differences, and add up. Look at the problem 216 − 174 (see Figure 6.16). With the *traditional algorithm for subtraction,* a student starts the problem starting in the ones column and regroups from right to left. With the *partial-differences algorithm,* a student starts in the problem in the greatest place value column and works to the ones column. The student interprets the digit in each column by its place value (e.g., the 2 in the tens place is interpreted as 20). After calculating all the partial differences, the student calculates the difference. Please note for partial differences, when the minuend is less than the subtrahend, the subtraction is interpreted with positive and negative integers (i.e., 1 ten minus 7 tens equals −6 tens or −60). With the *add-up* strategy, the student starts with the subtrahend and uses friendly numbers to add up to the minuend. As with several other strategies, one student may use different friendly numbers than another student (i.e., there is not one correct way to solve the problem).

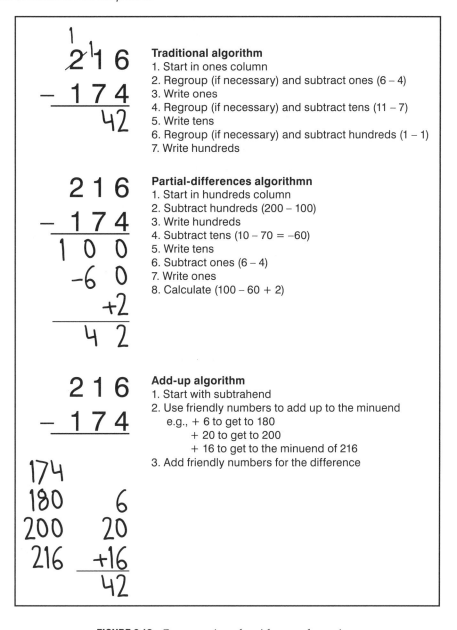

Traditional algorithm
1. Start in ones column
2. Regroup (if necessary) and subtract ones (6 – 4)
3. Write ones
4. Regroup (if necessary) and subtract tens (11 – 7)
5. Write tens
6. Regroup (if necessary) and subtract hundreds (1 – 1)
7. Write hundreds

Partial-differences algorithmn
1. Start in hundreds column
2. Subtract hundreds (200 – 100)
3. Write hundreds
4. Subtract tens (10 – 70 = –60)
5. Write tens
6. Subtract ones (6 – 4)
7. Write ones
8. Calculate (100 – 60 + 2)

Add-up algorithm
1. Start with subtrahend
2. Use friendly numbers to add up to the minuend
   e.g., + 6 to get to 180
      + 20 to get to 200
      + 16 to get to the minuend of 216
3. Add friendly numbers for the difference

FIGURE 6.16. Computation algorithms: subtraction.

This add-up strategy may be helpful for students experiencing mathematics difficulty who understand addition more than subtraction.

Multiplication

For multiplication, some of the more popular computation strategies include the traditional algorithm, partial products, and the area model. Look at the problem 27×34 (see Figure 6.17). With the *traditional algorithm for multiplication,* a student starts the problem in the ones column and multiplies the ones first. With the *partial-products algorithm,* a student starts with the greatest place value column and works to the ones column. The student interprets the digit in each column by its place value (e.g., the 3 in the tens place is interpreted as 30). After calculating all the partial products, the student adds the partial products for the product. The *area model* is another representation of the partial products algorithm. Here, the student makes a table for a two-digit factor and another two-digit factor (i.e., two rows and two columns) and writes each factor in expanded form. After multiplying, the student adds together all the partial products for a product.

Division

With division, students may employ the traditional algorithm or partial quotients. Look at the problem $298 \div 16$ (see Figure 6.18). Students using the *traditional algorithm for division* start the problem by determining how many groups of 16 can be made with 2 hundreds. If 2 hundreds cannot be divided into 16 equal groups, the student considers how many groups of 16 can be made with 29 tens. Figure 6.18 displays the rest of division with the traditional algorithm. With the *partial-quotients algorithm,* a student uses friendly numbers to make groups of 16. First, the student determines an approximate number of groups of 16 that can be made with 298. In this example, the student knows that 16×10 is 160. The student writes 10 to the right of the vertical line drawn down from the long division symbol. Then, the student subtracts $298 - 160$ for a difference of 138. Next, the student repeats the process again by determining an approximate number of groups of 16 that can be created with 138. After getting to a difference that is less than 16 (i.e., the divisor), the student adds all the partial quotients for the quotient. A remainder, when applicable, is the difference that is less than the divisor.

Conclusion

Fluency with number combinations and computation is necessary and makes many other mathematics skills easier. For example, fluency with multiplication number combinations can help with determining common denominators between fractions. Fluency with both number combinations and computation can make operations with decimals and within algebra an easier task as well. As discussed in this chapter, to intensify intervention, teachers must ensure that students are taught the concepts behind the

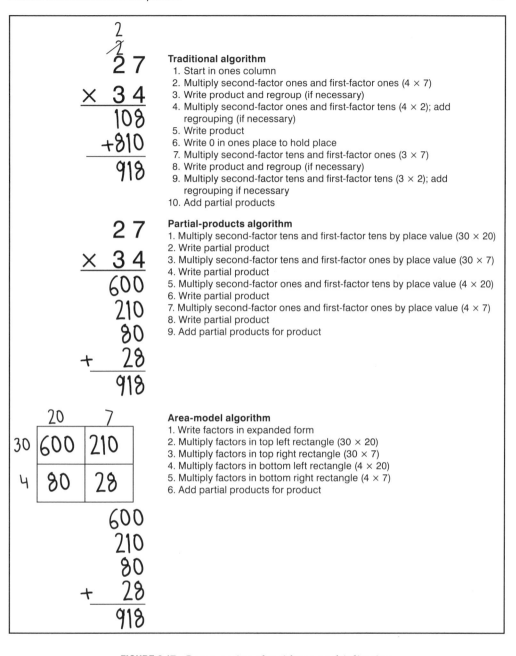

Traditional algorithm
1. Start in ones column
2. Multiply second-factor ones and first-factor ones (4 × 7)
3. Write product and regroup (if necessary)
4. Multiply second-factor ones and first-factor tens (4 × 2); add regrouping (if necessary)
5. Write product
6. Write 0 in ones place to hold place
7. Multiply second-factor tens and first-factor ones (3 × 7)
8. Write product and regroup (if necessary)
9. Multiply second-factor tens and first-factor tens (3 × 2); add regrouping if necessary
10. Add partial products

Partial-products algorithm
1. Multiply second-factor tens and first-factor tens by place value (30 × 20)
2. Write partial product
3. Multiply second-factor tens and first-factor ones by place value (30 × 7)
4. Write partial product
5. Multiply second-factor ones and first-factor tens by place value (4 × 20)
6. Write partial product
7. Multiply second-factor ones and first-factor ones by place value (4 × 7)
8. Write partial product
9. Add partial products for product

Area-model algorithm
1. Write factors in expanded form
2. Multiply factors in top left rectangle (30 × 20)
3. Multiply factors in top right rectangle (30 × 7)
4. Multiply factors in bottom left rectangle (4 × 20)
5. Multiply factors in bottom right rectangle (4 × 7)
6. Add partial products for product

FIGURE 6.17. Computation algorithms: multiplication.

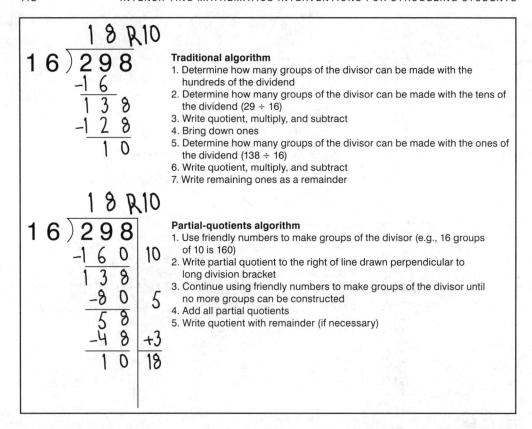

Traditional algorithm
1. Determine how many groups of the divisor can be made with the hundreds of the dividend
2. Determine how many groups of the divisor can be made with the tens of the dividend (29 ÷ 16)
3. Write quotient, multiply, and subtract
4. Bring down ones
5. Determine how many groups of the divisor can be made with the ones of the dividend (138 ÷ 16)
6. Write quotient, multiply, and subtract
7. Write remaining ones as a remainder

Partial-quotients algorithm
1. Use friendly numbers to make groups of the divisor (e.g., 16 groups of 10 is 160)
2. Write partial quotient to the right of line drawn perpendicular to long division bracket
3. Continue using friendly numbers to make groups of the divisor until no more groups can be constructed
4. Add all partial quotients
5. Write quotient with remainder (if necessary)

FIGURE 6.18. Computation algorithms: division.

operations. Another part of intensification requires that teachers model and allow time for students to practice building fluency with number combinations and efficiency solving computation problems. Many times, intensification involves providing more explicit modeling examples and many more practice opportunities for students. In some cases, intensification may involve unraveling false assumptions and reteaching mathematics. Intensification should be based on student needs and should aim to help students understand foundational concepts and procedures in mathematics.

REFERENCES

Baroody, A. J. (2003). The development of adaptive expertise and flexibility: The integration of conceptual and procedural knowledge. In A. J. Baroody & A. Dowker (Eds.), *The development of arithmetic concepts and skills: Constructing adaptive expertise* (pp. 1–33). Mahwah, NJ: Erlbaum.

Bliss, S. L., Skinner, C. H., McCallum, E., Saecker, L. B., Rowland-Bryant, E., & Brown, K. S. (2010). A comparison of taped problems with and without a brief post-treatment assessment on multiplication fluency. *Journal of Behavioral Education, 19*(2), 156–168.

Burns, M. K. (2005). Using incremental rehearsal to increase fluency of single-digit multiplication facts with children identified as learning disabled in mathematics computation. *Education and Treatment of Children, 28,* 237–249.

Calhoon, M. B., Emerson, R. W., Flores, M., & Houchins, D. E. (2007). Computational fluency performance profile of high school students with mathematics disabilities. *Remedial and Special Education, 28*(5), 292–303.

Chong, S. L., & Siegel, L. S. (2008). Stability of computational deficits in math learning disability from second through fifth grades. *Developmental Neuropsychology, 33*(3), 300–317.

Codding, R. S., Archer, J., & Connell, J. (2010). A systematic replication and extension of using incremental rehearsal to improve multiplication skills: An investigation of generalization. *Journal of Behavioral Education, 19*(1), 93–105.

Cook, B. G., & Schirmer, B. R. (2003). What is special about special education?: Overview and analysis. *Journal of Special Education, 37*(3), 200–205.

Fuchs, L. S., Compton, D. L., Fuchs, D., Paulsen, K., Bryant, J. D., & Hamlett, C. L. (2005). The prevention, identification, and cognitive determinants of math difficulty. *Journal of Educational Psychology, 97*(3), 493–513.

Fuchs, L. S., Powell, S. R., Hamlett, C. L., Fuchs, D., Cirino, P. T., & Fletcher, J. M. (2008). Remediating computational deficits at third-grade: A randomized field trial. *Journal of Research on Educational Effectiveness, 1*(1), 2–32.

Fuchs, L. S., Powell, S. R., Seethaler, P. M., Cirino, P. T., Fletcher, J. M., Fuchs, D., & Hamlett, C. L. (2010). The effects of strategic counting instruction, with and without deliberate practice, on number combination skill among students with mathematics difficulties. *Learning and Individual Differences, 20*(2), 89–100.

Fuchs, L. S., Powell, S. R., Seethaler, P. M., Cirino, P. T., Fletcher, J. M., Fuchs, D., . . . Zumeta, R. O. (2009). Remediating number combination and word problem deficits among students with mathematics difficulties: A randomized control trial. *Journal of Educational Psychology, 101*(3), 561–576.

Garnett, K. (1992). Developing fluency with basic number facts: Intervention for students with learning disabilities. *Learning Disabilities Research and Practice, 7*(4), 1–14.

Geary, D. C. (2004). Mathematics and learning disabilities. *Journal of Learning Disabilities, 37*(1), 4–15.

Geary, D. C., Hamson, C. O., & Hoard, M. K. (2000). Numerical and arithmetical cognition: A longitudinal study of process and concept deficits in children with learning disability. *Journal of Experimental Child Psychology, 77*(3), 236–263.

Gersten, R., & Chard, D. (1999). Number sense: Rethinking arithmetic instruction for students with mathematical disabilities. *Journal of Special Education, 33*(1), 18–28.

Gersten, R., Chard, D. J., Jayanthi, M., Baker, S. K., Morphy, P., & Flojo, J. (2009). Mathematics instruction for students with learning disabilities: A meta-analysis of instructional components. *Review of Educational Research, 79*(3), 1202–1242.

Gilmore, C. K., & Papadatou-Pastou, M. (2009). Patterns of individual differences in conceptual understanding and arithmetical skill: A meta-analysis. *Mathematical Thinking and Learning, 11*(1), 25–40.

Grafman, J. M., & Cates, G. L. (2010). The differential effects of two self-managed math instruction procedures: Cover, copy, and compare versus copy, cover, and compare. *Psychology in the Schools, 47,* 153–165.

Jitendra, A. K., Rodriguez, M., Kanive, R., Huang, J., Church, C., Corroy, K. A., & Zaslofsky, A. (2013). Impact of small-group tutoring interventions on the mathematical problem solving and achievement of third-grade students with mathematics difficulties. *Learning Disability Quarterly, 36*(1), 21–35.

Joseph, L. M., Konrad, M., Cates, G., Vajcner, T., Eveleigh, E., & Fishley, K. M. (2012). A meta-analytic review of the cover–copy–compare and variations of this self-management procedure. *Psychology in the Schools, 49*(2), 122–136.

Kearney, C. A., & Drabman, R. S. (1993). The write–say method for improving spelling accuracy in children with learning disabilities. *Journal of Learning Disabilities, 26*(1), 52–56.

Konrad, M., & Joseph, L. M. (2014). Cover–copy–compare: A method for enhancing evidence-based instruction. *Intervention in School and Clinic, 49*(4), 203–210.

Kornell, N. (2009). Optimising learning using flashcards: Spacing is more effective than cramming. *Applied Cognitive Psychology, 23*(9), 1297–1317.

Kornell, N., & Bjork, R. A. (2008). Optimising self-regulated study: The benefits—and costs—of dropping flashcards. *Memory, 16*(2), 125–136.

McCallum, E., Skinner, C. H., & Hutchins, H. (2004). The taped-problems intervention: Increasing division fact fluency using a low-tech self-managed time-delay intervention. *Journal of Applied School Psychology, 20*(2), 129–147.

McCallum, E., Skinner, C. H., Turner, H., & Saecker, L. (2006). The taped-problems intervention: Increasing multiplication fact fluency using a low-tech, classwide, time-delay intervention. *School Psychology Review, 35*(3), 419–434.

National Governors Association (NGA) Center for Best Practices & Council of Chief State School Officers (CCSSO). (2010). *Common Core State Standards for mathematics.* Washington, DC: Authors.

Nelson, G., & Powell, S. R. (2018). Computation error analysis: Students with mathematics difficulty compared to typically achieving students. *Assessment for Effective Intervention, 43*(3), 144–156.

Poncy, B. C., Skinner, C. H., & Jaspers, K. E. (2007). Evaluating and comparing interventions designed to enhance math fact accuracy and fluency: Cover, copy, and compare versus taped problems. *Journal of Behavioral Education, 16*(1), 27–37.

Powell, S. R., Fuchs, L. S., Fuchs, D., Cirino, P. T., & Fletcher, J. M. (2009). Effects of fact retrieval tutoring on third-grade students with math difficulties with and without reading difficulties. *Learning Disabilities Research and Practice, 24*(1), 1–11.

Schutte, G. M., Duhon, G. J., Solomon, B. G., Poncy, B. C., Moore, K., & Story, B. (2015). A comparative analysis of massed vs. distributed practice on basic math fact fluency growth rates. *Journal of School Psychology, 53*(2), 149–159.

Shin, M., & Bryant, D. P. (2015). A synthesis of mathematical and cognitive performances of students with mathematics learning disabilities. *Journal of Learning Disabilities, 48*(1), 96–112.

CHAPTER 7

Extending Students' Knowledge of Fractions as Relational Quantities

Teaching for Understanding

JESSICA H. HUNT and KATHERINE E. LEWIS

LEARNING OUTCOMES

After studying this chapter, you will be able to answer the following questions:

1. How do students reason or think about fractions?
2. What are assessment and instruction practices for fractions?
3. How can teachers use what students know to promote learning?

Students need experiences that build conceptual understanding of rational numbers, such as fractions, throughout their lives. A conceptual understanding of fractions contributes to students' *rational number sense,* a complex understanding of the varying forms of rational numbers such as fractions, ratio, rates, percentages, and decimals. The importance of fractions is evident in the Common Core State Standards for Mathematics (CCSSM; National Governors Association [NGA] Center for Best Practices & Council of Chief State School Officers [CCSSO], 2010), where understanding fractions is emphasized and re-emphasized throughout elementary school and is tied to other forms of rational numbers and proportional reasoning in middle school. Textbooks, online applications, and technology offer educators many tools to draw from to support students' reasoning. Yet, experience taught us that educators need to navigate these tools with the students' understanding in mind.

In this chapter, we begin by describing varying ways students reason about fractions. We describe difficulties that students experience, key points of understanding, and possible ways of reasoning. Next, we offer educators ideas for assessment and pedagogy to use in their classrooms based on frameworks of student thinking. Our hope is to share insight into student thinking such that educators can use this critical knowledge to consider learning goals (Hunt & Stein, 2020; National Council of Teachers of Mathematics [NCTM], 2014) and plan instruction. We end the chapter by providing several instructional activities that can help educators intervene at the outer edges of students' knowledge. In this kind of instruction, educators empower students to develop a conceptual foundation upon which to develop deeper understanding of mathematics.

Students' Reasoning about Fractions

Educators know that many students have difficulty learning fractions throughout elementary and middle school. Two difficulties tend to stand out. First, when comparing fractions, students may argue that $\frac{1}{10}$ is greater than $\frac{1}{4}$ because 10 is a larger whole number than four. Similarly, students may misuse whole-number reasoning and procedures for fractions (Mack, 1995) and argue, for example, that $\frac{1}{2} + \frac{1}{4} = \frac{2}{6}$. Both examples provide clear evidence that students are not reasoning about fractions as "numbers in their own right" (Hackenberg, 2007, p. 28). Other researchers argue that students' difficulties may center on overgeneralizing whole-number magnitudes (see Ni & Zhou, 2005) or that whole-number composites are not yet reorganized in such a manner that is useful for fraction knowledge (see Steffe & Olive, 2010).

One possible source of these difficulties is instruction. Part–whole teaching approaches, when used alone, often present prepartitioned shapes or linear segments and ask students to respond by indicating a requested number of parts or segments as a fractional quantity. Procedures for finding equivalent fractions are often presented next, followed by the four operations: adding, subtracting, multiplying, and dividing. The problem with this approach is that it does not build understanding of fractions as quantities (Hackenberg, 2007; Lamon, 1993, 2007). To facilitate fractional knowledge in a way that builds rational number sense, educators must have a goal for learning (Simon, 1995), give sufficient time and opportunity from which students can develop a conceptual basis to build more sophisticated notions of fractions, and plan rich, accessible instruction (CAST, 2011). Students must know the following:

- Fractions are numbers that have magnitude determined by the relationship of the numerator and denominator (Lamon, 2007). For example, to know that $\frac{3}{5}$ is greater than $\frac{3}{7}$, students need to understand that denominators refer to the size of the fractional parts ("fifths" means that five repetitions of a certain size part fill a whole, while "sevenths" means that seven repetitions of a certain size part fill the same size whole) *and* that numerators refer to the number of parts being considered (three $\frac{1}{5}$-sized parts versus three $\frac{1}{7}$-sized parts).

- Fractions can exist as parts and wholes (e.g., 1 out of 2) but also as measures (e.g., $\frac{1}{2}$ of a mile), ratios (e.g., 1 adult to 2 children), operators (e.g., making $\frac{1}{2}$ of a recipe), and quotients (e.g., 3 ÷ 4 =) (Behr, Lesh, Post, & Silver, 1983; Charalambous & Pitta-Pantazi, 2007; Kieran, 1988; Kieren, 1976, 1980, 1993; Lamon, 1993, 2007). Students' understanding grows in sophistication to include considerations of "how much" as opposed to only "how many" (e.g., Siegler et al., 2010; Steffe & Olive, 2010).

• Fractions can be represented in different ways, including words ("three-fourths"), symbols (¾), and models (area, linear, set models; Lesh, Post, & Behr, 1987) as well as through varying contexts.

Students' Development of Fraction Knowledge and Reasoning

It is possible that different understandings of fraction concepts develop at different times and/or orders depending on the tasks posed, student backgrounds and experiences, and other factors that occur in the midst of instruction and experience (e.g., Hunt, MacDonald, & Silva, 2019; Hunt, Silva, & Lambert, 2019; Lewis, 2014, 2016). What we describe in this section are ways of thinking evident across nearly 50 clinical interviews with students with mathematics difficulties and varying disabilities (Hunt, 2014; Hunt, Welch-Ptak, & Silva, 2016) and confirmed in later research (Hunt, Martin, et al., 2020). We align this with one existing literature base that describes how the learning of fractions could develop (e.g., Confrey, Maloney, Nguyen, & Rupp, 2014; Cramer, Post, & delMas, 2002; Empson & Levi, 2011; Piaget, Inhelder, & Szeminska, 1960; Steffe & Olive, 2010; Streefland, 1993). We present the following framework: (1) *no partitioning*, (2) *utilizing one-half*, (3) *anticipatory partitioning*, and (4) *relational composite partitioning*.

No Partitioning

In this way of reasoning, students begin to consider notions of equal and sharing through their experiences (e.g., sharing items at lunch). Sometimes, students may not understand the need for numbers that are not whole. In these instances, students may add more objects, make unequal shares, or throw away the remainder (Empson & Levi, 2011; Piaget et al., 1960). Students may equally share 6 cookies between two or three students but may not yet equally share 7 cookies between 2 students. It is possible that these students may be focused on whole-number ideas such as one-to-one correspondence, equality, and counting (Mack, 1995) along with notions of "fair" versus "equal," but do not yet see a need to create fractions.

Utilizing One-Half

Through engaging in problem solving (MP1; NGA & CCSSO, 2010), students first begin to consider the idea of nonwhole numbers in the context of "half," the fraction ½, or the action of making two parts. Two students sharing one stick of clay for an art project or five small sandwiches shared equally between two students are examples of situations that create a need for fractions (Davydov & Tsvetkovich, 1991; Empson & Levi, 2011; Steffe & Olive, 2010; Streefland, 1993). The focus of the students' activity is often an attempt to *partition,* or cut up, the one original item (e.g., the clay stick) or the one remaining item (e.g., the fifth sandwich). Students may cut the final sandwich into two equal parts that exhaust the whole, two unequal parts that exhaust the whole, or two equal parts that do not exhaust the whole (Hackenberg, 2013; Piaget et al., 1960). As students become more sophisticated with their partitioning, they will begin to focus on the equality of the parts and ensure that the entire whole is exhausted. The partitioning and coordination of created fractional units (Wilkins, Norton, & Boyce, 2013) provides ample opportunities for students to attend to precision (MP6; NGA & CCSSO, 2010).

Students who are able to successfully partition items into halves and coordinate the parts with the whole often attempt to extend this approach to create other numbers of parts. One characteristic of this kind of understanding is that students often approach a partitioning task by using doubling and halving to consider other fractional units (Fosnot & Dolk, 2002; Hiebert & Tonnessen, 1978; Piaget et al., 1960; Pothier & Sawada, 1983). Students are therefore successful in creating two parts, four parts, and eight parts and will likely partition one whole item into three unequal-sized parts if prompted. Students might begin to connect partitioning of the whole with the number of sharers through a variety of ways (Hunt, Tzur, & Westenskow, 2016; Hunt, Welch-Ptak, & Silva, 2016; Hunt, Westenskow, Silva, & Welch-Ptak, 2016) that show a nascent linking of the number of sharers with one item or several items (3.NF.A.1; NGA & CCSSO, 2010).

Anticipatory Partitioning

When students begin to turn their attention to partitioning one whole (or each whole in problems involving multiple wholes) into other amounts (Empson & Levi, 2011; Steffe & Olive, 2010) they have begun to engage in anticipatory partitioning. That is, students must anticipate not only the number of parts to create but also the size of each part with respect to the whole (3.NF.A.1; NGA & CCSSO, 2010). For example, to partition a bar of clay into three parts, the student needs to *unitize,* or specify, one whole as a quantifying unit and anticipate how the clay will be *partitioned,* or cut up, to make three equal shares. Students might repeatedly adjust the partitions to achieve equally sized parts (Steffe & Olive, 2010; Tzur, 2007; Tzur & Hunt, 2015). As opposed to only partitioning one whole to make three pieces, students are building what will be a later anticipation of the *size* of one part contained in or out of three parts *iterated,* or repeated, three times relative to the whole (Tzur, 1999, 2007). As students repeat this activity across multiple learning situations (e.g., share among four, share among five), they begin to anticipate the inverse size relation among unit fractions (e.g., $\frac{1}{4} > \frac{1}{5}$ because $4 < 5$; 3.NF.A.3.D; NGA & CCSSO, 2010).

Students then begin to use the fractional parts they create to produce nonunit fractions (m/n; 4.NF.B.3; NGA & CCSSO, 2010) or whole units (n/n) through iteration. Students who anticipate how a nonunit fraction could be partitioned into a variety of parts can make sense of composing and decomposing whole units and nonunit fractions in a variety of ways (e.g., $\frac{4}{5} = \frac{1}{5} + \frac{1}{5} + \frac{1}{5} + \frac{1}{5}$; $\frac{1}{5} + \frac{2}{5} + \frac{1}{5} = \frac{4}{5}$; 4.NF.B.3.B; NGA & CCSSO, 2010). Students who engage in these ways of partitioning and iterating begin to see one part as separate from yet contained within one whole and can begin to consider the magnitude of parts relative to each other and to the whole (Mack, 1995; Tzur, 2007). For example, a student understands ahead of activity that partitioning a whole into five parts produces a uniquely sized part such that one part repeated five times reproduces the whole. Students may also begin to count with unit fractions in ways that extend past one whole ($\frac{1}{3} + \frac{1}{3} + \frac{1}{3} + \frac{1}{3} = \frac{4}{3}$) and may be on the way toward constructing a multiplicative coordination of fractional units outside of one whole (Tzur, 1999).

Relational Composite Partitioning

Students who flexibly reason about fractions are able to consider fractions across a number of contexts and representations as fractions (i.e., measures, ratios, operators; Kieren, 1993) and begin to link the additive composition of unit fractions to a multiple of a unit fraction (4.NF.B.3.B; NGA & CCSSO, 2010). For example, students might consider the resulting quantity when three friends each consume $\frac{1}{5}$ of one whole birthday cake as $3 \times \frac{1}{5}$ or the amount of flour used in each batch of a recipe as $\frac{7}{3}$ if it takes $\frac{1}{3}$ cup of flour and seven batches of the recipe are made (4.NF.B.4.A; NGA & CCSSO, 2010). Within these contexts, it becomes important for students to consider the whole (Lamon, 2007; Tzur, 1999). They know ahead of activity that six repetitions of a unit whose size is $\frac{1}{3}$ creates two whole units and that each whole unit contains three one-third-sized units. In this way, students coordinate the fractional units at three levels (Hackenberg, 2007). Furthermore, students begin to use similar reasoning to understand multiples of non-unit fractions (e.g., relating three iterations of $\frac{2}{5}$ to six iterations of $\frac{1}{5}$) with and without context (Tzur, 1999; 4.NF.B.4.B, 4.NF.B.4.C; NGA & CCSSO, 2010).

Students who are able to consider fractions as relational composites can also partition and manipulate fractional quantities and link the results of combining partitioning and iteration as a relational division (Empson, Junk, Dominguez, & Turner, 2006; Lamon, 2005). For instance, results of previous sharing activity become distributive as students consider a fractional quantity as the result of dividing the numerator by the denominator (MP8; 5.NF.B.3; NGA & CCSSO, 2010). Here, students begin to reunitize their notions of a whole. That is, they can consider more than one object as "the whole" and negotiate meaning of fractions with respect to that whole. For example, if students are given a scenario involving two whole cups of flour partitioned into thirds, students might unitize the two cups as one whole and imagine groups of two-thirds across the two whole cups of flour as one-third of all the flour. They can also switch back to consider this quantity as two-thirds of one whole cup of flour. Reunitizing the whole (Lamon, 2005) across contexts (e.g., elapsing time, distance, rates) and representations (e.g., area, linear, set, tabular) enables students to see equivalent relationships in proportional reasoning later.

We have provided a narrative of how children can come to understand fractions as quantities and how children should be able to flexibly manipulate and conceptualize fractional quantities when understanding fractions as relational composites. In order to determine how children think, we recommend using assessment and instruction that employs clinical interviews and an adaptive or responsive form of teaching to identify the boundaries of what students know. Then teaching begins from a deep understanding of children's knowledge and promotes learning within the boundaries of children's understanding to support advancement of knowledge toward a learning goal. In the following sections of the chapter, we supply a process for educators to assess and instruct.

Assessment and Instruction

In order to ensure that assessment and instruction are paired in such a way that knowledge advances, educators must use what they know about the development of fraction conceptions. Educators should be mindful that children's notions of fractions do not necessarily begin at the point of the adult's goal for children's learning. In many ways, the literature base concerning all children's mathematical thinking is incomplete. However, what we do know about using children's thinking in instruction is that the goal should not be for children to solve one kind of problem (e.g., addition with unlike denominators).

Instead, educators must promote sense making (NCTM, 2014) and develop a comprehensive learner profile of student strengths (McLeskey et al., 2017). To do that, assessing what students currently understand and who they are is an essential first step. After that, educators can support development by refining the varying ways of reasoning we described earlier by using tasks and pedagogy that make sense in the contexts in which they are teaching, whether that is in classrooms with a large number of students, smaller-group instructional formats, or even one-on-one. Important across all of these models of instruction is the engagement of students in learning situations that facilitate learning not only through the child's own cognition but also through interaction.

Clinical Interviews

Clinical interviews (Ginsburg, 1997) can be useful to educators, as they uncover what a student "knows" and how a student understands a topic. In this way, clinical interviews provide a respectful, flexible sense of students' present performance and *why* students may be performing as observed or assessed. Clinical interviews vary in their format yet tend to include the following:

1. A plan for the tasks, tools, and probing questions to ask students
2. A way to start the interview
3. A way to interpret student thinking
4. A way to document what was found out about the thinking to guide instruction

On the next page, we list a set of problem tasks and questions that teachers might use to begin the clinical interview to assess students' thinking about fractions. Then we supply a way to start the interview and a reproducible that educators can use to interpret students' thinking and/or ask questions of students' responses. We tie the section together with a graphic that includes possible variations of students' thinking that educators can look for across the tasks and that can help them plan instruction.

Tasks, Tools, and Possible Questions

This particular set of situations is designed to help you as an educator better understand student thinking about the ways of thinking we described earlier (i.e., no partitioning, utilizing one-half, anticipatory partitioning, and relational composite partitioning) (Hunt, 2015/2020). Table 7.1 shows the tasks, tools to have available, and questions to ask.

The first column lists the tasks. Many of the tasks are based on equal sharing, and we leave the context of some of these tasks open. You will need to create or alter the context of these tasks to attach to students' sense making and interests. One idea is to ask students to visualize items and contexts that make sense to them. You can suggest contexts, yet you need to be ready to alter these contexts if they do not make sense to students. For example, if students do not know what banana bread is or do not seem interested in sharing clay bars, it would not be appropriate to use these contexts in the interview. Alter the context to fit the backgrounds of the students you are working with.

The second column lists the stage of thinking we described earlier to align to the mathematics that each task may support. The third column lists possible tools to have for student use during the interview. Sometimes, a representation is supplied. Begin with the supplied representation and, should you find that it is not accessible to students, follow the directions on the chart to alter the representation to increase access for the student. You might also ask students to solve the task with both representations to see not only what they are thinking but also what they are operating with (e.g., tangible items, drawn representations).

The fourth and fifth columns list questions to ask during the interview. Problem tasks are written to elicit thinking. Questions are prepared to accompany tasks and encourage the student to elaborate on sense making. This is not a time to teach, or lead, students to a particular solution, so resist the urge to tell or to teach during the clinical interview. Table 7.1 lists the questions you should use as you pose each task to students during the clinical interview. There are questions listed to ask after each task. There are also questions listed to ask if students seem stuck. If students are still stuck after using the questions, praise their effort and move on to the next task.

Starting the Interview with Students

You can begin the interview by explaining to students what will happen as they interact with the tasks and why it is important. The best way to do this is to state, simply and honestly, your purpose for posing the tasks. Getting students to show you their thinking can be difficult. For instance, students might believe it is their role not to show their thinking in mathematics but instead to mimic the thinking of the teacher (Hunt & Empson, 2015). These perceptions could affect the way students initially interact with the

TABLE 7.1. Clinical Interview Tasks, Questions, and Tools

Task	Stage or Action Assessed	Tools or Supplied Representation	Possible Questions	
			Always Ask	Ask If Student Is Stuck
1. Eight share 4 (add a context that makes sense to the child)	N/A (access point)	Unifix cube; paper rectangles that can be drawn on or torn up; "ones" blocks from base-ten materials; paper squares. All of the above tools should be available. The student chooses what to use.	"How many [context] does each person get?" "How do you know that is the right amount?" "Can you solve the problem another way?"	"Show me how you share those." "What does 'fair' mean to you?"
2. Two share 5; four share 9 (add a context that makes sense to the child)	Unitize Partition		"How much [context] for each person? How do you know that?" "Can you solve the problem another way?"	"Can you picture the [context] in front of you? What would they look like?" "What if everyone wanted to get all that they could?"
3. Equally share one item, even parts (add a context that makes sense to the child)	Unitize Partition Iterate	Supplied representations: Draw an 8.5" × 2" rectangle and a 4" × 4" square. If representation is inaccessible: Use 8.5" × 2" paper strip and 4" × 4" square. If using paper, the child should be asked to equally share without folding the paper.	"Can you draw one out of [2, 4; 3, 5] equal parts of the [add a context]?" "How do you know that is the size of the equal share for one out of [2, 4; 3, 5] people?" "Can you solve the problem another way?"	"Do you share things at home? What do you share?" "Can you use what you know about sharing at home to help you share the [context]?"
4. Equally share one item, odd parts (add a context that makes sense to the child)	Unitize Partition Iterate			
5. Order fractions	Result of partition Result of iteration	Arrange the parts in order from small to large: $\frac{1}{7}$ $\frac{1}{4}$ $\frac{1}{11}$ $\frac{1}{3}$	"Your friend cuts the following sized parts from one whole. Put the parts in order. Explain and justify." "Is there another way to explain why you are right?"	[This is an altered task] "Two [context] are exactly the same size. One has [7, 5] equal parts, and the other has [8, 9] equal parts."

	Concept	Task / Materials	Prompts	Follow-up prompts
Smallest $\frac{1}{\square}$ $\frac{1}{\square}$ $\frac{1}{\square}$ $\frac{1}{\square}$ Largest				"In which [context] are the parts larger? Why is that the right answer?"
6. Build up from a unit or nonunit fraction (add a context that makes sense to the child)	Coordinate partition and iterate / Coordinate units	Three friends each eat ⅕ of one [context]. Each batch of a recipe takes ⅓ cup of flour. Seven batches of the recipe are made.	"How much of one [context] did the friends eat? How do you know that?" "How much flour is needed? How do you know that?" a. and b. "Can you solve the answer in another way?"	"What does it mean to have [one-third; one-fifth] of a [context]? Can you use what you know about [⅓; ⅕] to help you here?" "Can you draw it out somehow?"
7. Equally share multiple items / 3 share 5 / 7 share 4	Coordinate partition and iterate / Coordinate units	Unifix cube; paper rectangles that can be drawn on or torn up; "ones" blocks from base-ten materials; paper squares. All of the above tools should be available. The student chooses what to use.	"How much of one [context] does each person get? How do you know?" Then ask, "How much of all of the [context] does one person get? How do you know?" Then ask, "Can you solve the problem another way?"	"Can you picture the [context] in front of you? What would they look like?" "Can you use another tool to help you show the problem?"
8. Reunitize the whole; unit coordinate	Coordinate units	[Re-create on larger paper; circle two of the parts below]	"Name the fraction quantity in several ways." "How do you know that is the right answer?"	"How much of one whole rectangle is that? How do you know?" Then ask, "How much of all of the rectangles is that? How do you know?"

mathematics tasks. So it is important to put students at ease in order to gain a window into their mathematical thinking. Do not present the tasks as a test. Reading the following to students (you can personalize the ideas to your own classroom or situation) can be helpful for providing a safe environment where they will feel comfortable showing you their thinking.

> "Today we are going to solve several mathematics problems to help me better understand how you think about mathematics. You may think some problems are simple while others are kind of tough. As you think about each one, you can use any of these tools [reference the tools you've prepared] that you like or even your fingers! There are a lot of different ways to think about each problem, and I am not looking for a 'right' or 'wrong' answer. I am just interested in how you think. If you are not sure, just let me know. Sometimes I might ask you questions so that I can understand what you mean a little better. Are you ready to help me out?"

How to Keep Records of Student Thinking

We understand that educators such as you work in different settings and will use the tasks in different ways. For example, some educators may pose the tasks to individual students, while others may work with groups of several students at one time. For each task in Table 7.1, consider how the student is demonstrating partitioning, iterating, and unitizing. We suggest that you use Table 7.2 to keep track of student reasoning, or you can create a way to notate that makes sense to you. It is certainly possible that students could demonstrate answers and explanations that align with more than one of the ways of reasoning we have written about. This is okay. You can still get a sense of how the student is thinking and what stage of reasoning is dominant.

Teaching at the Boundaries: Using What Students Know to Promote Learning

After completing a clinical interview and assessing a student's reasoning, educators can provide intervention that involves (1) mathematical learning situations that the students can access and (2) questioning and task constraints done at the boundary of what students know (e.g., Ulrich, Tillema, Hackenberg, & Norton, 2014). In this section, we provide examples of learning situations and explicit pedagogical moves that can support students' fractional reasoning to grow. The learning situations that we provide are experiences that students need to engage with and advance their understanding of fractions. We supply these situations alongside possible learning goals (see Figure 7.1, left side) such that educators can use the ideas to systematically design instruction (McLeskey et al., 2017).

The learning situations we suggest are purposive. That is, they are designed to support and promote *possible* ways that student development of fractions might show up and develop over time. We do not suggest that the proposed learning situations are

TABLE 7.2. Characteristics of Thinking Found across the Tasks

	No Partitioning	Utilizing One-Half	Anticipatory Partitioning	Relational Composite Partitioning
	• Adds more objects to make equal shares • Throws away "extra" or "remainders" • Makes unequal shares within one object	• Repeatedly halves to partition an object or objects • May successfully create 2, 4, or 8 parts yet have difficulty in creating 3 parts • When making 3 parts, may attend to equality of parts or using up the entire object, but not both at one time	• When partitioning for 3 people, repeatedly adjusts the parts to achieve equality • Repeats a created part across the whole to test its value or size • Quantifies the result of equal sharing multiple ways ($\frac{3}{4} = \frac{1}{4} + \frac{1}{4} + \frac{1}{4}$, $\frac{3}{4} = \frac{2}{4} + \frac{1}{4}$) • Quantifies unit fractions within one whole and outside of one whole using counting or addition; may lose sight of one whole	• Quantifies unit fractions within one whole and outside of one whole using multiplication • Uses unit fractions as inputs to make other fractions (uses one-thirds to make one-sixths; uses one-thirds to make two-thirds) • Repeats unit fractions across wholes without losing the bounds of one whole (e.g., four one-thirds do not become one-fourths)
Number of Tasks Where Activity Is Observed				
Dominant Representations				

the only ones educators might consider. The instructional situations suggested here explore fractions in a variety of different contexts. By encouraging engagement across a variety of instructional situations, students are granted access to refining and elaborating their understanding of and performance in fractions, in terms of both the complexity and the contexts in which students might make sense of their own reasoning.

Preparing for and Designing Instruction

Goals for Learning and Learning Situations

Look at Table 7.2 and notice where the majority of student reasoning is occurring across the tasks. Using the bulleted information in Table 7.2 alongside the narrative provided in the beginning of the chapter, assess which area(s) of the trajectory appear(s) evident in students' thinking and where thinking tends to converge (i.e., observable evidence of how a student is thinking).

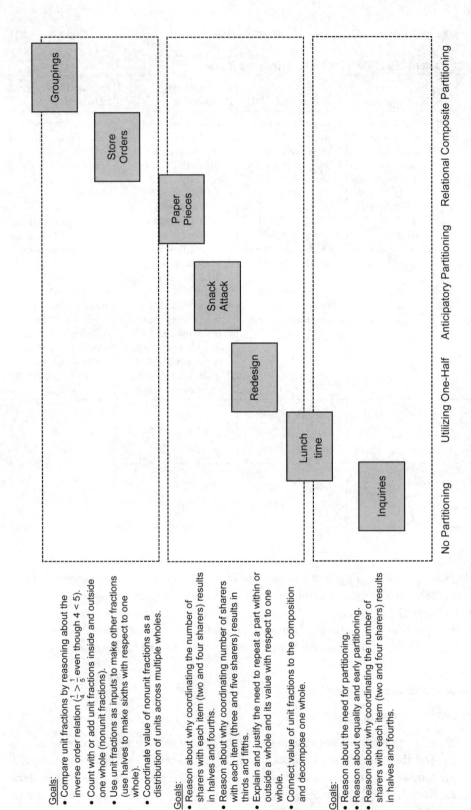

Goals:
- Compare unit fractions by reasoning about the inverse order relation ($\frac{1}{4} > \frac{1}{5}$ even though 4 < 5).
- Count with or add unit fractions inside and outside one whole (nonunit fractions).
- Use unit fractions as inputs to make other fractions (use halves to make sixths with respect to one whole).
- Coordinate value of nonunit fractions as a distribution of units across multiple wholes.

Goals:
- Reason about why coordinating the number of sharers with each item (two and four sharers) results in halves and fourths.
- Reason about why coordinating number of sharers with each item (three and five sharers) results in thirds and fifths.
- Explain and justify the need to repeat a part within or outside a whole and its value with respect to one whole.
- Connect value of unit fractions to the composition and decompose one whole.

Goals:
- Reason about the need for partitioning.
- Reason about equality and early partitioning.
- Reason about why coordinating the number of sharers with each item (two and four sharers) results in halves and fourths.

FIGURE 7.1. Synopsis of reasoning, possible instructional goals and situations, and pathways.

Next, consider the learning goals listed at the left-hand side of Figure 7.1, and consider a goal and a corresponding learning situation that align with the student's current ways of knowing fractions and yet is challenging for students. This means that you must select a learning situation that is within the area of reasoning that was dominant in the clinical interview. The selected learning situation must bring forward the student's current thinking so you can promote it to advance in instruction toward an instructional goal; for example, "Anticipatory Partitioning" was the dominant area, so "Paper Pieces" is selected as the learning situation with the goal of "Explain and justify the need to repeat a part within or outside a whole and test its value with respect to one whole."

Then, immerse the student in the learning situation. Watch how the student solves the task and use teacher questioning to support students to take note of and advance their own thinking (Hunt, Tzur, & Westenskow, 2016; Hunt, Westenskow, et al., 2016; Hunt & Tzur, 2017). We give suggestions for teacher questioning in the description of each learning situation. You should notice and respond to students' evolving thinking, using and adapting the learning situations when necessary toward the learning goal (McLeskey et al., 2017; Simon, 1995) to promote a rich understanding. You should not take what is pictured in Figure 7.1 as a cue to move through the tasks as pictured. The learning situations should be changed as student thinking changes (Hunt, Valentine, Bryant, Pfannenstiel, & Bryant, 2016; Hunt, Westenskow, et al., 2016).

Finally, re-evaluate student learning on a consistent basis. Although you can get some indication of where student thinking may originate, it is important to acknowledge that student thinking advances, or not, in real time, context, and experience (Simon, 1995). We provide ideas, but you should respond to student thinking in your classroom communities and contexts (Hunt, Valentine, et al., 2016). For example, you might begin with the "Lunchtime" situation on page 135 because you felt the student needed to reason about the need for partitioning. Yet, in practice, you might find that a more appropriate learning goal is to reason about why coordinating the number of sharers with each (three and five sharers) results in thirds and fifths. Students should be given access to making multiple connections between and among the various ideas summarized in Figure 7.1 and unpacked in the following sections.

Instructional Practices

All learning situations that we describe here are infused with instructional practices proven to be very beneficial for improving performance and/or understanding for all students (i.e., Tier 1). Specifically, we describe how educators can encourage the use of a variety of strategies for solving problems (see Woodward et al., 2012). Research converges on the effectiveness of giving students opportunities to use multiple-solution strategies and compare/contrast their solutions to promote problem-solving flexibility (see Star & Rittle-Johnson, 2009). We also propose ways to adjust learning situations to respond to students through access to varying means of representation, engagement, and expression (e.g., CAST, 2011; Hunt, Silva, & Lambert, 2019; Lewis, 2017). Providing ways for students to make connections between the tasks supports students to extend their thinking toward more sophisticated notions of fractions.

In certain situations, we infuse practices found to be beneficial for Tier 2 and Tier 3 instruction. We describe four practices to intensify instruction. First, we provide targeted feedback on language comprehension and understanding of the iterative and relational nature of unit fractions with respect to one whole (see Gersten et al., 2009) after robust conceptual foundations for later abstractions (Simon et al., 2010) are constructed. Second, all learning situations include opportunities for representations, such as concrete materials, drawings, or number sentences to organize and represent the mathematical situations (see Carpenter, Fennema, Franke, Levi, & Empson, 2014) and to bridge symbolic notation to student reasoning (see Tzur et al., 2013; Xin, Wiles, & Lin, 2008). Third, questioning is included to help students reflect on their own problem-solving activity using explanations of their own reasoning (see Hunt & Tzur, 2017; Siegler, 1995; Zhang, Xin, Harris, & Ding, 2014) or regulation of the word-problem-solving process (see Hunt & Vasquez, 2014). Finally, we include instructional prompting (see Hunt & Tzur, 2017) as facilitators.

Implementing Instruction

One powerful learning situation to promote fractions begins with equal sharing (Empson & Levi, 2011; Fosnot & Dolk, 2002; Hunt & Empson, 2015; Streefland, 1993). Begin with situations that result in whole-number shares and then move to situations where students can see a need to create fractions. Using situations that involve two and four sharers may support students to use knowledge of these numbers to connect whole-number reasoning to partitioning. Later, educators might use situations that involve a need to make an odd number of parts from a whole number of parts. Then educators need to consider tasks that empower students to use created fractional parts to think about the size of nonunit fractions and wholes, compare fractional parts, and coordinate fractional units across wholes. In the rest of this section, we list possible tasks that can help students build their understanding. A reproducible is included for the second task.

Inquiries

Present a variety of scenarios where students make judgments about in which situation they would get more to eat (Lamon, 2005). Begin by posing a situation where three items are shared by two students and four items are shared by four students. Then pose a situation where two items are shared by four students and three items are shared by seven students. Next, pose a situation where five items are shared by six people and three items are shared by twelve people. Finally, pose a situation where two items are shared by eight students and three items are shared by five students. Present the representations of each situation so students can see the groupings. Students consider these situations to attach notions of "two" and "four" to partitioning and quantities. The situations are designed for students to take note of situations where students receive a whole number of items, quantities involving one-half or one-fourth, or some other quantity. These situations help students unitize and consider early notions of partitions using two and four.

Lunchtime

Ask students if they have ever shared food at lunchtime (or use another meaningful context for sharing). Pose situations such as two sharers and three items or four sharers and ten items (Empson, 2003; Empson & Levi, 2011; Streefland, 1993). Begin with two or four sharers to gather evidence of if and/or how students use their ideas about "two" and "four" to reason about partitioning and creating fractions. If students show one way to partition, ask them to solve the problem another way. A partial conception students may evidence in the situation is a difficulty seeing different ways to partition the items. Address this by varying the ways in which the sandwiches are served (e.g., one at a time, all at once) (Streefland, 1993). The situation can be extended using the question of four friends sharing 13 sandwiches.

This learning situation can be intensified for Tier 2 and Tier 3 interventions in the following ways. First, have representational options, such as tearable rectangles or paper and pencil, available for students to use during problem solving. If students are having difficulty using a representation, suggest a similar representation that matches the students' original activity (e.g., suggesting students draw a square to partition if they describe a drawn circle to be problematic; Hunt & Vasquez, 2014). Similarly, should you see that students' drawings do not match the situation (e.g., the student might draw three sharers and two items as opposed two sharers and three items), ask questions about their drawing and how it relates to the problem situation (Hunt & Empson, 2015). Finally, ask questions to promote self-explanations (Hunt & Tzur, 2017; Siegler, 1995; Zhang et al., 2014). For example, ask students to describe what they are doing as they are doing it (Hunt & Tzur, 2017; Hunt, Tzur, & Westenskow, 2016; Hunt, Valentine, et al., 2016). Or, if students created four parts in the last two items in four sharers and 10 items, ask them how they might use that same thinking to consider four items and 13 sharers. A reproducible of the task can be found in Figure 7.2.

Redesign

In this learning situation, students are asked to use measurement to reason about the midpoint of a wall, hall, or whiteboard, in order to support their understanding of the fraction ½. If educators want to use the idea of measuring a wall or finding the midpoint of a board, we suggest they introduce the task as a kind of problem in which the result is something tangible. For instance, students could be asked to find the middle of a bulletin board to position a picture. Students may use a multitude of methods to achieve their goal. We suggest that educators constrain the activity and not allow the use of a standardized means of measurement because students will have to use some informal way to measure. For example, if students reason about the midpoint of a hallway, they could use their feet, hands, or some other way of measuring to express the entire length. Students can connect the number of feet or hand lengths to consider the total length and then the midpoint. They may also talk about why measurements can change (e.g., a longer foot versus a shorter foot). Students can begin to reason about the number

Instructions: *Friends are sharing food at their lunch tables. For each situation, show your thinking using drawings, words, and symbols.*

1. At the first table, two friends share three small sandwiches equally. How many sandwiches does each friend eat?

2. At the second table, four friends share 10 small sandwiches equally. How many sandwiches does each friend eat?

Extension: *What if there was a third table with four friends and 13 sandwiches? How many sandwiches does each friend eat? Is this more or less than what each friend eats at the first table?*

FIGURE 7.2. Lunchtime task starter.

of unit lengths in each half and the number of unit lengths in the whole (Davydov & Tsvetkovich, 1991).

Tower Tails

To support students who can utilize one-half but struggle with other partitions, it may be helpful to extend their experiences with measurement to provoke the need for an odd number of parts. Ask students to consider how to measure out two equal parts of a tall tower, then four equal parts, and finally, three equal parts. Challenge students to use various ways of reasoning. Provide varying tangible or drawn representations that students find realistic (e.g., a water tower, a milk carton, a cooler). Supply measuring tools shorter than the whole. Students will use a variety of problem-solving strategies. For example, students might find the midpoint of the tower or use one part and adjust its height by repeating it or stacking it against the whole to test the preciseness of the height. This last strategy is preferable as it supports iteration of the part with respect to the whole. If iteration is observed, challenge students to use the magnitude of the previously created part (e.g., the length of one out of two parts) to consider the next part (e.g., one out of four parts) and to justify their decisions (Tzur & Hunt, 2015).

This situation can be intensified in the following ways. First, should students not independently use a separate item to estimate the size of one part; suggest that the size of the part is a particular size (e.g., "I think this length represents one-half of the height of the tower"), and see if students use this part in some way to reason about the size of one out of three parts (or use the size of one out of four equal parts to consider the size of one out of five equal parts). Promoting self-explanations (Hunt & Tzur, 2017; Siegler, 1995; Zhang et al., 2014) is essential. Ask students to describe how they adjust the magnitude of the parts and why (Tzur & Hunt, 2015). Moreover, begin asking students how much taller or shorter to make the part and why. This challenges students to attend to precision. Finally, you should help students understand the vocabulary and notation involved in each instance (e.g., one out of seven parts is called one-seventh of the tower because it takes seven repetitions of the part to re-create the entire height of the tower; one out of nine parts is called one-ninth because it takes nine repetitions of the part to re-create the entire height of the tower). However, you should only introduce terminology after you see evidence that students know how to adjust each part and why (see Hunt, Tzur, & Westenskow, 2016).

Paper Pieces

We continue with equal sharing and add two additional means of engagement that support students to consider how to combine the fraction parts they create in activity. That is, we use number choices that produce a fractional result less than one alongside problems that use a fraction as a factor in a multiplication problem. Pose the following problems:

- "Four students share three strips of ribbon for a project. How much ribbon does each student use?"
- "Five students each use ½ of one whole piece of construction paper in class to write on for an assignment. How much paper is used?"

We have returned to using two or four as a number of parts to create unit fractions through partitioning or repeating a unit fraction. However, you should also try including problems with a common factor, such as a number that is accessible to promote reflection and conversation, especially in Tier 1 and Tier 2 environments.

This situation can be intensified in the following ways. First, students should be challenged to put the fractional parts back together with respect to one whole. Second, you should help students understand the vocabulary and notation involved in each instance (e.g., one out of two parts is called one-half because it takes two repetitions of the part to produce one whole; one out of four parts is called one-fourth because it takes four repetitions of the part to create one whole). Third, to promote learning toward the goal of anticipatory partitioning for odd sharers, include additional problems that involve three parts or five parts (or using $\frac{1}{3}$ or $\frac{1}{5}$ as a factor in contextualized multiplication problems that result in quantities greater than and less than one whole). Promote self-explanations: make sure the explanations are coming from the student's reasoning and ideas and not the teacher's (see Hunt & Tzur, 2017; Hunt, Tzur, & Westenskow, 2016; Hunt, Martin, et al., 2020). Finally, if students make drawings of the fractional parts inside of one whole but not outside, continue posing problems until you see a shift in their representations.

Store Orders

In this task, we return to the need to measure with the constraint of having only one part to measure from, such as a part of a sandwich, an ounce of nuts at a grocery store, or different-sized cups of a container of water (Olive & Vomvoridi, 2006). Ask students to say how many times the part of a sandwich, ounce of nuts, or cups of water are needed to remake the whole and explain and justify how they know. You might begin from two and then four parts (sandwich parts out of a whole), five and then ten parts (medium and small cups of water), and three and then six parts (pounds of different kinds of bulk food items placed in packages). This activity helps students consider the size of one part relative to one whole. You should help students understand the notation involved in each instance (e.g., one out of two parts is called one-half; one out of four parts is called one-fourth).

Next, ask students how many times they would need to use, for example, the small cup to have the same amount of water as the medium-sized cup. Or ask how many times they might need to use one-fourth of one whole sandwich to have the same amount as one-half of one whole sandwich. In the same way, ask students how many packages of bulk food items (e.g., trail mix in $\frac{1}{10}$ of one-pound or sunflower seeds in $\frac{1}{5}$ of one-pound bags). Student might first visualize the quantities and then draw them out in multiple ways.

Groupings

In this task students are asked to reason about the quantity created when a certain sized unit is repeated some number of times within and beyond one whole. For example, ask students to visualize and then draw an amount that is two or three times the amount of a bulk food item placed in packages of $\frac{1}{6}$ of one pound. Then ask students to think about double that quantity ($2 \times \frac{1}{6}$) or triple that quantity ($3 \times \frac{1}{6}$), and reason about the result. Next, ask students to consider six times ⅖ or four times ⅗. Finally, the situations support students to think about connections to equivalence by reconsidering the whole (e.g., naming each amount with respect to 1 pound as "the whole" or 2 pounds as "the whole").

You should use knowledge of your own students and classrooms along with data collected from the clinical interview to alter the ideas offered here to fit your needs. Students need to have opportunities to make connections between these related contexts. Respond to the needs of your students. These are only suggestions for what you could do; you should alter these ideas as needed to fit the individual needs of students and community needs of classrooms.

Conclusion

Fractions help develop rational number sense that students need to understand topics like ratio, rates, and proportions that support algebraic reasoning later and careers in STEM education. Our intent in this chapter is to support educators' navigation of curriculum tools from a lens of student thinking. In this chapter, we began by describing varying ways students reason about fractions. We described difficulties students experience, key points of understanding, and a possible pathway of development educators could use to plan assessment and instruction. Several instructional activities are supplied as task starters to help educators intervene at the outer edges of students' knowledge. In these ways, our hope is to empower students to develop a conceptual foundation upon which to develop deeper understanding of mathematics.

ACKNOWLEDGMENT

This material is based on work supported by the National Science Foundation, Grant No. 1708327.

REFERENCES

Behr, M. J., Lesh, R., Post, T., & Silver, E. A. (1983). Rational number concepts. In R. Lesh & M. Landau (Eds.), *Acquisition of mathematics concepts and processes* (pp. 91–126). New York: Academic Press.

Carpenter, T. P., Fennema, E., Franke, M. L., Levi, L., & Empson, S. B. (2014). *Children's mathematics: Cognitively guided instruction.* Portsmouth, NH: Heinemann.

CAST. (2011). *Universal design for learning guidelines version 2.0.* Wakefield, MA: Author.

Charalambous, C. Y., & Pitta-Pantazi, D. (2007). Drawing on a theoretical model to study students' understandings of fractions. *Educational Studies in Mathematics, 64*(3), 293–316.

Confrey, J., Maloney, A. P., Nguyen, K. H., & Rupp, A. A. (2014). Equipartitioning: A foundation for rational number reasoning. In A. P. Maloney, J. Confrey, & K. H. Nguyen (Eds.), *Learning over time: Learning trajectories in mathematics education* (pp. 61–96). Charlotte, NC: Information Age.

Cramer, K. A., Post, T. R., & delMas, R. C. (2002). Initial fraction learning by fourth- and fifth-grade students: A comparison of the effects of using commercial curricula with the effects of using the rational number project curriculum. *Journal for Research in Mathematics Education, 33*(2), 111–144.

Davydov, V. V., & Tsvetkovich, Z. H. (1991). On the objective origin of the concept of fractions. *Focus on Learning Problems in Mathematics, 13*(1), 13–64.

Empson, S. B. (2003). Low-performing students and teaching fractions for understanding: An interactional analysis. *Journal for Research in Mathematics Education, 34*(4), 305–343.

Empson, S. B., Junk, D., Dominguez, H., & Turner, E. (2006). Fractions as the coordination of multiplicatively related quantities: A cross-sectional study of children's thinking. *Educational Studies in Mathematics, 63*(1), 1–28.

Empson, S. B., & Levi, L. (2011). *Extending children's mathematics: Fractions and decimals.* Portsmouth, NH: Heinemann.

Fosnot, C. T., & Dolk, M. (2002). *Young mathematicians at work: 3. Constructing fractions, decimals, and percents.* New York: Heinemann.

Gersten, R., Beckmann, S., Clarke, B., Foegen, A., Marsh, L., Star, J. R., & Witzel, B. (2009). *Assisting students struggling with mathematics: Response to Intervention (RTI) for elementary and middle schools* (NCEE 2009-4060). Washington, DC: National Center for Education Evaluation and Regional Assistance, Institute of Education Sciences, U.S. Department of Education. Retrieved from *https://ies.ed.gov/ncee/wwc/Docs/PracticeGuide/rti_math_pg_042109.pdf.*

Ginsburg, H. (1997). *Entering the child's mind: The clinical interview in psychological research and practice.* New York: Cambridge University Press.

Hackenberg, A. J. (2007). Units coordination and the construction of improper fractions: A revision of the splitting hypothesis. *Journal of Mathematical Behavior, 26*(1), 27–47.

Hackenberg, A. J. (2013). The fractional knowledge and algebraic reasoning of students with the first multiplicative concept. *Journal of Mathematical Behavior, 32*(3), 538–563.

Hiebert, J., & Tonnessen, L. H. (1978). Development of the fraction concept in two physical contexts: An exploratory investigation. *Journal for Research in Mathematics Education, 9*(5), 374–378.

Hunt, J. H. (2014). Effects of a supplemental intervention focused in equivalency concepts for students with varying abilities. *Remedial and Special Education, 35*(3), 135–144.

Hunt, J. H. (2020). *Tasks and tools: Uncovering children's initial concepts of fractions.* Unpublished manuscript, North Carolina State University. (Original work written 2015)

Hunt, J. H., & Empson, S. B. (2015). Exploratory study of informal strategies for equal sharing problems of students with learning disabilities. *Learning Disability Quarterly, 38*(4), 208–220.

Hunt, J. H., MacDonald, B. L., & Silva, J. (2019). Gina's mathematics: Thinking, tricks, or "teaching"? *Journal of Mathematical Behavior, 56,* 100707.

Hunt, J. H., Martin, K., Khounmeuang, A., Silva, J., Patterson, B., & Welch-Ptak, J. (2020). Design, development, and initial testing of asset-based intervention grounded in trajectories of student fraction learning. *Learning Disabilities Quarterly.* [Epub ahead of print]

Hunt, J. H., Silva, J., & Lambert, R. (2019). Empowering students with specific learning disabilities: Jim's concept of unit fraction. *Journal of Mathematical Behavior, 56,* 100738.

Hunt, J., & Stein, M. K. (2020). Constructing goals for student learning through conversation. *Mathematics Teacher: Learning and Teaching PK–12, 113*(11), 904–909.

Hunt, J. H., & Tzur, R. (2017). Where is difference?: Processes of mathematical remediation through a constructivist lens. *Journal of Mathematical Behavior, 48,* 62–76.

Hunt, J. H., Tzur, R., & Westenskow, A. (2016). Evolution of unit fraction conceptions in two fifth-graders with a learning disability: An exploratory study. *Mathematical Thinking and Learning, 18*(3), 182–208.

Hunt, J. H., Valentine, C., Bryant, D. P., Pfannenstiel, K. H., & Bryant, B. R. (2016). Supplemental mathematics intervention: How and why special educators intensify intervention for students with learning disabilities. *Remedial and Special Education, 37*(2), 78–88.

Hunt, J. H., & Vasquez, E., III. (2014). Effects of ratio strategies intervention on knowledge of ratio equivalence for students with learning disability. *Journal of Special Education, 48*(3), 180–190.

Hunt, J. H., Welch-Ptak, J. J., & Silva, J. M. (2016). Initial understandings of fraction concepts evidenced by students with mathematics learning disabilities and difficulties: A framework. *Learning Disability Quarterly, 39*(4), 213–225.

Hunt, J. H., Westenskow, A., Silva, J., & Welch-Ptak, J. (2016). Levels of participatory conception of fractional quantity along a purposefully sequenced series of equal sharing tasks: Stu's trajectory. *Journal of Mathematical Behavior, 41*, 45–67.

Kieran, C. (1988). Two different approaches among algebra learners. In A. F. Coxford (Ed.), *The ideas of algebra, K–12* (pp. 91–96). Hillsdale, NJ: Erlbaum.

Kieren, T. E. (1976). On the mathematical, cognitive, and instructional foundations of rational numbers. In R. A. Lesh & D. A. Bradford (Eds.), *Number and measurement: Papers from a research workshop* (pp. 101–144). Columbus, OH: ERIC.

Kieren, T. E. (1980). The rational number construct: Its elements and mechanisms. In T. E. Kieren (Ed.), *Recent research on number learning* (pp. 125–149). Columbus, OH: ERIC.

Kieren, T. E. (1993). Rational and fractional numbers: From quotient fields to recursive understanding. In T. P. Carpenter, E. Fennema, & T. A. Romberg (Eds.), *Rational numbers: An integration of research* (pp. 49–84). Hillsdale, NJ: Erlbaum.

Lamon, S. (1993). Ratio and proportion: Connecting content and student's thinking. *Journal for Research in Mathematics Education, 24*(1), 41–61.

Lamon, S. J. (2005). *Teaching fractions and ratios for understanding: Essential content knowledge and instructional strategies for teachers.* Mahwah, NJ: Erlbaum.

Lamon, S. J. (2007). Rational numbers and proportional reasoning: Towards a theoretical framework for research. In F. Lester (Ed.), *Second handbook of research on mathematics teaching and learning* (pp. 629–667). Reston, VA: NCTM.

Lesh, R., Post, T., & Behr, M. (1987). Representations and translations among representations in mathematics learning and problem solving. In C. Janvier (Ed.), *Problems of representation in the teaching and learning of mathematics* (pp. 33–40). Hillsdale, NJ: Erlbaum.

Lewis, K. E. (2014). Difference not deficit: Reconceptualizing mathematical learning disabilities. *Journal for Research in Mathematics Education, 45*(3), 351–396.

Lewis, K. E. (2016). Understanding mathematical learning disabilities as developmental difference: A fine-grained analysis of one student's partitioning strategies for fractions. *Infancia y Aprendizaje, 39*(4), 812–857.

Lewis, K. E. (2017). Designing a bridging discourse: Re-mediation of a mathematical learning disability. *Journal of the Learning Sciences, 26*(2), 320–365.

Mack, N. K. (1995). Confounding whole-number and fraction concepts when building on informal knowledge. *Journal for Research in Mathematics Education, 26*(5), 422–441.

McLeskey, J., Barringer, M.-D., Billingsley, B., Brownell, M., Jackson, D., Kennedy, M., . . . Ziegler, D. (2017, January). *High-leverage practices in special education.* Arlington, VA: Council for Exceptional Children & CEEDAR Center.

National Council of Teachers of Mathematics (NCTM). (2014). *Principles to actions: Ensuring mathematics success for all.* Reston, VA: Author.

National Governors Association (NGA) Center for Best Practices & Council of Chief State School Officers (CCSSO). (2010). *Common Core State Standards for mathematics*. Washington, DC: Authors.

Ni, Y., & Zhou, Y. (2005). Teaching and learning fraction and rational numbers: The origins and implications of whole number bias. *Educational Psychologist, 40*(1), 27–52.

Olive, J., & Vomvoridi, E. (2006). Making sense of instruction on fractions when a student lacks necessary fractional schemes: The case of Tim. *Journal of Mathematical Behavior, 25*(1), 18–45.

Piaget, J., Inhelder, B., & Szeminska, A. (1960). *The child's conception of geometry*. New York: Basic Books.

Pothier, Y., & Sawada, D. (1983). Partitioning: The emergence of rational number ideas in young students. *Journal for Research in Mathematics Education, 14*(4), 307–317.

Siegler, R. S. (1995). How does change occur: A microgenetic study of number conservation. *Cognitive Psychology, 28*(3), 225–273.

Siegler, R., Carpenter, T., Fennell, F., Geary, D., Lewis, J., Okamoto, Y., . . . Wray, J. (2010). *Developing effective fractions instruction for kindergarten through 8th grade: A practice guide* (NCEE #2010-4039). Washington, DC: National Center for Education Evaluation and Regional Assistance, Institute of Education Sciences, U.S. Department of Education. Retrieved from *https://ies.ed.gov/ncee/wwc/Docs/PracticeGuide/fractions_pg_093010.pdf*.

Simon, M. A. (1995). Reconstructing mathematics pedagogy from a constructive perspective. *Journal for Research in Mathematics Education, 26*(2), 114–145.

Simon, M., Saldanha, L., McClintock, E., Akar, G. K., Watanabe, T., & Zembat, I. O. (2010). A developing approach to studying students' learning through their mathematical activity. *Cognition and Instruction, 28*(1), 70–112.

Star, J. R., & Rittle-Johnson, B. (2009). It pays to compare: An experimental study on computational estimation. *Journal of Experimental Child Psychology, 102*, 408–426.

Steffe, L. P., & Olive, J. (2010). *Children's fractional knowledge*. New York: Springer.

Streefland, L. (1993). Fractions: A realistic approach. In T. P. Carpenter, E. Fennema, & T. A. Romberg (Eds.), *Rational numbers: An integration of research* (pp. 289–326). Hillsdale, NJ: Erlbaum.

Tzur, R. (1999). An integrated study of children's construction of improper fractions and the teacher's role in promoting that learning. *Journal for Research in Mathematics Education, 30*(4), 390–416.

Tzur, R. (2007). Fine grain assessment of students' mathematical understanding: Participatory and anticipatory stages in learning a new mathematical conception. *Educational Studies in Mathematics, 66*(3), 273–291.

Tzur, R., & Hunt, J. H. (2015). Iteration: Unit fraction knowledge and the French fry tasks. *Teaching Children Mathematics, 22*(3), 149–157.

Tzur, R., Johnson, H. L., McClintock, E., Xin, Y. P., Si, L., Woodward, J., . . . Jin, X. (2013). Distinguishing schemes and tasks in children's development of multiplicative reasoning. *PNA, 7*(3), 85–101.

Ulrich, C., Tillema, E. S., Hackenberg, A. J., & Norton, A. (2014). Constructivist model building: Empirical examples from mathematics education. *Constructivist Foundations, 9*(3), 328–339.

Wilkins, J. L., Norton, A., & Boyce, S. J. (2013). Validating a written instrument for assessing students' fractions schemes and operations. *The Mathematics Educator, 22*(2), 31–54.

Woodward, J., Beckmann, S., Driscoll, M., Franke, M., Herzig, P., Jitendra, A., . . . Ogbuehi, P. (2012). *Improving mathematical problem solving in grades 4 through 8: A practice guide* (NCEE 2012-4055). Washington, DC: National Center for Education Evaluation and Regional

Assistance, Institute of Education Sciences, U.S. Department of Education. Retrieved from *http://ies.ed.gov/ncee/wwc/PracticeGuide.aspx?sid=16.*

Xin, Y. P., Wiles, B., & Lin, Y. Y. (2008). Teaching conceptual model-based word problem story grammar to enhance mathematics problem solving. *Journal of Special Education, 42*(3), 163–178.

Zhang, D., Xin, Y. P., Harris, K., & Ding, Y. (2014). Improving multiplication strategic development in children with math difficulties. *Learning Disability Quarterly, 37*(1), 15–30.

CHAPTER 8

Intensifying Mathematics Word-Problem-Solving Interventions for Students with or at Risk for Mathematics Difficulties

ASHA K. JITENDRA and JENNIFER KRAWEC

LEARNING OUTCOMES

After studying this chapter, you will be able to answer the following questions:

1. How is mathematical word-problem solving described, and what are the critical components for understanding and solving word problems?

2. What are word-problem-solving challenges for students with mathematics difficulties?

3. What are instructional approaches that contribute to success in word-problem solving?

4. How can interventions be intensified in Tier 2 and Tier 3 for students with or at risk for mathematics difficulties?

5. What are potential misconceptions and solutions related to word-problem solving?

The purpose of this chapter is to describe instructional practices that provide support in word-problem solving for students with or at risk for mathematics difficulties (MD). First, we describe mathematical word-problem solving and the critical components linked to the ability to understand and solve word problems. Second, we describe the challenges that students with or at risk for MD have in solving word problems. Third, we describe the unique features of instructional approaches that contribute to word-problem-solving performance. Fourth, we describe ways to intensify interventions for Tier 2 and Tier 3 students with mathematics difficulties. Last, we discuss misconceptions and solutions related to word-problem solving to help teachers teach and students to learn from solving word problems.

Mathematics interventions must be effective for all students, including students with or at risk for MD. This focus is consistent with national educational policy embodied by the Common Core State Standards for Mathematics (CCSSM; National Governors Association [NGA] Center for Best Practices & Council of Chief State School Officers [CCSSO], 2010) that requires all students to develop proficiency in mathematics. Moreover, the framework for CCSSM requires students to engage in mathematical practices such as *making sense of problems, reasoning abstractly and quantitatively, looking for and making use of structure, modeling with mathematics,* and *attending to precision.* Importantly, the CCSSM requires students to connect the standards of mathematical practice to the standards for mathematical content. Meeting these standards creates significant challenges for students with or at risk for MD.

Mathematical Word-Problem Solving and Critical Components

The ability to think mathematically is a critical skill, and the CCSSM focus on problem solving is especially important in an increasingly competitive job market where the demand for mathematics-intensive science and engineering jobs are outpacing overall job growth three to one (National Mathematics Advisory Panel, 2008). Student difficulties in acquiring higher-order thinking skills such as problem solving and reasoning (e.g., Hunt & Vasquez, 2014) inhibit opportunities to pursue mathematics-related careers. Given the importance of problem solving across the school years, the CCSSM at the primary level emphasizes addition and subtraction word-problem solving in the context of length, time, and money using objects, drawings, and symbols to represent the unknown. In the upper elementary grades, the focus shifts to word-problem solving using all four operations in the context of mathematical concepts such as whole-number multiplication and division, fractions, measurement conversions, perimeter, and volume. At this level, students are expected to solve problems with the support of drawings and symbols and to begin using letters to represent the unknown. By secondary grades, word-problem-solving skills are developed around the complex mathematical concepts of ratios and proportional relationships, rational numbers, and linear functions. Across grades (kindergarten to high school), the CCSSM makes explicit that students should be developing the key mathematical practices (e.g., reasoning abstractly and quantitatively, looking for and making use of structure, modeling with mathematics) that build proficiency in problem solving.

Mathematical word problems are "typically composed of a mathematics structure embedded in a more or less realistic context" (Depaepe, De Corte, & Verschaffel, 2010, p. 152). Word problem solving is a complex, multifaceted process that comprises two phases—problem representation and problem solution (Mayer, 1999). Key features of the problem representation phase involve the ability to read the problem with the goal of understanding the problem situation and to identify the relevant numerical and linguistic information and quantitative relations in the problem in order to represent the problem situation. The problem solution phase entails creating a plan to solve the problem, executing that plan, aligning the solution with the original problem situation, and determining the reasonableness of the mathematical outcome (Depaepe et al., 2010; Mayer & Hegarty, 1996). Given what we know about word-problem solving, what issues do students with MD and mathematics learning disabilities (MLD) exhibit when solving word problems?

Word-Problem-Solving Challenges for Students with MD

Students have persistent difficulties with word-problem solving as they experience cognitive skill deficits in working memory, language, and attentive behavior, which interferes with their ability to effectively integrate cognitive (e.g., attention, memory, language) and metacognitive processes (e.g., self-questioning, self-monitoring, self-evaluation) necessary for successful word-problem solving. These students struggle not only with the abstract formal structures of mathematics but also with the reading/language element of word problems (Andersson, 2008; Fuchs et al., 2010). As Rothman and Cohen (1989) noted, proficiency in mathematical problem solving requires learning its language, which includes both symbolic (mapping objects to meaning) and communicative (situating/sharing meaning in context) functions. It is clear that instruction should address the language used in mathematics so that students with or at risk for MD understand what it is that the problem is asking as well as how to solve it (Woodward et al., 2012). This would mean identifying the academic terms (*more than, less than*) and vocabulary (e.g., *addition, addend, sum, subtraction, minuend, subtrahend, difference, multiplication, factor, product, equal groups, division, dividend, divisor, quotient, ratio, proportion, percent, percent change, interest, scale factor*) that are essential for teaching a given unit on word-problem solving.

In addition to the language component of mathematical problem solving, students with or at risk for MD struggle to make sense of the problem, identify the critical information, and create a representation that accurately reflects the problem situation (Boonen, van der Schoot, van Wesel, de Vries, & Jolles, 2013; Schumacher & Fuchs, 2012). Although these students' difficulty with word problems extends beyond computation, this component of problem solving cannot be ignored: research on the problem-solving performance of students who struggle with both computational and word-problem-solving difficulties reveals poor outcomes for these students despite explicit problem-solving instruction (Jitendra, Rodriguez, et al., 2013; Schumacher & Fuchs, 2012). Thus, for students with dual deficits in computation and problem solving, it is necessary to integrate knowledge of foundational mathematics content (e.g., understanding the base-ten system to represent numbers, computation strategies) with effective word-problem-solving instruction.

For secondary grade students, in addition to problem solving and computational skills, it is crucial that they acquire understanding of complex mathematical content to be able solve grade-level word problems. For example, the CCSSM requires middle school students to *analyze proportional relationships and use them to solve real-world and mathematical problems* such as the following: "If a person walks ½ mile in each ¼ hour, compute the unit rate as the complex fraction ½ ÷ ¼ miles per hour, equivalently 2 miles per hour" (7.RP.A.1; NGA & CCSSO, 2010). This type of problem requires that students understand unit rate, rational numbers, and the concepts of ratios and rates in addition to the computational and problem-solving skills necessary to solve it.

Unique Features of Instructional Approaches That Contribute to Success in Word-Problem Solving

Findings from several research syntheses indicate that effective interventions for facilitating mathematics word-problem solving for students with or at risk for MD include the following characteristics: (1) providing explicit instruction to teach mathematical concepts and procedures (e.g., Gersten, Chard, et al., 2009; Xin & Jitendra, 1999); (2) teaching students to use heuristics (Gersten, Chard, et al., 2009); (3) encouraging students to think aloud while solving a problem (Gersten, Chard, et al., 2009); (4) using visual representations of mathematical ideas (Gersten, Chard, et al., 2009; Zhang & Xin, 2012); and (5) providing a range of examples and sequencing examples (e.g., concrete to abstract; Gersten, Chard, et al., 2009).

Additionally, Gersten, Beckmann, and colleagues (2009) recommend that to enhance these students' learning outcomes, problem-solving interventions should focus on common underlying structures so that students not only gain problem-solving proficiency but also better understand the underlying mathematical ideas that are present in word problems. Thus, the focus of this chapter is on intervention studies priming the problem structure: schema-based instruction (SBI; see Jitendra, Dupuis, et al., 2013; Jitendra, Harwell, Dupuis, & Karl, 2017), schema-broadening instruction (e.g., Fuchs et al., 2008; Fuchs, Malone, et al., 2016), and conceptually based model problem solving (COMPS; Xin et al., 2011). Although these approaches varied in terms of their explicit or implicit emphasis on specific instructional components (e.g., transfer, schematic diagrams), a common feature was teaching students to move beyond the superficial features of a problem (e.g., cover story) to categorize problems by problem type or schema (e.g., *compare, proportion*) on the basis of their mathematical structure (Gersten, Beckmann, et al., 2009).

The SBI approach focuses on (1) identifying the underlying problem structure (i.e., additive structure—*change, group, compare*; multiplicative structure—*ratio, proportion, percent*) by focusing on key elements and relations between elements (e.g., *part–part–whole*) in the problem; (2) using a schema diagram to represent the problem situation; and (3) selecting an appropriate solution method to solve the problem. The schema-broadening approach teaches students to (1) identify the underlying problem structure (i.e., additive structure—*change, total, difference*; multiplicative structure—*grouping, splitting*) using concrete materials and role playing; (2) sort word problems by problem type; and (3) transfer their learning to problems that appeared novel due to variation in problem features different from the original problem (e.g., irrelevant information, missing information in different position, information presented in charts, graphs, pictures). The COMPS approach emphasizes (1) identifying the underlying problem structure (i.e., additive structure—*part–part–whole, additive compare*; multiplicative structure—*equal groups [EG], multiplicative compare*) by focusing on key elements (unit rate, number of units, and total or product for EG problems) and mathematical relations in the equation and (2) using prompt cards to facilitate organizing information using the conceptual model diagram (Xin & Zhang, 2009).

Schema-Based Instruction

Since the initial studies of SBI that focused on teaching elementary school students to solve arithmetic word problems (e.g., Jitendra et al., 1998; Jitendra, Dupuis, et al., 2013), SBI has been developed to enhance the ability of middle school students to understand the underlying mathematical concepts and meaningfully represent problems involving ratios, proportions, and percent in order to solve them. The SBI approach to solving word problems is unique in two ways. First, SBI is a multicomponent intervention that incorporates the following four components: (1) identifying the structure of a problem, (2) using visual schematic representations to meaningfully represent problems (i.e., show how quantities in a word problem are related), (3) applying problem-solving procedures grounded in reasoning, and (4) using metacognitive skills to monitor and reflect on the problem-solving processes.

A primary focus of SBI is unpacking the problem structure (e.g., *change, group, compare; ratio, proportion, percent*), which can facilitate understanding of the problem situation, especially the relationships (e.g., part–part–whole) between quantities in the problem and serve as the basis for problem solution. Much of the work on word-problem solving in elementary grades has focused on arithmetic word problems—namely, addition and subtraction of integers. Figure 8.1 shows the three problem types that characterize the additive problem structure. A *change* problem consists of a starting quantity, and a direct or implied action causes either an increase or a decrease in that quantity. The three quantities in the *change* problem represent the beginning, change, and ending and entail the same object identity (e.g., pounds of wool). In contrast, a *group* problem involves combining two distinct small groups (parts) to form a large group (whole). The relationship between quantities in the problem is a part–part–whole relationship, which is static (i.e., no action is evoked). A *compare* problem involves the comparison of two disjoint sets (compared and referent). Similar to the *group* problem, the relationship between the two sets in the *compare* problem is static.

In contrast, proportion word problems involve the multiplicative structure. Figure 8.2 shows the following problem types: (1) *ratio*—a comparison of any two quantities (part to whole or part to part) that expresses a multiplicative relationship between two quantities in a single situation; (2) *percent*—a ratio that compares a number to 100; (3) *percent change*—one quantity in the problem either increases or decreases by a certain percentage; (4) *proportion*—a statement of equality between two ratios/rates that allows us to think about the ways that two situations are the same; (5) *scale drawing* (represents a real object)—a type of proportion problem that describes the scale of a drawing (ratio of the size of the drawing to the actual size of the object) and scale factor (the value of the ratio of the drawing to the actual size of the object); and (6) *simple interest*—interest paid or calculated on only the original amount (principal) of an account or loan.

Problem Representation	Problem Solution
Change: José and his father have gathered 10 pounds of wool from a sheep. So far, some of the wool has been used to make a sweater. Now there are 5 pounds of wool left. How many pounds of wool have been used? 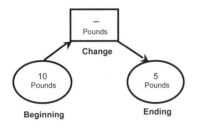	Number sentence: 10 – ? = 5 *(We can solve this problem by thinking about the fact or number families. We know the greater number in this subtraction problem. So, we can subtract the lesser number from the greater number [10 – 5 = ?] to solve for ?. Alternatively, we can think addition to solve this problem: 5 + ? = 10.)* Answer: 5 pounds of wool have been used.
Group: Farmer Jake has 88 animals on his farm. He only has horses and goats. There are 49 horses on the farm. How many goats are on the farm? 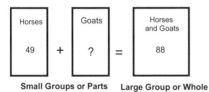	Number sentence: 49 + ? = 88 *(We can solve this addition problem or write a subtraction problem: 88 – 49 = ?, and solve for ?)* Answer: There are 39 goats on the farm.
Compare: A redwood tree can grow to be 85 meters tall. A Douglas fir can grow to be 15 meters taller. How tall can the Douglas fir grow? 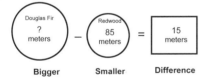	Number sentence: ? – 85 = 15 *(We can solve this problem by thinking about how addition and subtraction are related. We don't know the greater number in this subtraction problem. So, we can write an addition problem, 85 + 15 = ?, and solve for ?)* Answer: The Douglas fir can grow to be 100 meters.

FIGURE 8.1. Solving one-step and two-step problems involving change, group, and compare schemata. From Jitendra (2007, pp. 32–33, 78, 117, 158). Copyright by PRO-ED. Reprinted with permission.

Problem Type	Example of Problem
Ratio 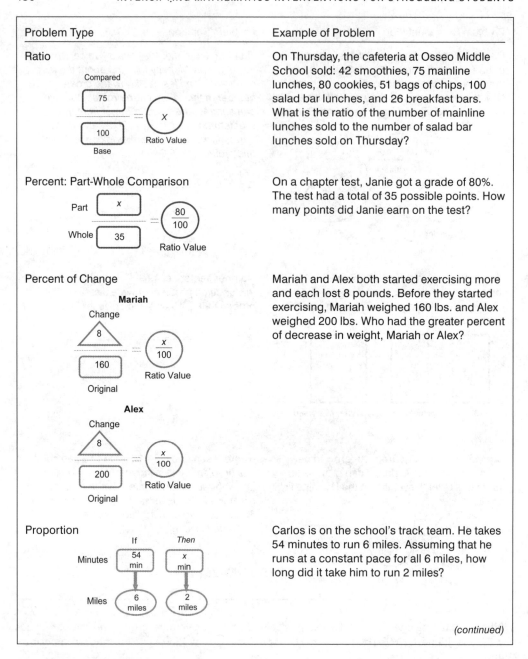	On Thursday, the cafeteria at Osseo Middle School sold: 42 smoothies, 75 mainline lunches, 80 cookies, 51 bags of chips, 100 salad bar lunches, and 26 breakfast bars. What is the ratio of the number of mainline lunches sold to the number of salad bar lunches sold on Thursday?
Percent: Part–Whole Comparison	On a chapter test, Janie got a grade of 80%. The test had a total of 35 possible points. How many points did Janie earn on the test?
Percent of Change	Mariah and Alex both started exercising more and each lost 8 pounds. Before they started exercising, Mariah weighed 160 lbs. and Alex weighed 200 lbs. Who had the greater percent of decrease in weight, Mariah or Alex?
Proportion	Carlos is on the school's track team. He takes 54 minutes to run 6 miles. Assuming that he runs at a constant pace for all 6 miles, how long did it take him to run 2 miles?

(continued)

FIGURE 8.2. Proportion problem types and visual schematic representations. From Jitendra and Star (2016). Copyright by A. K. Jitendra and J. R. Star. Reprinted with permission.

Problem Type	Example of Problem
Scale Drawing 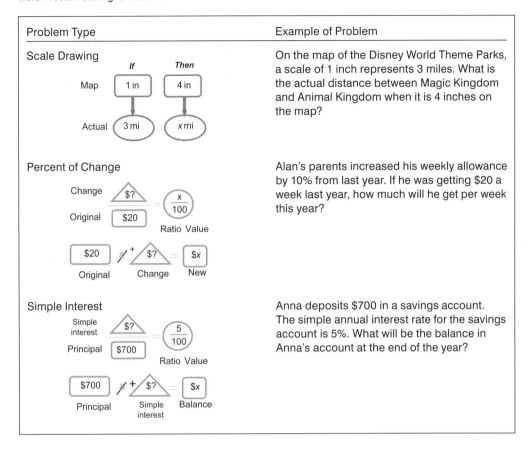	On the map of the Disney World Theme Parks, a scale of 1 inch represents 3 miles. What is the actual distance between Magic Kingdom and Animal Kingdom when it is 4 inches on the map?
Percent of Change	Alan's parents increased his weekly allowance by 10% from last year. If he was getting $20 a week last year, how much will he get per week this year?
Simple Interest	Anna deposits $700 in a savings account. The simple annual interest rate for the savings account is 5%. What will be the balance in Anna's account at the end of the year?

FIGURE 8.2. *(continued)*

A second component of SBI is using visual schematic diagrams as representations. In the SBI approach, teachers model their mathematical thinking using "think-alouds" as they represent quantities and their relationships for word problems. Consider the following *compare* problem: "A redwood tree can grow to be 85 meters tall. A Douglas fir can grow to be 15 meters taller. How tall can the Douglas fir grow?" The quantities in the word problem—bigger (compared), smaller (referent), and difference sets—and the relationships between quantities can be seen in the *compare* schematic diagram. Instruction focuses on translating contextual information (nonmathematical) in the problem text to meaningfully represent the problem by showing how quantities in the problem are related. Teachers cue students to the linguistic expression "taller" (translated to mean "taller" than the redwood tree) in the relational sentence ("A Douglas fir can grow to be 15 meters taller.") to understand that the problem involves a comparison of two sets. Next, teacher prompts highlight that the relational sentence not only describes the difference (i.e., 15 meters) between the two things compared (i.e., height of the Douglas fir and height of the redwood tree) but also helps identify the compared or bigger set (height of the Douglas fir) and the referent or smaller set (height of the redwood tree).

Last, information in the remaining verbal text is used to identify the known or smaller quantity (85 meters) and the unknown or bigger quantity (? meters) to represent in the *compare* diagram (see Figure 8.1). The completed *compare* diagram represents the following quantities and their relationships: (1) the Douglas fir represents the bigger set (? meters), (2) the redwood tree represents the smaller set (85 meters), and (3) the difference between the Douglas fir and the redwood tree is 15 meters. Translating the relationship to numerical expression requires one to understand the operation meaning. Although the relationship between quantities can be seen as a comparison of the bigger and smaller quantities so that the operation required is subtraction (? − 85 = 15), this relationship can be translated to mean that the bigger quantity is the result of joining the difference and smaller quantities. So, the numerical expression is 15 + 85. See Figure 8.2 for schematic representations of ratio, percent, percent of change, proportion, scale drawing, and simple interest problems.

The third component of SBI is applying problem-solving procedures grounded in reasoning. Again, using think-alouds, teachers help students think systematically about solving word problems by focusing on problem schema identification, representation, planning, and solution (see Marshall, 1995; Mayer, 1999). Consider the following problem in Figure 8.1: "Farmer Jake has 88 animals on his farm. He only has horses and goats. There are 49 horses on the farm. How many goats are on the farm?" Although a step-by-step approach is used to teach problem solving, the emphasis is on quantitative reasoning, which involves recognizing the relevant quantities in a problem and using reasoning to identify the relationship between them. As such, SBI is used to (1) *find the problem type* by reading and paraphrasing the problem, as well as using the word-problem context (e.g., two small groups—horses, goats; a large group—animals or horses and goats) to understand the problem situation (a *group* problem); (2) *organize information and represent the word problem* using the *group* diagram by finding the known (a total of 88 animals, 49 are horses) and unknown quantities (? goats) and identifying the statement in the word problem that expresses a relationship (part–part–whole) between quantities; (3) *plan how to solve* the problem by translating the relationship between quantities in the problem to numerical representations (e.g., 49 + ? = 88 or 88 − 49 = ?); and (4) *solve the problem* (e.g., one way to solve 49 + ? = 88 is as follows: 49 + 1 = 50; 50 + 30 = 80; 80 + 8 = 88. So 1 + 30 + 8 = 39) and check the solution (e.g., if 88 is the large-group amount, then the answer 39 representing one of the two small-group amounts seems reasonable).

The problem solution phase for word-problem solving involving ratios, proportions, and percent consists of first estimating the answer before solving the problem using a strategy (e.g., unit rate, equivalent fractions, cross products) that is most efficient based on the quantities in the problem, and then evaluating if the estimate is close to the exact answer and checking whether the answer makes sense. For example, for the proportion problem in Figure 8.2, students estimate that if Carlos runs 6 miles in 54 minutes, he should run 2 miles in less than 54 minutes. Using number sense, students reason that half of 6 is 3; if he ran 3 miles, this would be half of running 6 miles. But he is running 2 miles, so this is *less than* half of 6. Half of 54 is 27, so the estimate is that Carlos will run 2 miles in less than 27 minutes. Next, students translate the visual representation into a mathematics equation: $54/6 = x/2$. Then they test two strategies (unit rate, equivalent fractions) to see which works best with this problem. For example, using the unit rate strategy, students reason up or down to analyze the relationship between the two quantities. The question to ask is this: 6 times what number equals 54? Because $6 \times 9 = 54$, then to find x, they multiply the denominator (2) in the second ratio also by 9 to find the numerator (x). So the answer is 18 because $9 \times 2 = 18$.

Fourth, SBI embeds *metacognitive* (the ability to understand and monitor one's thinking) activities such as analyzing the problem, monitoring strategy use, and evaluating the outcome within the word-problem-solving context. Teachers use questions that can scaffold a solution process by encouraging students to regulate their strategy knowledge during the problem-solving processes: (1) problem comprehension (e.g., "How do you know what type of a problem it is?"), (2) problem representation (e.g., "What schematic diagram best fits this problem type to represent information in the problem?"), (3) planning (e.g., "How can you solve this problem?"), and (4) problem solution (e.g., "Is the answer reasonable given the question asked?").

Another unique feature of the SBI approach is that it includes effective instructional practices (e.g., systematic and explicit instruction, opportunities for student response and feedback; e.g., Gersten, Chard, et al., 2009). For example, the SBI program supports student learning in the following ways: (1) teacher-mediated instruction followed by paired partner learning and independent learning activities and (2) student-constructed diagrams that eventually replace the external visual schematic representations. Teacher-mediated instruction entails using think-alouds and prompts to make instruction explicit and visible and clarify student thinking. Partner learning activities provide many opportunities for students to practice solving word problems. For example, a think–pair–share model is used to have students first think about the problem type independently and then work with a partner to model the problem situation using representations and solve it before sharing their solutions and explanations with the whole group. This practice of verbalizing the strategy steps during partner work and publicly with the whole group is important as it allows the teacher to monitor student understanding and provide instructive feedback to support students (Hattie & Timperley, 2007) and enables students to express their own thinking and listen to the ideas of their peers. Additionally, because problem comprehension is particularly difficult for many students with or at risk for MD, the SBI program provides external visual schematic diagrams as they translate and integrate information in the problem into the representation before they are taught to construct their own. Ongoing progress monitoring or assessment of student response to instruction in the elementary grades is another feature of the SBI program.

Numerous studies of SBI have been conducted to evaluate its effectiveness for enhancing students' word-problem-solving performance. Studies with elementary students with or at risk for MD have demonstrated that SBI is more effective than a general strategy instruction (i.e., typical textbook instruction) or standards-based instruction (e.g., Jitendra et al., 1998; Jitendra, Dupuis, et al., 2013). Results of studies with middle school students also provide evidence of the efficacy of SBI for students with or at risk for MD taught in small groups when compared to students who received a contrasting word-problem-solving instruction (Xin, Jitendra, & Deatline-Buchman, 2005). More recently, when teachers implemented SBI in real classrooms for the same amount of time typically scheduled by schools to teach ratios and proportional relationships, results indicated that SBI was more effective than typical classroom instruction in improving the learning of students with MD and/or reading difficulties (Jitendra, Dupuis, Star, & Rodriguez, 2016; Jitendra et al., 2017). Furthermore, intensifying the design and delivery of SBI (e.g., individualized instruction) for elementary and middle school students with or at risk for MD led to substantial improvements in word-problem-solving performance (e.g., Jitendra, DiPipi, & Perron-Jones, 2002; Jitendra & Hoff, 1996). Intensifying instruction consisted of modeling/think-alouds and practice built throughout a unit of lessons, individualized intervention implementation provided 5 days a week for 45 minutes each session, mathematics vocabulary (e.g., compare terms such as *more than* and *less than*) reviewed within the context of lessons, direct questioning interspersed throughout lessons (e.g., "What kind of a problem is this? How do you know?"), fading of schematic diagrams, and progress monitoring every 2 weeks.

Schema-Broadening Instruction

The early work on schema-broadening instruction categorized problem types based on solution path. The authors identified four problem types (*shopping list, half, buying bag,* and *pictograph*) from a school district's mathematics textbook (e.g., shopping-list problems involve the purchase of a number of items and one must determine the total cost; Fuchs et al., 2003). Students were also explicitly taught to recognize those problem types in novel problems that had different features, including vocabulary, question format, and irrelevant information (Fuchs, Fuchs, Finelli, Courey, & Hamlett, 2004). More recent versions of schema-broadening instruction focus on mathematically agreed-upon arithmetic word-problem types (e.g., *change, total, difference*; Fuchs et al., 2008, 2009; Fuchs, Schumacher, et al., 2016), which align with the problem schemata specified in Jitendra, Dupuis, and colleagues (2013); for example, the *difference* problem schema in schema-broadening instruction is almost identical to Jitendra, Dupuis, and coauthors' *compare* problem schema in SBI, which involves comparing two quantities to determine the difference amount.

Schema-broadening instruction has also been extended to rational numbers using both additive and multiplicative structures. Additive fraction word problems involve an increase or decrease in the change quantity (e.g., "Maria bought 1¼ pounds of candy. Later she bought another ¼ of a pound of candy. How many pounds of candy does Maria have?"; Fuchs, Schumacher, et al., 2016, p. 627). Multiplicative fraction word problems involve *grouping* (multiplication) or *splitting* (measurement division) word problems. *Grouping* problems require students to make units from the fractions given (e.g., "Keisha wants to make 8 necklaces for friends. For each necklace, she needs ½ of a yard of string. How many yards of string does Keisha need?"; Fuchs, Schumacher, et al., 2016, p. 627), whereas *splitting* problems require that students make fractions from units (e.g., "Matthew has 2 watermelons. He cuts each watermelon into fifths. How many pieces of watermelon does Matthew have?"; Fuchs, Schumacher, et al., 2016, p. 627).

Schema-broadening instruction can be implemented in a tutoring format and has been shown to be effective for students with MD as well as those with mathematics and reading difficulties. In the tutoring sessions, students receive an introductory unit on foundational skills (e.g., adding and subtracting numbers using a number line, solving problems with and without regrouping) before being introduced to schema-broadening instruction to solve *change, total,* and *difference* problem types. Instruction consists of the following features: (1) use of concrete materials and role play to teach the underlying problem structure, (2) explicit teaching for transfer using problems with unexpected features (irrelevant information, unknown information in different positions, two-digit operands, and format) within the taught problem type, and (3) a review of the three problem types using a sorting activity. Additionally, explicit teaching of language comprehension and relational terms and understanding the equal sign as a relational term are incorporated into schema-broadening instruction (Powell et al., 2015; Powell & Fuchs, 2010).

Schema-broadening instruction for teaching students to solve fraction word problems is similar to solving word problems involving whole-number addition and subtraction. Students are taught to identify the problem type, represent the underlying structure using representations (number sentences and arrays), and recognize the transfer features (e.g., different vocabulary or question) to solve novel problems. The instructional sequence for additive fraction word problems involving an increase or decrease in the change quantity is as follows: "(a) underline the unknown, (b) circle the start and increase [or decrease] value, (c) write a number sentence to represent the structure of increase [or decrease] [word problems], and (d) solve for the unknown and write a numerical answer and word label" (Fuchs, Schumacher, et al., 2016, p. 637). The instructional sequence for multiplicative fraction word problems involving multiplication and measurement division is as follows: (a) underline the unknown; (b) determine the units and size of each fractional piece and label them "U" and "S"; (c) create an array that represents the splitting word-problem type; (d) use the array information to show how each unit is divided into fractional pieces (e.g., if each unit was divided into fifths, ⅕ was recorded for each piece of each unit); and (e) solve for the unknown and write the complete answer (Fuchs, Schumacher, et al., 2016).

It is worth noting that results of fraction word-problem-solving intervention studies showed that schema-broadening instruction is more effective than standard textbook instruction and a self-explaining comparison condition on both additive and multiplicative fraction word-problem solving (Fuchs, Malone, et al., 2016; Fuchs, Schumacher, et al., 2016). Importantly, researchers noted that at posttest, students with MD who received word-problem instruction in fractions erased a large pretest achievement gap between themselves and their not-at-risk peers.

Conceptual Model-Based Problem Solving

Several studies of COMPS focused on teaching elementary school students to solve arithmetic problems involving both additive and multiplicative problem structures. Xin, Wiles, and Lin (2008) categorized additive problems as part–part–whole (PPW) and additive compare (AC) problem types involving five subtypes: *combine* (e.g., "Christine has 5 apples. John has 4 apples. How many apples do they have all together?"); *change–join* (e.g., "Christine had 5 apples. John gave her 4 more apples. How many apples does Christine have now?"); *change–separate* ("Christine had 9 apples. Then she gave away 4 apples. How many apples does she have now?"); *compare–more* ("Christine has 9 apples. She has 5 more apples than John. How many apples does John have?"); and *compare–less* ("Christine has 9 apples. John has 4 less apples than Christine. How many apples does Christine have?") (Xin et al., 2008, p. 170).

Problems involving the multiplicative problem structure included *equal groups* (EG) describing the number of equal sets or units (e.g., "A school arranged a visit to the museum in Lafayette Town. It spent a total of $667 buying 23 tickets. How much does each ticket cost?") and *multiplicative compare* (MC) problems, which compared two quantities wherein one quantity was a multiple or part of the other quantity ("It rained 147 inches in New York one year. In Washington, D.C., it rained only 21 inches during the same year. The amount of rain in New York is how many times the amount of rain in Washington, D.C.?") (Xin et al., 2008, p. 170).

COMPS instruction for the four problem types (PPW, AC, EG, and MC) occurred in two phases: problem–structure instruction and problem–solution instruction. During problem–structure instruction, students learn to recognize the problem type (PPW, AC, EG, or MC) using stories without unknowns and represent the relevant elements using the conceptual model diagram. The purpose of this instruction is to allow students to visualize the generalized problem relations in the problem situation (e.g., part–part–whole; factor–factor–product).

In the problem–solution phase, students apply a four-step problem-solving procedure to solve word problems with unknown quantities. Figure 8.3 shows problem-type-specific prompt cards to guide problem representation. For example, to solve the EG problem presented earlier, students are prompted to use their prompt cards to *detect* the problem structure (i.e., step 1). The three elements in the EG word problem—cost of each ticket (unit rate), total cost of $667 (product), and 23 tickets (number of units)—align with the EG problem type, which describes a number of equal units. In step 2, students are taught to *organize* the information in the problem using the conceptual model EG diagram (see Figure 8.3). That is, using the prompts (e.g., "Which sentence or question tells about a Unit Rate [number of items in each unit]?"; Xin & Zhang, 2009, p. 433), students use a letter as a variable to represent the unknown quantity in the square (unit rate), write "23" in the circle (number of units), and "$667" in the triangle (product). Step 3 of COMPS instruction requires that students *transform* the diagram into a meaningful equation by removing the box shapes and labels, leaving only the numbers, the operation, and the variable (e.g., $a \times 23 = \$667$).

In step 4, students *solve* for the unknown, which requires understanding how to manipulate the equation (e.g., unit rate × number of units = total [product]) to isolate the unknown. In this example, students must isolate the variable and solve for the unknown by dividing ($667 ÷ 23 = 29). Additionally, COMPS incorporates evidence-based instructional practices such as explicit instruction, frequent teacher–student interactions, and ongoing student performance feedback. It is important to note that in the early stages

---

Equal Groups (EG)

An *EG* problem describes number of equal sets or units

UNIT Rate	# of Units	Product

☐ × ○ = △

EG WP Story Grammar Questions

☐ **Which sentence or question tells about a <u>Unit Rate</u> (# of items in each unit)?** Find the unit rate and write it in the Unit Rate box.

○ **Which sentence or question tells about the <u># of Units</u> or sets (i.e., quantity)?** Write that quantity in the circle next to the unit rate.

△ **Which sentence or question tells about the <u>Total</u> (# of items) or product?** Write that number in the triangle on the other side of the equation.

Multiplicative Compare (MC)

An *MC* describes one quantity as a multiple or part of the other quantity

Referent unit	Multiplier	Compared/Product

☐ × ○ = △

MC WP Grammar Questions

○ **Which sentence (or question) describes one quantity as a multiple or part of the other?** Detect the two things (people) being compared and name the *referent unit* (benchmark) in the diagram. Fill in the relation (e.g., "12 times") in the circle.

☐ **What is the benchmark quantity?** Write that quantity in the referent unit box.

△ **What is the compared quantity or product?** Write that quantity in the triangle on one side of the equation by itself.

FIGURE 8.3. Models for equal groups and multiplicative compare problem types. From Xin et al. (2011, p. 387). Copyright 2011 by Taylor & Francis Group, LLC. Reprinted with permission.

of COMPS implementation, teachers demonstrate how to solve the problems (see Xin & Zhang, 2009, for an excerpt from the teacher scripts to solve EG and MC problems). As students gain proficiency in solving word problems, teacher support in terms of prompts is provided only as needed.

The effectiveness of COMPS has been validated for elementary students with MD. Positive benefits were seen for COMPS-tutored students compared to students taught general heuristics for problem solving (Xin et al., 2011). When intensifying instruction for these students using COMPS instruction delivered individually or in pairs, students demonstrated substantial growth in word-problem solving involving whole numbers and geometry (e.g., Hord & Xin, 2015; Xin & Zhang, 2009).

Intensifying Interventions in Tier 2 and Tier 3 for Students with or at Risk for MD

The three research-based approaches described in the preceding sections are beneficial in improving the problem-solving performance of elementary and secondary students with or at risk for MD, particularly when instruction in Tier 1 is not effective and more intensive Tier 2 or Tier 3 intervention is necessary. To address the needs of these students, researchers developed Tier 1 interventions to incorporate evidence-based instructional design principles (e.g., Jitendra et al., 2016; Powell et al., 2015) and then purposefully intensified instructional design and delivery for Tier 2 or Tier 3 interventions in several ways. First, all three approaches to word-problem solving included explicit modeling of lessons initially followed by sufficient opportunities for practice and review built into lessons. Explicit word-problem-solving instruction also targeted language comprehension and understanding of relational terms (more–less, older–younger). In addition, schema-broadening instruction (Powell et al., 2015; Powell & Fuchs, 2010) and COMPS (Xin et al., 2011; Xin & Zhang, 2009) emphasized understanding of the equal sign, which is addressed in first grade (1.OA.D.7: *Understand the meaning of the equal sign and determine if equations involving addition and subtraction are true of false*; NGA & CCSSO, 2010). Furthermore, teacher-directed questioning was included to help students generate self-explanations as to why fractions differed in magnitude. To support these self-explanations, the teacher first models high-quality explanations and identifies important features of quality explanations; then, during students' explanations, they are prompted to elaborate on their response in light of the important features previously discussed (see Fuchs, Malone, et al., 2016).

Second, all three intervention approaches included representations such as concrete materials, visual-schematic diagrams, number sentences, or arrays to help organize and represent the mathematical information in the problems. Third, all three approaches included procedural facilitators/supports, including problem-solving checklists and instructional prompts such as "Which sentence tells us about a unit rate?" (Xin & Zhang, 2009, p. 440). Fourth, SBI and schema-broadening interventions in third grade included foundational concepts and skills (e.g., understanding the base-ten number system, addition and subtraction categories, using a number line to add and subtract numbers, strategies for checking work) that are addressed in earlier grades or focused on underlying concepts such as ratios/rates (e.g., Jitendra et al., 2017; Xin et al., 2011), which are necessary for successful arithmetic and proportion word-problem solving. The inclusion of foundational concepts and skills in Tier 2 and Tier 3 interventions is critical, as struggling students likely have gaps in conceptual understanding that, if left unaddressed, will prevent them from reaching proficiency.

Additionally, intervention implementation of these approaches occurred in a whole-class format, in small groups, or one-on-one. When students received individualized or small-group instruction, instruction occurred 3 to 5 days per week for 25–45 minutes per session.

Potential Misconceptions and Solutions

It is critical that interventionists not only understand effective instructional approaches to improve the word-problem-solving performance of students with MD but also have knowledge of the potential misconceptions in teaching word-problem solving that may impede student growth. Next, we describe some misconceptions and solutions to effective problem solving.

A "Key Words" Approach to Teaching Problem Solving

The *key word approach* continues to be widely used by many teachers even though it does not help students become successful problem solvers (Riccomini, Hwang, & Morano, 2016). This approach teaches students to use a particular operation whenever a word problem contains certain words or phrases (e.g., addition is the operation whenever the question in the word problem includes *in all*). The key word approach has limited value for at least two reasons. Key words are misleading and do not always produce correct solutions when the operation suggested by the key word is applied; many word problems do not contain key words that might be connected to a particular operation (Karp, Bush, & Dougherty, 2014). Instead of relying on key words, it is important to get students thinking systematically about solving problems by focusing on the mathematical structure to make sense of the problem situation that is critical to solve the problem.

A Visual Approach to Teaching Problem Solving

Many textbooks encourage students to use diagrams to represent and solve mathematical word problems. However, students with or at risk for MD often demonstrate difficulties in using representations to express their mathematical thinking. Specifically, they have difficulty understanding and using textbook-provided representations on their own, and their self-constructed representations either neglect the relevant details or include unnecessary information (Woodward et al., 2012). These types of self-constructed representations are considered pictorial representations in that the visual appearance of elements in a word problem is highlighted rather than the relevant details (Boonen et al., 2013). For example, consider the following problem: "There are 4 adults and 2 children who need to cross the river. A small boat is available that can hold either 1 adult or 1 or 2 small children. Everyone can row the boat. How many one-way trips does it take for all of them to cross the river?" (Woodward et al., 2012, p. 30). A pictorial representation of this problem may include illustrations such as the boat and the river with people waiting on the shore to cross the river, which is ineffective because it does not help identify the mathematical structure of the problem to move students toward an accurate solution plan (Hegarty & Kozhevnikov, 1999; Krawec, 2014). On the other hand, a visual schematic representation includes all relevant information and the relation between key elements in the problem. For this problem, a visual schematic representation would depict the number of trips and the boat occupants on each trip to get all adults and children across the river.

Teachers can develop relevant visual schematic representations that integrate the solution-relevant text elements (Boonen et al., 2013) to illustrate the problem or incorporate into their lessons the ones developed by researchers in the three intervention approaches described earlier. Alternatively, teachers can focus on specific aspects of student representations that were correct and follow up by asking guiding questions to modify their diagrams such that the representation includes the relevant details without the unnecessary information. Also, teacher explanations can focus on the difference between relevant and irrelevant features of the problem and emphasize that the goal of a diagram is to highlight the relations among quantities that are important to solve the problem (see Woodward et al., 2012).

A Cross-Products Method to Solving Proportion Word Problems

Although multiple methods are available for solving proportion problems and particular methods are more efficient than others for solving specific problems, the standard procedure taught in schools is the *cross-multiplication algorithm*. The lack of opportunity to compare and contrast among different types of approaches may lead to students relying exclusively on a small set of problem-solving strategies and focusing on rote memorization without understanding them. In contrast, "some of the alternative approaches exploit available integer multiplicative relationships and thereby reduce computational demands" (Berk, Taber, Gorowara, & Poetzl, 2009, p. 113). Teachers should ensure that students have experienced conceptual methods (e.g., unit rate, equivalent fractions) before presenting symbolic methods such as the *cross-product algorithms* for solving proportional problems and develop students' procedural flexibility by purposefully selecting a variety of strategies to compare side by side as it can help them understand and effectively solve problems. When students lack the prerequisite knowledge (i.e., poor recall of multiplication and division facts), taking time to ask them to write down the facts before solving problems or changing the numbers in the problem to focus on the problem solving rather than on the computation is important to support student learning (see also Woodward et al., 2012).

In closing, teaching mathematical word-problem solving to students with or at risk for MD requires a shift from focusing on surface features such as story context or key words, creating pictorial representations that depict the problem visually but do not emphasize the relationships between quantities in the problem, or using rote procedures such as the cross-product algorithm. Instead, it is important to have students identify the problem structure or problem type, use well-chosen representations that show the relevant details in the problem, and apply procedures that are understood.

REFERENCES

Andersson, U. (2008). Mathematical competencies in children with different types of learning difficulties. *Journal of Educational Psychology, 100*, 48–66.

Berk, D., Taber, S. B., Gorowara, C. C., & Poetzl, C. (2009). Developing prospective elementary teachers' flexibility in the domain of proportional reasoning. *Mathematical Thinking and Learning, 11*(3), 113–135.

Boonen, A. J. H., van der Schoot, M., van Wesel, F., de Vries, M. H., & Jolles, J. (2013). What underlies successful word problem solving?: A path analysis in sixth grade students. *Contemporary Educational Psychology, 38*, 271–279.

Depaepe, F., De Corte, E., & Verschaffel, L. (2010). Teachers' approaches towards word problem solving: Elaborating or restricting the problem context. *Teaching and Teacher Education, 26*, 152–160.

Fuchs, L. S., Fuchs, D., Finelli, R., Courey, S. J., & Hamlett, C. L. (2004). Expanding schema based transfer instruction to help third graders solve real-life mathematical problems. *American Educational Research Journal, 41*, 419–445.

Fuchs, L. S., Fuchs, D., Prentice, K., Burch, M., Hamlett, C. L., Owen, R., & Schroeter, K. (2003). Enhancing third-grade students' mathematical problem solving with self-regulated learning strategies. *Journal of Educational Psychology, 95*, 306–315.

Fuchs, L. S., Geary, D. C., Compton, D. L., Fuchs, D., Hamlett, C. L., Seethaler, P. M., . . . Schatschneider, C. (2010). Do different types of school mathematics development depend on different constellations of numerical versus general cognitive abilities? *Developmental Psychology, 46*, 1731–1746.

Fuchs, L. S., Malone, A. S., Schumacher, R. F., Namkung, J., Hamlett, C. L., Jordan, N. C., . . . Changas, P. (2016). Supported self-explaining during fraction intervention. *Journal of Educational Psychology, 108*, 493–508.

Fuchs, L. S., Powell, S. R., Seethaler, P. M., Cirino, P. T., Fletcher, J. M., Fuchs, D., . . . Zumeta, R. O. (2009). Remediating number combination and word problem deficits among students with mathematics difficulties: A randomized control trial. *Journal of Educational Psychology, 101*, 561–576.

Fuchs, L. S., Schumacher, R. F., Long, J., Namkung, J., Malone, A. S., Wang, A., . . . Changas, P. (2016). Effects of intervention to improve at-risk fourth graders' understanding, calculations, and word problems with fractions. *The Elementary School Journal, 116*, 625–651.

Fuchs, L. S., Seethaler, P. M., Powell, S. R., Fuchs, D., Hamlett, C. L., & Fletcher, J. M. (2008). Effects of preventative tutoring on the mathematical problem solving of third-grade students with math and reading difficulties. *Exceptional Children, 74*, 155–173.

Gersten, R., Beckmann, S., Clarke, B., Foegen, A., Marsh, L., Star, J. R., & Witzel, B. (2009). *Assisting students struggling with mathematics: Response to Intervention (RTI) for elementary and middle schools* (NCEE 2009-4060). Washington, DC: National Center for Education Evaluation and Regional Assistance, Institute of Education Sciences, U.S. Department of Education. Retrieved from *https://ies.ed.gov/ncee/wwc/Docs/PracticeGuide/rti_math_pg_042109.pdf*.

Gersten, R., Chard, D. J., Jayanthi, M., Baker, S. K., Morphy, P., & Flojo, J. (2009). Mathematics instruction for students with learning disabilities: A meta-analysis of instructional components. *Review of Educational Research, 79,* 1202–1242.

Hattie, J., & Timperley, H. (2007). The power of feedback. *Review of Educational Research, 77,* 81–112.

Hegarty, M., & Kozhevnikov, M. (1999). Types of visual-spatial representations and mathematical problem solving. *Journal of Educational Psychology, 91,* 684–689.

Hord, C., & Xin, Y. P. (2015). Teaching area and volume to students with mild intellectual disability. *Journal of Special Education, 49,* 118–128.

Hunt, J. H., & Vasquez, E., III. (2014). Effects of ratio strategies intervention on knowledge of ratio equivalence for students with learning disability. *Journal of Special Education, 48,* 180–190.

Jitendra, A. K. (2007). *Solving math word problems: Teaching students with learning disabilities using schema-based instruction.* Austin, TX: PRO-ED.

Jitendra, A., DiPipi, C. M., & Perron-Jones, N. (2002). An exploratory study of schema-based word-problem-solving instruction for middle school students with learning disabilities. *Journal of Special Education, 36,* 23–38.

Jitendra, A. K., Dupuis, D. N., Rodriguez, M. C., Zaslofsky, A. F., Slater, S., Cozine-Corroy, K., & Church, C. (2013). A randomized controlled trial of the impact of schema-based instruction on mathematical outcomes for third-grade students with mathematics difficulties. *The Elementary School Journal, 114,* 252–276.

Jitendra, A. K., Dupuis, D. N., Star, J. R., & Rodriguez, M. C. (2016). The effects of schema-based instruction on the proportional thinking of students with mathematics difficulties with and without reading difficulties. *Journal of Learning Disabilities, 49,* 354–367.

Jitendra, A. K., Griffin, C., McGoey, K., Gardill, C., Bhat, P., & Riley, T. (1998). Effects of mathematical word problem solving by students at risk or with mild disabilities. *Journal of Educational Research, 91,* 345–356.

Jitendra, A. K., Harwell, M. R., Dupuis, D. N., & Karl, S. R. (2017). A randomized trial of the effects of schema-based instruction on proportional problem solving for students with mathematics problem-solving difficulties. *Journal of Learning Disabilities, 50,* 322–336.

Jitendra, A. K., & Hoff, K. (1996). The effects of schema-based instruction on the mathematical word-problem-solving performance of students with learning disabilities. *Journal of Learning Disabilities, 29,* 422.

Jitendra, A. K., Rodriguez, M., Kanive, R. G., Huang, J.-P., Church, C., Corroy, K. C., & Zaslofsky, A. F. (2013). The impact of small-group tutoring interventions on the mathematical problem solving and achievement of third grade students with mathematics difficulties. *Learning Disability Quarterly, 36,* 21–35.

Jitendra, A. K., & Star, J. R. (2016). *Solving ratio, proportion, and percent problems using schema-based instruction.* Eugene: Center on Teaching and Learning, University of Oregon. Retrieved from *https://dibels.uoregon.edu/market/sbi.*

Karp, K. S., Bush, S. B., & Dougherty, B. J. (2014). 13 rules that expire. *Teaching Children Mathematics, 21*(1), 18–25.

Krawec, J. (2014). Problem representation and mathematical problem solving of students of varying math ability. *Journal of Learning Disabilities, 47,* 103–115.

Marshall, S. P. (1995). *Schemas in problem solving.* New York: Cambridge University Press.

Mayer, R. E. (1999). *The promise of educational psychology: Vol. 1. Learning in the content areas.* Upper Saddle River, NJ: Merrill Prentice Hall.

Mayer, R. E., & Hegarty, M. (1996). The process of understanding mathematics problems. In R. J. Sternberg & T. Ben-Zeev (Eds.), *The nature of mathematical thinking* (pp. 29–53). Hillsdale, NJ: Erlbaum.

National Governors Association (NGA) Center for Best Practices & Council of Chief State School Officers (CCSSO). (2010). *Common Core State Standards for mathematics.* Washington, DC: Authors.

National Mathematics Advisory Panel. (2008). *Foundations for success: Final report of the National Mathematics Advisory Panel.* Washington, DC: U.S. Department of Education.

Powell, S. R., & Fuchs, L. S. (2010). Contribution of equal-sign instruction beyond word-problem tutoring for third-grade students with mathematics difficulty. *Journal of Educational Psychology, 102,* 381–394.

Powell, S. R., Fuchs, L. S., Cirino, P. T., Fuchs, D., Compton, D. L., & Changas, P. C. (2015). Effects of a multitier support system on calculation, word problem, and prealgebraic performance among at-risk learners. *Exceptional Children, 81*(4), 443–470.

Riccomini, P. J., Hwang, J., & Morano, S. (2016). Developing mathematical problem solving through strategic instruction: Much more than a keyword. In B. G. Cook, M. Tankersley, & T. J. Landrum (Eds.), *Instructional practices with and without empirical validity* (pp. 39–60). Bingley, UK: Emerald Group.

Rothman, R. W., & Cohen, J. (1989). The language of math needs to be taught. *Academic Therapy, 25,* 133–142.

Schumacher, R. F., & Fuchs, L. S. (2012). Does understanding relational terminology mediate effects of intervention on compare word problems? *Journal of Experimental Child Psychology, 111,* 607–628.

Woodward, J., Beckmann, S., Driscoll, M., Franke, M., Herzig, P., Jitendra, A., . . . Ogbuehi, P. (2012). *Improving mathematical problem solving in grades 4 through 8: A practice guide* (NCEE 2012-4055). Washington, DC: Institute of Education Sciences, U.S. Department of Education. Retrieved from *http://ies.ed.gov/ncee/wwc/PracticeGuide.aspx?sid=16.*

Xin, Y. P., & Jitendra, A. K. (1999). The effects of instruction in solving mathematical word problems for students with learning problems: A meta-analysis. *Journal of Special Education, 32,* 207–225.

Xin, Y. P., Jitendra, A. K., & Deatline-Buchman, A. (2005). Effects of mathematical word problem-solving instruction on middle school students with learning problems. *Journal of Special Education, 39,* 181–192.

Xin, Y. P., Wiles, B., & Lin, Y. Y. (2008). Teaching conceptual-model-based word problem story grammar to enhance mathematics problem solving. *Journal of Special Education, 42,* 163–178.

Xin, Y. P., & Zhang, D. (2009). Exploring a conceptual model-based approach to teaching situated word problems. *Journal of Educational Research, 102,* 427–442.

Xin, Y. P., Zhang, D., Park, J. Y., Tom, K., Whipple, A., & Si, L. (2011). A comparison of two mathematics problem-solving strategies: Facilitate algebra-readiness. *Journal of Educational Research, 104*(6), 381–395.

Zhang, D., & Xin, Y. P. (2012). A follow-up meta-analysis for word-problem-solving interventions for students with mathematics difficulties. *Journal of Educational Research, 105,* 303–318.

CHAPTER 9

Algebra

BARBARA J. DOUGHERTY, DIANE PEDROTTY BRYANT, JIHYUN LEE,
and BRIAN R. BRYANT

LEARNING OUTCOMES

After studying this chapter, you will be able to answer the following questions:

1. How can algebra be defined or described?
2. What are the critical foundational concepts and skills for algebra?
3. What are specific guidelines for teaching algebra?
4. How can interventions be intensified for Tier 2 and Tier 3?

Have your students ever asked you, "When are we going to use algebra?" Many teachers, especially at the middle and high school levels, have heard this question countless times. For many students who struggle learning mathematics, including students with disabilities, this is not an unusual question. Why do you think this is true? There are many reasons for this type of question from our students. Here are a few reasons. First, if you said these students are usually frustrated about not understanding the important critical foundational content for algebra such as fractions, decimals, and percent and thus are unmotivated to learn algebra, then you would be correct. Second, if you said these students often lack automatic retrieval of solutions for basic facts, which are needed for proficiency with whole-number computation, then you would be correct. Third, if you thought that specific concepts and skills related to geometry and measurement are lacking, then you are right again! Does it surprise you that students should also be proficient in understanding specific aspects of geometry and measurement? (See Table 9.1 for more information about the Benchmarks for the Critical Foundations of Algebra [National Mathematics Advisory Panel (NMAP), 2008].) The takeaway message for elementary and middle school mathematics teachers and mathematics interventionists is that students must be proficient with the Critical Foundations of Algebra to be more successful with algebra coursework. In fact, according to the NMAP's (2008) survey findings of 743 Algebra I teachers, foundations of algebra were "weak." Specific areas identified for improvement were basic mathematics skills, rational numbers, and word-problem solving. Algebra I teachers rated "unmotivated students" and teaching to "mixed ability groupings" as major challenges.

Why is there such a focus on the critical foundations for success in algebra? Can you identify times when you use your knowledge of algebra to make decisions in situations? Perhaps you identified more algebraic knowledge than you had thought about previously. Now, identify a description of algebra and then see how your description is reflected in the position statement of the National Council of Teachers of Mathematics (NCTM; 2014): "Algebra is a way of thinking and valuing structure with integrated sets of concepts, procedures, and applications [that enable] . . . students to generalize, model, and analyze situations that are purely mathematical or ones that arise in real-world phenomena." Algebra provides a systematic way to investigate relationships and helps to describe, organize, and understand the world. Our use of this knowledge, whether consciously or unconsciously, is important to understand, and it is equally important to ensure our students can identify situations in which algebra is used and to answer their question, "When are we going to use algebra?"

Problems with patterns (rules)—that is, repeated-numbers arrangements—are a good way for students to apply their understanding of how patterns are created to solve problems. Students must understand how to analyze problems for patterns and generate solutions based on the pattern. Students must understand the meaning of the equals sign, which represents a balanced quantitative relationship and can be thought of as expressions on both sides of the equals sign as meaning "same as." Teachers must check students' understanding about algebraic concepts, particularly as the understandings are related to misconceptions. The reader of this chapter should review the misconceptions definition and description in Chapter 1 and look for evidence of misconceptions about algebraic ideas. For example, misconceptions about algebraic concepts and skills stem from erroneous understanding of the core of a pattern, which repeats and extends a repeating pattern. For instance, according to Bamberger, Oberdorf, and Schultz-Ferrell (2010), teachers need to watch for students who cannot repeat a pattern sequence and extend a pattern, which increases by a designated amount. Regarding the equals sign, Bamberger and colleagues noted that some students think the equals sign means they need to perform an operation to arrive at a solution rather than understanding that the equals sign shows a relationship, not an operator.

The purpose of this chapter is to provide an overview of algebraic concepts and skills, including the critical foundations of algebra, to provide guidelines for teaching algebraic concepts and skills, and to give examples of how algebra interventions can be intensified for Tier 2 and Tier 3. We have chosen to organize this chapter with an overview of the critical foundational topics, and more specifically with a focus on pertinent topics related to algebra instruction, including (1) algebraic thinking across the grades; (2) algebraic number sense; (3) concept of variable; (4) algebraic expressions, equations, and inequalities; and (5) functions.

Concepts and Skills for Algebra

Critical Foundations of Algebra

The NMAP (2008) was appointed by then-president George W. Bush with members whose expertise spanned different fields but all with connections to algebra. Specifically, the NMAP identified the Critical Foundations of Algebra, including categories to promote proficiency or fluency with the concepts and skills, such as whole numbers, fractions, and aspects of geometry and measurement. The concepts and skills for the three categories represent topics that are difficult for struggling learners, including students with disabilities, resulting in a decided disadvantage of not being prepared sufficiently compared to their typically achieving peers to tackle and generalize or transfer this content knowledge to algebra. A list of the critical foundations is shown in Table 9.1.

TABLE 9.1. Critical Foundations of Algebra

Fluency with Whole Numbers

1. By the end of grade 3, students should be proficient with the addition and subtraction of whole numbers.

2. By the end of grade 5, students should be proficient with multiplication and division of whole numbers.

Fluency with Fractions

1. By the end of grade 4, students should be able to identify and represent fractions and decimals and compare them on a number line or with other common representations of fractions and decimals.

2. By the end of grade 5, students should be proficient with comparing fractions and decimals and common percent, and with the addition and subtraction of fractions and decimals.

3. By the end of grade 6, students should be proficient with multiplication and division of fractions and decimals.

4. By the end of grade 6, students should be proficient with all operations involving positive and negative integers.

5. By the end of grade 7, students should be proficient with all operations involving positive and negative fractions.

6. By the end of grade 7, students should be able to solve problems involving percent, ratio, and rate and extend this work to proportionality.

Geometry and Measurement

1. By the end of grade 5, students should be able to solve problems involving perimeter and area of triangles and all quadrilaterals having at least one pair of parallel sides (i.e., trapezoids).

2. By the end of grade 6, students should be able to analyze the properties of two-dimensional shapes and solve problems involving perimeter and area and analyze the properties of three-dimensional shapes and solve problems involving surface area and volume.

3. By the end of grade 7, students should be familiar with the relationship between similar triangles and the concept of the slope of a line.

Note. From NMAP (2008).

Algebraic Thinking across the Grades

According to Seeley (2004), "Algebraic thinking includes recognizing and analyzing patterns, studying and representing relationships, making generalizations, and analyzing how things change." The Common Core State Standards for Mathematics (CCSSM; National Governors Association [NGA] Center for Best Practices & Council of Chief State School Officers [CCSSO], 2010]) include the algebra domain for high school level, yet elementary students can learn key algebraic concepts and skills, such as algebraic aspects of problem solving and equations and pattern generalization (Kaput, 2008). For instance, elementary students should learn about and become proficient or fluent with addition and the related subtraction facts and multiplication and the related division facts. Unfortunately, teaching arithmetic in elementary school and algebra in secondary school separately has not allowed students to develop algebraic thinking deeply (Blanton et al., 2015). Instead, elementary and secondary educators need to understand that the instructional content about algebraic concepts and skills spans the grades from kindergarten to grade 12.

Algebraic Concepts and Skills in Grades K–2

In kindergarten, students learn to represent and solve addition and subtraction problems within 10 with objects, drawing, verbal expressions, equations, or expressions. Students also need to know how to *decompose* (take apart) numbers equal to or less than 10 into pairs in multiple ways (K.OA; NGA & CCSSO, 2010). In grade 1, the standards include representing and solving addition and subtraction problems within 20 with objects, drawing, verbal expressions, or equations with a symbol that represents the unknown number in problems. Additionally, students should understand and apply properties of operations (i.e., commutative property and associative property of addition) and the meaning of the equals sign used in equations, including addition and subtraction (1.OA; NGA & CCSSO, 2010).

Algebraic Concepts and Skills in Grades 3–5

In grade 3, students need to solve multiplication and division problems, interpret products and whole-number quotients of whole numbers, solve multiplication and division word problems within 100 by using drawings and a symbol for the unknown number in situations involving equal groups, and identify the unknown whole number in an equation involving multiplication and division (3.OA; NGA & CCSSO, 2010). In grade 4, students learn how to interpret multiplication equations as comparisons, solve multiplication and division word problems containing multiplicative comparison, represent and solve multistep word problems with whole numbers using the four operations and equations with a letter for the unknown number, and assess reasoning of the answers using computation and estimation (4.OA; NGA & CCSSO, 2010). Finally, in grade 5, students interpret and write numerical expressions using symbols, such as parentheses, brackets, and braces; generate numerical patterns using given rules;

identify relationships between terms; and graph the corresponding pairs on a coordinate plane (5.OA; NGA & CCSSO, 2010).

Algebraic Concepts and Skills in Grades 6–8

The standards about the number system for grade 6 include (1) applying and extending understanding of multiplication and division to division of fractions; (2) computing with multidigit numbers fluently and identifying common factors and multiples; and (3) applying and extending understanding of numbers to the rational number system, such as positive and negative numbers, absolute numbers, and ordering numbers, by using number lines or graphs (6.NS; NGA & CCSSO, 2010). In grade 7, the standards about the number system include applying and extending operations understanding with fractions to addition, subtraction, multiplication, and division of rational numbers (7.NS; NGA & CCSSO, 2010). In grade 8, the standards about the number system include knowing irrational numbers (e.g., every number has decimal expansion) and approximating irrational numbers by rational numbers (8.NS; NGA & CCSSO, 2010).

Algebraic Concepts and Skills in High School

The domain of algebra at the high school level includes standards about (1) seeing structure in expressions, (2) arithmetic with polynomials and rational expressions, (3) creating equations, and (4) reasoning with equations and inequalities.

Algebraic Number Sense

The NCTM (2000) defined *number sense* as "moving from the initial development of basic counting techniques to more sophisticated understandings of the size of numbers, number relationships, patterns, operations, and place value" (p. 79). The number sense concept was additionally operationalized as the ability to comprehend number magnitude, use multiple representations to solve problems, and employ mental computation to find estimates and solutions to problems (Gersten & Chard, 1999).

Children's number sense awareness is important across the grades and the CCSSM domains (NGA & CCSSO, 2010). For example, Jordan, Glutting, and Ramineni (2010) explained that for young children, counting, knowledge of number, and arithmetic operations require a good understanding of number and quantity in the early years. For older students, such as middle-grade students, Mazzocco and Devlin (2008) found in their studies on rational number sense with students with mathematics learning disabilities (MLD) and students without MLD that students with MLD had weaker rational number understanding than students without MLD. Students were asked to name fractions and decimals, to rank-order fraction and decimal quantities, and to identify equivalent quantities for fractions ($\frac{1}{2} = \frac{2}{4}$), decimals (e.g., $\frac{1}{2} = 0.5$), and ratios (e.g., $0.25 = \frac{1}{4}$). Compared to students without MLD, students with MLD showed difficulties with naming decimals, rank-ordering decimals and fractions, and identifying correctly equivalent ratios, all skills that require a sense of number and quantity. Meanwhile, students without MLD could name decimals and equivalent pairs correctly, but much like their peers with MLD the students without MLD could not correctly rank-order decimals and fractions, which is a skill that involves understanding the magnitude of given rational numbers to assist with the rank-ordering task.

What can teachers do to address number sense problems? Houlihan and O'Riordan (2018) offer examples of number sense and algebra, such as giving students a number line with the end points 0 and 100 and asking them to locate a given number on the number line in relation to 0 and 100. For instance, given a number line, if students are given the number 50, we would predict that "50" would be placed in about the middle of the number line. This number-placement task would become increasingly difficult with other numbers, such as 20, 65, and 80, to name a few. Houlihan and O'Riordan (2018) also provide a list of ideas for remediating number sense.

Concept of Variable

Recently, the focus of school algebra shifted from isolated abstract concepts in secondary school to a strand of algebraic thinking and problem solving that begins from the earliest years (Wilkie, 2016). This shift is based on developing a deeper and broader view of algebra learning at school (Wilkie, 2016). Also, the CCSSM (NGA & CCSSO, 2010) emphasized developing students' algebraic thinking, including the use of variables as early as kindergarten.

Many research findings support introduction of the use of variables and variable notation in the early grades as well (Brizuela, 2016; Brizuela, Blanton, Sawrey, Newman-Owens, & Murphy Gardiner, 2015). For example, a previous research finding supported the notion that students in elementary grades can grasp variable and variable notation in processing generalizations (Brizuela et al., 2015). Thus, the use of variables and variable notation can be useful for students to express algebraic thinking in many different ways. However, constructing the concepts of variable can be complicated because the term *variable* can have a different role and meaning depending on the context in which it is used.

Specific Types of Roles of a Variable

Variables are an essential part in learning algebra, and variable notation is a versatile tool for expressing generalizations (Brizuela et al., 2015). The concept of a variable has five different roles: a placeholder for a numerical value, a varying quantity, an unknown number, a parameter, and a generalized number (Arcavi, Drijvers, & Stacey, 2017; Blanton, Levi, Crites, Dougherty, & Zbiek, 2011).

The first role of variables is a placeholder for a numerical value. For example, the letter a in the statement $a^2 - 2a$ is a placeholder in an algebraic process, because $a^2 - 2a$ is an expression, not an equation to solve. The role of the variable a is an abstract or arbitrary symbol to be manipulated.

The second role of variables is a varying quantity. For example, the letters x and y in the equation $2x = y$ can have many values that make the equation true. However, the values of x and y do not randomly vary. The value of y is always two times the value of x.

The third role of variables is an unknown number. For example, the letter x in the equation $3x - 2 = x + 2$, is an unknown, but a fixed number. The variable x cannot be any arbitrary value. By solving the equation, we can find the value of x that makes the equation true (i.e., $x = 2$).

The fourth role of variables is to represent a parameter. For example, the letter b in the equation $y = bx$ represents a parameter. As you can see in this example, the value of the parameter determines the characteristics of other quantities. If each bicycle has two tires, we can write this relationship as $y = 2x$. If each bicycle has three tires, we can write this relationship as $y = 3x$. If we generalize the number of tires on each bicycle to b tires, we can express the relationship between bicycle and tires as $y = bx$. The variable b is considered a parameter because it determines the function of the other variables, x and y.

The fifth role of variables is as generalized numbers. In the example $x + y = y + x$, where x and y represent real numbers, the letters x and y represent a generalized pattern. The equation can represent that the sum of two numbers are the same if the order of two numbers is changed, regardless of the two addends' values. If students know this role of variable, students can communicate this generalization efficiently by using $x + y = y + x$ without using many examples of sums of two numbers (e.g., $1 + 2 = 2 + 1$, $3 + 5 = 5 + 3$, and $2 + 4 = 4 + 2$).

Algebraic Expressions, Equations, and Inequalities

The relationships between quantities are foundational as early as kindergarten when students are first introduced to the equals sign. The equals sign is used to show that two quantities represent the same amount. This is essential in developing algebraic reasoning because, as students move forward, they must be able to interpret the equivalence notion expressed with the equals sign (Carpenter, Levi, & Farnsworth, 2000).

However, in many cases, students' first experience with the equals sign is when they see it written in an equation such as $1 + 2 = 3$. Because students see many equations written in this way (that is, the addition [or subtraction] expression on the left and the answer on the right), they may overgeneralize that the equals sign is an operator, indicating that they need to do something. They may also view it as indicating that the "answer comes next" rather than thinking of it as a relational symbol (Knuth, Alibali, Hattikudur, McNeil, & Stephens, 2008). Thus, they are likely to not be able to see the truth or validity of an equation such as $3 = 1 + 2$.

As students move to middle grades, they must be able to apply their understanding of equivalence to interpreting equations of the type $2x - 10 = 3x + 7$. This becomes problematic if students do not understand the meaning of the equals sign when two expressions are shown to be equivalent (Byrd, McNeil, Chesney, & Matthews, 2015; 6.EE and 7.EE; NGA & CCSSO, 2010).

Developmental Sequence

To better students' understanding of expressions, equations, and inequalities, the developmental sequence should provide a progression that builds from an intuitive approach to a more formal one. This understanding affords students the opportunity to build from their previous knowledge to new ideas. *Possible misconceptions* include (1) variables are objects rather than quantities; (2) if a value for a variable is substituted into two expressions and the result is the same value, then the expressions are equivalent; (3) expressions are equations; and (4) there are prescribed steps that must be done to find the solution to an equation.

Expressions, which are a sentence with a minimum of two numbers and at least one mathematics operation, can be introduced as a way to represent a generalization related to particular patterns or properties. The use of a variable allows the pattern to be extended to any term and provides a symbolic representation of it. Using geometric representations supports a visual and physical representation. Consider the following problem. How would you solve it? What mathematical thinking will students need to do?

> Sixteen blocks are needed to build a four-step double staircase like the one below. How many blocks will be needed to build a double staircase of similar shape with 50 steps? (Dougherty, Zenigami, & Matsumoto, 2003, pp. 1–9)

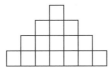

In this problem, students would first need to consider what the previous staircases look like. If they use square tiles to model the problem, they can begin to see a growth pattern. If y is used to represent the number of the term in the pattern, students can write y_2 to represent the number of tiles needed for any staircase. The variable in this case represents a generalized quantity. Figure 9.1 shows the development of the staircase pattern.

As students are able to write expressions to represent a pattern, they also *evaluate expressions,* which means a number is substituted for the variable and the computations

FIGURE 9.1. Previous staircase representations.

are performed to get a numerical value for the expression. This includes using the order of operations as well.

At this point, students should start to consider equivalent expressions. *Equivalent expressions* are two or more expressions whose values are equal for all replacements of the variable or variables. Thus, $3(2c + 2)$ is equivalent to $6c + 6$, $6(c + 1)$, or $2(3c + 3)$. At this point, equations may be introduced so that students write $3(2c + 2) = 2(3c + 3)$, for example.

Evaluating expressions is the first step in learning how to solve equations and inequalities. When students have developed some proficiency in evaluating expressions and finding equivalent expressions, they can be introduced to solving equations with a predict-and-test method. For example, find a value of x for which $3x - 2 = 2x + 1$. By using an equation like this, students can link their understanding of the equals sign with their experience in evaluating expressions. This allows them to begin an intuitive understanding of what it means to solve an equation.

To further this intuitive understanding, the next step in the sequence would be to use a table to record values of the expressions with a given value of a variable. For example, using the equation $3x - 2 = 2x + 1$, a table might look like the one shown in Table 9.2.

The table shows that the two expressions are the same value when $x = 3$. This reinforces the concept of the equals sign and also gives students an opportunity to think about the relationship between the two expressions when $x < 3$ and when $x > 3$. Notice that if $x < 3$, $3x - 2 < 2x + 1$. If $x > 3$, $3x - 2 > 2x + 1$.

Next, using diagrams and physical materials builds students' understanding of what it means to solve an equation. In Figure 9.2, students can show how a value for the variable is found by using a diagrammatic approach. It is important to show the resulting equation with the diagram so that students see the symbolic representation to make strong connections. Note that the balance helps students to link the solution method to the properties of equality. Additionally, the equation and the solution process can be modeled with physical materials such as square tiles and two-color chips or with Algebra Tiles™.

Finally, this progression moves to equivalent equations. In Figure 9.2, *equivalent equation*, which contains algebraic equations that have identical solutions and results

TABLE 9.2. Two Expressions, Same Value, When $x = 3$

x	$3x - 2$	$2x + 1$
-2	-8	-3
-1	-5	-1
0	-2	1
1	1	3
2	4	5
3	7	7
4	10	9

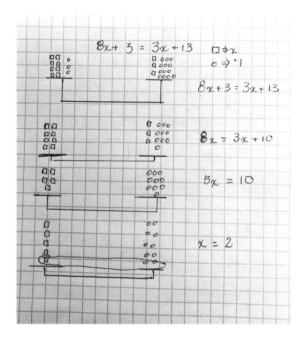

FIGURE 9.2. Diagrammatic approach for finding a variable.

from performing an action with the diagram, is the more formal approach to solving an equation. It is often the case that students are taught steps, such as first subtract the constants and then divide by the *coefficient*, which is a number used to multiply a variable (e.g., 4x means 4 times x, and x is a variable, so 4 is a coefficient). Although those steps will find a solution, students do not understand why they are doing the steps and can then misapply them. Try using each of these methods to solve the equation $3x + 4 = x + 5$.

Functions

Relations are ordered pairs of numbers, such as (1, –2) and (–5, 7). *Functions* are a special kind of relation; they are a relation such that for each first number of an ordered pair, there is exactly one second number. That is, no two ordered pairs in a set have the same first number and different second numbers. Functions can be represented in multiple ways, including a table, a graph, and an equation. Possible misconceptions include that (1) any graph is a function, and (2) each ordered pair results in two points: one representing the x-coordinate and one representing the y-coordinate.

To support students' understanding of functions, they should begin by graphing points related to physical phenomena. For example, the Knotty Problem (Figure 9.3) is one in which students can see the relationship between the two quantities represented in the x- and y-coordinates (Dougherty et al., 2003, pp. 5–25). They can discuss what happens as more knots are tied in relation to the length of the rope. It is interesting to note that this relationship is the fundamental principle of slope.

Materials: Rope (about 1 yard), a meter stick or metric tape, graph paper, notebook paper, ruler

1. You will collect data showing how the length of a rope changes as you tie more knots in it. Before your group begins, discuss what you expect to find out. Write your group's prediction about what you think will happen.

2. Measure the length of the rope before you tie any knots, and record the length in the table below. Tie one knot in the rope, measure the new length, and record it in the data table. Continue tying knots in the rope, measuring, and recording data until you have nine knots.

Number of Knots	Length of Rope (cm)
0	
1	
2	
3	
4	
5	
6	
7	
8	
9	

FIGURE 9.3. Knotty Problem.

Additionally, the relationships that are evident in the Knotty Problem are modeled with physical materials so that students experience a linear function through a hands-on approach. Beginning with an activity of this type promotes an understanding of how to graph an ordered pair and then interpret the graph that results.

Continuing to develop the idea of functions using similar tasks would be appropriate for a Tier 2 or Tier 3 class. The physical modeling allows access across a diverse group of learners and creates a context for discussing the relationships. Additionally, it brings together multiple representations of the mathematics: physical (rope), diagrammatic (graph), and symbolic (equation). In the next section, we discuss instructional guidelines for teaching algebraic thinking.

Instructional Guidelines for Teaching Algebra

When teaching algebra, there are several guidelines that you can follow as you plan lessons for students with MLD and mathematics difficulties (MD). These guidelines are applicable to the CCSSM (NGA & CCSSO, 2010) mathematics domains. Several instructional guidelines are discussed with examples (Van de Walle, Karp, & Bay-Williams, 2019).

The *first guideline* is to include modeling the mathematical concepts as a means for helping students to better understand what they are learning. What does modeling the mathematics mean? Modeling mathematics is described as an object, picture, or drawing to show the concept (Van de Walle et al., 2019). Importantly, it is common for several representations to be used together during instruction such as concrete and symbolic.

Modeling mathematics begins in kindergarten where students are expected to use manipulatives, pictures, and drawings to represent simple equations (e.g., 2 + 1 = ?), for example, the actions of addition and subtraction (i.e., putting together and adding to for addition and taking apart or taking away for subtraction; K.OA; NGA & CCSSO, 2010). As students progress through the grades and the mathematical ideas for domains become more challenging, especially for students with MLD and MD, other types of models can be used to help students explore and represent mathematics problems and verbalize their understandings of the mathematics. For instance, students use rectangular arrays as a pictorial representation for showing multiplication of a whole number of up to four digits by a one-digit whole number (4.NBT; NGA & CCSSO, 2010). In sixth grade, students use visual fraction models to represent a problem (6.NS; NGA & CCSSO, 2010), and in high school, students calculate and interpret the average rate of change of a function shown symbolically or as a table (i.e., pictorial representation; F-IF; NGA & CCSSO, 2010). Modeling functions includes verbal, symbolic, graphical, and tabular translations of functional relationships as illustrated in Figure 9.4 (Bryant & Bryant, 2014). These translations are important for teachers to incorporate into instruction to help students represent mathematical ideas in different ways.

Thus, modeling mathematics is highly recommended as a way for students to represent their understandings of mathematical ideas (Cirillo, Pelesko, Felton-Koestler, & Rubel, 2016). The reader is referred to the CCSSM (NGA & CCSSO, 2010) for other examples of the use of mathematical models.

The *second guideline* refers to teaching and using appropriate vocabulary for algebra. According to Hughes, Powell, and Stevens (2016), teachers must use precise mathematical language during instruction. Teachers must also expect their students to use mathematical language when talking about the mathematics with their peers or in whole-group instruction. When a student talks about or verbalizes the mathematics, the students should be expected to use appropriate vocabulary for algebra. If a student misuses a term or uses a word familiar to the student but not mathematically correct, then the teacher must provide a correction. For instance, if a student says the coefficient is a variable, then a possible correction strategy could be "A coefficient is a number used to multiply a variable. What is an example?" Figure 9.5 is a list of steps for problem solving.

Word Walls are a great activity for students to practice new vocabulary terms that are used in a unit, chapter, or specific activity. Words are chosen from the current topic of study for the Word Wall. The words are displayed in large letters and posted on a wall.

Verbal: Sally sells seashells by the seashore for $2 each.

Symbolic: $y = 2x$ where x represents the number of seashells sold, and y represents the amount of money Sally earns. Graphical and tabular are provided.

Graphical:

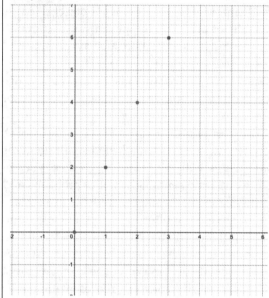

Tabular:

x	y
0	0
1	2
2	4
3	6

FIGURE 9.4. Translations for representations.

STAR Strategy Steps

1. Search—Read the problem and engage in activities to promote understanding (e.g., highlighting key words).

2. Translate—Convert the word problem to a number sentence (e.g., draw a visual representation of the problem, paraphrasing the problem).

3. Answer—Solve the problem using tools from the translate step; students know the math operations to use and the sequence of implementation steps.

4. Review—Check calculations; students check for clearly written digits and correct use of place value.

FIGURE 9.5. STAR strategy steps (Maccini & Hughes, 2000).

Wortd Walls should include words that students use frequently when reading and writing. For additional resources on vocabulary terms for the grade levels and other activities, see *www.doe.virginia.gov/instruction/mathematics/professional_development/institutes/index.shtml*. Figure 9.6 shows a vocabulary activity. The takeaway is that vocabulary related to algebra, or any matheatics domain for that matter, must be taught explicitly prior to instruction and then students should be expected to apply their vocabulary knowledge to instruction.

Word Steps

What is the word?

Describe it in your own words.

Give three examples of the word (use pictures or words).

FIGURE 9.6. Word steps.

The *third guideline* focuses on using cognitive and metacognitive strategies to teach algebraic concepts. Simply stated, cognitive strategies refer to using processes such as experiences, thoughts, and sensory input for acquiring knowledge. Cognitive strategies can be used to comprehend, process, remember, and apply information. Metacognitive strategies can be paired with cognitive strategies to assist students in applying the cognitive strategies using self-questioning and self-regulation and teaching students how to think about the academic content (Montague, Krawec, Enders, & Dietz, 2011). Witzel and Little (2016) identified three cognitive and metacognitive strategies that can be used to teach algebra using mnemonics, which are a useful technique especially for students with MLD and MD who can benefit from the mnemonics tools.

The first mnemonic, which can be applied to solving algebra problems, is the ASSOC strategy: Ask if any numbers or letters are grouped by parentheses; See how the numbers or letters are grouped within the parentheses; Same numbers/letters, symbols, and total?; One, two, three, or more numbers/letters or symbols?; Can be all addition or all multiplication symbols (Witzel & Little, 2016). The second mnemonic, ISOLATE, can be used to solve equations: Identify the location of the variable or unknown; Subtract, add, multiply, or divide parts of the expression to isolate the unknown with its coefficient and sign; Organize the equation to balance across the equations sign, so that each operation input is completed on both sides; List the equations and compute; Arrange final calculations to isolate the unknown; Try your calculation; Evaluate the answer (Witzel, 2005). The third mnemonic, which students can learn for solving one-variable equations, is DRAW (Mercer & Miller, 1992): Discover the variable, the operations, and what the left side of the equation equals; Read the equation, and combine like terms on each side of equation; Answer, or draw and check; Write the answer for the variable. See Figure 9.7 for an example of strategy steps.

Here are some tips for teaching the mnemonics. First, for students to be able to apply the mnemonics independently, they will need to say the name of the mnemonic, tell the letters, and state what each letter stands for so they can use the mnemonics for algebra instruction. Other instructional guidelines for teaching mnemonics include using explicit instruction, including modeling, to teach mnemonics, and offering many opportunities for students to show their understanding of mnemonics through direct application to algebraic problems. We recommend creating a poster with the mnemonic letters indicating what each letter means. Sometimes, teachers create bookmarks with the mnemonic letters and their meaning so that students can keep this information handy and use it both in the classroom and at home for homework. We now turn our attention to ways to intensify interventions for teaching struggling students. We focus on an example for Tier 2 intervention with a modification of the intervention for Tier 3 students.

Intensifying Interventions for Algebra

As a reminder from Chapter 1, response to intervention (RTI) is characterized as preventative models that include screening for at-risk students; high-quality, evidence-based

1. S—Search the word problem.
   (a) Read the problem carefully.
   (b) Ask yourself questions: "What facts do I know?" "What do I need to find?"
   (c) Write down facts.

2. T—Translate.
   (a) Choose a variable.
   (b) Identify the operation(s).
   (c) Represent the problem with the Algebra Lab Gear (concrete application).
   (d) Draw a picture of the representation (semiconcrete application). Write an algebraic equation (abstract application).

3. A—Answer the problem

Addition	Subtraction	Multiplication/Division
Same signs → Add #s & keep sign Different → signs find difference of #s & keep sign of # (farthest → from zero)	Add the opposite of the second term	Same signs → Add Different signs → Subtract

4. R—Review the solution.
   (a) Reread the problem.
   (b) Ask question, "Does the answer make sense?" "Why?"
   (c) Check answer.

FIGURE 9.7. STAR strategy. From The Access Center, *Using Mnemonic Instruction to Teach Math,* LD online.

intervention; progress monitoring; and tiered levels of intervention. RTI is usually characterized as having three tiers, Tier 1, Tier 2, and Tier 3, of prevention and intervention. We discuss an example of an intervention for Tier 2 students and how this intervention can be adjusted for Tier 3 students who require much more intensive instruction.

Tier 2 Intervention Example

This problem-solving strategy centers on solving word problems with integers. The intervention is a good example of the integration of problem solving, the algebra-readiness concept, a cognitive and metacognitive strategy, and the concrete–semiconcrete–abstract (CSA) routine discussed in Chapter 2. The reader should revisit the steps of the CSA routine and suggestions for how to slightly modify it before reading this intervention example. Also, explicit teaching practices were employed to teach the mnemonic (review explicit teaching practices in Chapter 1). Finally, review the ADAPT mnemonic's steps and adaptation categories in Chapter 1.

Maccini and Hughes (2000) studied the effects of a word-problem-solving strategy. The following is a description of the strategy and the instructional procedures used to teach the strategy to secondary students with learning disabilities (LD). The STAR strategy was taught to students and then they were expected to apply the strategy to solve word problems with integers. Review Figure 9.7 for the STAR mnemonic.

The CSA procedure was used to teach and implement the STAR strategy. By now, you should have reviewed the CSA routine in Chapter 2. As you may recall, the concrete phase involves manipulatives, the semiconcrete includes pictorial, and the abstract or symbolic focuses on numbers. For the concrete step, students worked with algebra tiles and a work mat, which had negative and positive areas. For the problem to represent, a temperature example was presented with –2°F as the beginning temperature of a day. Then the temperature rose to 9°F. The question asked, "What was the temperature in the afternoon?" Students then manipulated the tiles to show two zero pairs with +7 tiles remaining. In the semiconcrete step, the concrete manipulatives were replaced with a two-dimensional drawing (pictorial) representation of the algebra tiles. In the abstract step, numbers (abstract symbols) were used. Also, students were taught computational procedures for integer problems.

The STAR intervention occurred for 20 to 30 minutes a day, and progress was assessed twice a week (see Figure 9.7). Students were assessed on solving word problems with integers; the scoring consisted of assigning points to accurately or partially accurately answered items. Mastery was set at 80% accuracy for 2 consecutive days. Students were also assessed using a think-aloud protocol. Overall results showed that most students' scores improved in solving addition, subtraction, multiplication, and division integer word problems; mean percentage scores ranged from 91.4% to 98.3%. Scores on the use of the STAR strategy steps also showed marked improvement. Therefore, we suggest educators further examine the STAR strategy and consider implementing this when teaching word problems with integers to secondary-level students with LD. Because this word-problem-solving intervention was designed for and implemented with students with LD, adaptations may not be necessary; however, adaptions are likely for Tier 3 students due to their instructional needs.

Tier 3 Intervention Example

For intensifying interventions, we know that the duration of an instructional lesson will need to be extended to 45 minutes a day (ADAPT, Instructional Delivery category). The ADAPT Instructional Content may need adapting so that integer problems include only one operation at a time to mastery and then the problems can be mixed with computation involving the four operations. Work done during intervention time should include students spending time learning the strategy letters and what each letter represents to mastery and students thinking aloud all problems as they solve them (ADAPT, Instructional Delivery category). Remember that the hallmark of strategy instruction is student mastery of the strategy mnemonic and steps so that students can apply the strategy independently. The strategy steps should include a think-aloud process where students' thinking is made transparent because of student verbalizations of the steps.

Mastery could be adapted at 80% for 4 rather than 2 consecutive days (ADAPT, Instructional Delivery category).

Conclusion

In this chapter, we described these components and provide examples of activities to teach various aspects of algebra, such as a variable. We also provided an example of a cognitive and meta-cognitive strategy, STAR, for Tier 2 intervention and explained how the STAR intervention instructional delivery and instructional content could be adapted using the ADAPT framework. The examples of activities and the framework adaptation are intended to help readers understand how algebra can be taught to students with MLD and MD.

REFERENCES

Arcavi, A., Drijvers, P., & Stacey, K. (2017). *The learning and teaching of algebra*. New York: Routledge.

Bamberger, H. J., Oberdorf, C., & Schultz-Ferrell, K. (2010). *Math misconceptions*. Portsmouth, NH: Heinemann.

Blanton, M., Levi, L., Crites, T., Dougherty, B., & Zbiek, R. M. (2011). *Developing essential understanding of algebraic thinking for teaching mathematics in grades 3–5*. Reston, VA: National Council of Teachers of Mathematics.

Blanton, M., Stephens, A., Knuth, E., Gardiner, A. M., Isler, I., & Kim, J. S. (2015). The development of children's algebraic thinking: The impact of a comprehensive early algebra intervention in third grade. *Journal for Research in Mathematics Education, 46*(1), 39–87.

Brizuela, B. M. (2016). Variables in elementary mathematics education. *Elementary School Journal, 117*(1), 46–71.

Brizuela, B. M., Blanton, M., Sawrey, K., Newman-Owens, A., & Murphy Gardiner, A. (2015). Children's use of variables and variable notation to represent their algebraic ideas. *Mathematical Thinking and Learning, 17*(1), 34–63.

Bryant, D. P., & Bryant B. (2014). *Mathematics observation tool: Instructional practices and description*. Austin, TX: Psychoeducational Services.

Byrd, C. E., McNeil, N., Chesney, D. L., & Matthews, P. G. (2015). A specific misconception of the equal sign acts as a barrier to children's learning of early algebra. *Learning and Individual Differences, 38*, 61–67.

Carpenter, T. P., Levi, L., & Farnsworth, V. (2000). Building a foundation for learning algebra in the elementary grades. *In Brief, 1*(2), 1–4.

Cirillo, M., Pelesko, J. A., Felton-Koestler, M. D., & Rubel, L. (2016). Perspectives on modeling in school mathematics. In C. R. Hirsch & A. R. McDufie (Eds.), *Mathematical modeling and modeling mathematics* (pp. 87–96). Reston, VA: National Council of Teachers of Mathematics.

Dougherty, B. J, Zenigami, F., & Matsumoto, A. (2003). *Explorations in algebra*. Honolulu: Curriculum Research & Development Group, University of Hawaii.

Gersten, R., & Chard, D. (1999). Number sense: Rethinking arithmetic instruction for students with mathematical disabilities. *Journal of Special Education, 33*, 18–28.

Houlihan, B., & O'Riordan, M. (2018). *Number sense remediation in the upper grades.* Prides Crossing, MA: Landmark School.

Hughes, E. M., Powell, S. R., & Stevens, E. A. (2016). Supporting clear and concise mathematics language: Instead of that, say this. *Teaching Exceptional Children, 49,* 7–17.

Jordan, N. C., Glutting, J., & Ramineni, C. (2010). The importance of number sense to mathematics achievement in first and third grades. *Learning and Individual Differences, 20,* 82–88.

Kaput, J. J. (2008). What is algebra?: What is algebraic reasoning? In J. J. Kaput, D. W. Carraher, & M. L. Blanton (Eds.), *Algebra in the early grades* (pp. 5–17). Hillsdale, NJ: Erlbaum.

Knuth, E. J., Alibali, M. W., Hattikudur, S., McNeil, N. M., & Stephens, A. C. (2008). The importance of equal sign understanding in the middle grades. *Mathematics Teaching in the Middle School, 13*(9), 514–519.

Maccini, P., & Hughes, C. A. (2000). Effects of a problem-solving strategy on the introductory algebra performance of secondary students with learning disabilities. *Learning Disabilities Research and Practice, 15*(1), 10–21.

Mazzocco, M. M. M., & Devlin, K. T. (2008). Parts and "holes": Gaps in rational number sense among children with vs. without mathematical learning disabilities. *Developmental Science, 11*(5), 681–691.

Mercer, C. D., & Miller, S. P. (1992). Teaching students with learning problems in math to acquire, understand, and apply basic math act. *Remedial and Special Education, 13,* 19–35, 61.

Montague, M., Krawec, J., Enders, C., & Dietz, S. (2011). The effects of cognitive strategy instruction on math problem solving of middle-school students of varying abilities. *Journal of Educational Psychology, 106*(2), 469–481.

National Council of Teachers of Mathematics (NCTM). (2000). *Principles and standards for school mathematics.* Reston, VA: Author.

National Council of Teachers of Mathematics (NCTM). (2014). *Algebra as a strand of school mathematics for all students: Position paper.* Reston, VA: Author.

National Governors Association (NGA) Center for Best Practices & Council of Chief State School Officers (CCSSO). (2010). *Common Core State Standards for mathematics.* Washington, DC: Authors.

National Mathematics Advisory Panel (NMAP). (2008). *Foundations for success: The final report of the National Mathematics Advisory Panel.* Washington, DC: U.S. Department of Education.

Seeley, C. L. (2004, September). A journey in algebraic thinking. *NCTM News Bulletin.* Retrieved from *www.nctm.org/News-and-Calendar/Messages-from-the-President/Archive/Cathy-Seeley/A-Journey-in-Algebraic-Thinking.*

Van de Walle, J. A., Karp, K. S., & Bay-Williams, J. M. (2019). *Elementary and middle school mathematics: Teaching developmentally* (10th ed.). London: Pearson.

Wilkie, K. J. (2016). Students' use of variables and multiple representations in generalizing functional relationships prior to secondary school. *Educational Studies in Mathematics, 93*(3), 333–361.

Witzel, B. S. (2005). Using CRA to teach algebra to students with math difficulties in inclusive settings. *Learning Disabilities: A Contemporary Journal, 3*(2), 49–60.

Witzel, B. S., & Little, M. E. (2016). *Teaching elementary mathematics to struggling learners.* New York: Guilford Press.

CHAPTER 10

Use of Technology
for Intensifying Mathematics Intervention

MIN WOOK OK, MIKYUNG SHIN, BRIAN R. BRYANT,
and DIANE PEDROTTY BRYANT

LEARNING OUTCOMES

After studying this chapter, you will be able to answer the following questions:

1. What is Universal Design for Learning, and how do its guidelines, principles, and checkpoints assist teachers during interventions with struggling students?

2. What is the role of computer-assisted instruction in helping teachers meet the needs of struggling students?

3. What tips provide teachers with information as to how to evaluate and use computer-assisted instruction with their struggling students?

4. What are virtual manipulatives, and what is their role in providing intensive intervention for Tiers 2 and 3 for students with mathematics difficulties and mathematics learning disabilities?

Technology has evolved rapidly over the decades, as it has become an essential part of our everyday lives. Teachers and students use a variety of technology tools such as computers, tablets, and interactive whiteboards in today's K–12 classrooms. We know that technology can be a valuable instructional tool for all students, especially for students who have disabilities (Maccini, Gagnon, & Hughes, 2002). More specifically with regard to this chapter, technology, when combined with effective teaching, has been proven to improve students' learning in mathematics (Ok & Bryant, 2016). In fact, technology has become so important that the National Council of Teachers of Mathematics (NCTM, 2000) recommended that teachers use technology to help their students increase their mathematics knowledge and skills, and technology is emphasized in the Common Core

State Standards for Mathematics (CCSSM; National Governors Association [NGA] Center for Best Practices & Council of Chief State School Officers [CCSSO], 2010).

We have learned that technology can help teachers provide individualized instruction to better meet each student's unique learning needs. For example, teachers can adjust the difficulty levels and learning pace, and set personal goals for individual students to match their individualized education program (IEP) goals. Technology provides more practice opportunities or repeats instruction when needed, provides immediate feedback, and records students' progress (Shippen, Morton, Flynt, Houchins, & Smitherman, 2012). Because technology can be a valuable tool for teaching students with mathematics learning disabilities (MLD), the focus of this chapter is to provide information on how teachers can use technology to teach mathematics concepts and skills to struggling students who have great difficulty learning mathematics and who require intensive intervention. Although there are many aspects of technology that can be examined, we have chosen to focus on three technology-related areas that are being used to intensify instruction for struggling students: Universal Design for Learning, computer-assisted instruction, and virtual manipulatives.

Technology Application 1: Universal Design for Learning

The principles, guidelines, and checkpoints associated with Universal Design for Learning (UDL) have become increasingly popular with teachers as they make lessons accessible to all of their students. Although many teachers use UDL applications in their general education classes for whole-class work, UDL can also be used when they need to intensify instruction, such as when teachers differentiate instruction for small groups of struggling students. We pose two questions for consideration as you read this section of the chapter: How can teachers apply the UDL framework as instruction is intensified? How can technology be used for teaching and learning when using UDL?

UDL is defined in and supported by the Higher Education Opportunity Act of 2008.

> The term "universal design for learning" means a scientifically valid framework for guiding educational practice that (A) provides flexibility in the ways information is presented, in the ways students respond or demonstrate knowledge and skills, and in the ways students are engaged; and (B) reduces barriers in instruction, provides appropriate accommodations, supports, and challenges, and maintains high achievement expectations for all students, including students with disabilities and students who are limited English proficient. (Section 103[24])

UDL also was referenced as important instructional and assessment components in the Individuals with Disabilities Education Act Amendments of 2004 (IDEA, 2004), which provides guidance for special educators and general educators who might be developing Tier 2 supplemental lessons and Tier 3 intensive interventions. IDEA also encourages teachers, "to the extent possible, [to] use universal design principles in developing and administering any assessments (Section 300.160), and through technology (Section 300.704) to maximize its use to provide access to the general curriculum" (Kennedy, Thomas, Meyer, Alves, & Lloyd, 2014, p. 71).

The term *UDL* was first coined by David Rose and Anne Meyer (2002) as part of their work with the Center for Applied Special Technology (CAST), a not-for-profit research and development organization. Rose, Meyer, and their colleagues working at CAST suggested that it might be possible to extend Universal Design architectural concepts to the classroom. Over the next several years they offered the principles, guidelines, and checkpoints to help teachers make their lessons accessible to diverse students, including students with disabilities, through supports in lessons and assessments (Ok, Rao, Bryant, & McDougall, 2017). As shown in UDL guidelines developed by CAST (*http://udlguidelines.cast.org*), the principles are listed first, and then the guidelines are presented below each principle; checkpoints are embedded within the guidelines.

A frequently asked question regarding UDL involves whether the application of UDL is research based. In this regard, Rao, Ok, and Bryant (2014) conducted a review of the research and found a growing body of evidence that supports the application of UDL to help students learn and be able to access the curriculum. It is also important to note that technology, including assistive technology, can play an important role in UDL-related lessons; thus, we focus on UDL lessons that involve both instructional technology and assistive technology. *Assistive technology* is a general term that includes equipment (devices) and services that help people compensate for their disability-related challenges (Assistive Technology Act, 2004).

Applications of UDL to Tier 2 and Tier 3 Small-Group, Intensive Interventions

In the same way that teachers can apply UDL in whole-class instruction, teachers, interventionists, and other educators can apply UDL to three to five students in a small group. Small groups for instruction are typically associated with supplemental, Tier 2 instruction or more intensive, Tier 3 intervention. Figure 10.1 shows a sample lesson that can be used to teach small groups how to use grids to learn percentages (Bryant, Bryant, & Smith, 2019). The CAST UDL Lesson Builder (*http://lessonbuilder.cast.org*) was used to focus on five different UDL checkpoints. As can be seen in the lesson outline, elements of effective instruction, such as providing an anticipatory set, modeling, and presenting practice opportunities, help promote accessibility so that all students, including students with mathematics difficulties and MLD, can benefit from the instruction.

Applications of UDL as Teachers Differentiate Instruction

Most teachers recognize that UDL provides important information that they can use to help make their lessons accessible to most students. However, even when doing their best to help students learn, teachers find that some students continue to struggle and require "something more." In this way, UDL can be considered a useful umbrella that, for the most part, "shields" students from factors and influences that can interfere with

Title: Using Grids to Learn Percentages

Subject: Mathematics: Number and Operations—percentage

Grade Level: 6

Duration: 45 minutes

Unit Description: This lesson is part of a group of lessons that focus on the relationship among percentages, fractions, and decimals.

Lesson Description for Day: Prerequisite skills: Ability to communicate verbally.

Unit Goals: To understand the relationship among percentages, fractions, and decimals.

Lesson Goals: To introduce the concept of percentage using a 10×10 grid.

Misconception: In the Anticipatory Set, the relationship among percentages, fractions, and decimals is presented. Some students think the decimal point marks a symmetrical location in a decimal number. Instead, the decimal point separates the whole-number values that are less than 1.

Methods:

Anticipatory Set: Tell the students that the purpose of the day's lesson is to help them become familiar with the concept of a percentage to prepare for further lessons about the relationship among percentages, fractions, and decimals. They will need to understand how these concepts are related and ways for representing similar quantities.

Introduce and Model New Knowledge:
1. Introduce the mathematical term *percent* and the symbol that denotes percent. Explain that percent means one part in a hundred. Project onto a whiteboard pictures from online magazines that use percent and the % symbol to discuss sales (*Checkpoint 2.1: Clarify vocabulary and symbols*). Have students provide real-life examples of items that they and their family buy on sale and what bargains they look for, such as 50% off or an item is reduced by 25% and then the reduced price is later reduced by 25% (*Checkpoint 3.1: Activate supply background knowledge*).
2. Explain that they are going to use the concept of percent for planting a garden. Read the problem to the students: Ms. Sanchez is going to plant a garden this spring. She has a plot of land that she will partition into parts so that she can plant both flowers and vegetables. Ms. Sanchez knows that she wants more land devoted to flowers and that the remaining land will be for different types of vegetables. She decides to draw a grid on her interactive whiteboard to help her visualize what the garden might look like.
3. Show students models using the virtual manipulative grids of what Ms. Sanchez's garden might look like (*http://nlvm.usu.edu/en/nav/vlibrary.html*; *Checkpoint 5.2: Use multiple tools for construction and composition*).
4. Show a percentage and ask students what the grid would look like given the percentage, so that they can work from a number to shading a grid and from a shaded grid to providing a percentage, to help students become comfortable with using the virtual manipulatives (*Checkpoint 3.3: Guide information processing, visualization, and manipulation*).

Provide Guided Practice:
1. Have the students work in pairs at computer stations to use the virtual manipulative grid to create pictorial scenarios of what Ms. Sanchez's garden might look like.
2. Have student pairs share with each other their ideas and use the term *percent* as they describe their plot of land's partition (*Checkpoint 7.1: Optimize individual choice and autonomy*).

Provide Independent Practice: At the end of the lesson, give students scenarios for the garden, and have them show their gardens.

FIGURE 10.1. Sample lesson for small-group instruction. From Bryant, Bryant, and Smith (2019). Adapted with permission from Sage Publications.

learning. But in the same way that umbrellas can sometimes leak and allow rain to seep through, the UDL "umbrella" cannot be expected to account for "keeping out" all factors that can result in students not fully benefitting from instruction. In these cases, it is important to differentiate instruction, in other words, to adapt instruction so that each student's personal strengths and struggles are considered. There has been a lot of information provided to teachers to help them combine UDL and differentiated instruction. Table 10.1 shows useful examples of how UDL checkpoints can be matched to differentiation principles (Hall, Vue, Strangman, & Meyer, 2004). We have added sample technologies that can be used to support differentiated instruction.

As an example of an application for differentiation, consider Ms. Jackson, who is teaching a lesson to her algebra class on graphing. As Ms. Jackson looks at the lesson she will be teaching, she remembers that one of her students, Tiffany, struggled with yesterday's graphing introduction lesson. Tiffany often struggles dealing with Tier 1 or core content, so Ms. Jackson knows she must address Tiffany's learning needs while also receiving Tier 3, intensive intervention 4 days per week for 30 minutes each day. One of the issues that arose during the lesson was that a number of students, including Tiffany,

TABLE 10.1. Example of Aligning Differentiation Principles with UDL Checkpoints

Checkpoints	Differentiated Instruction Features/Technologies
Checkpoint 3.2: Highlight patterns, critical features, big ideas, and relationships	The teacher provides multiple examples throughout the lesson with multiple models, practice activities, and additional math problems. *Technology:* Virtual manipulatives
Checkpoint 3.2: Highlight patterns, critical features, big ideas, and relationships	The teacher highlights critical features of the mathematics by stopping and calculating, checking in with students, and modeling behavior. *Technology:* Calculator
Checkpoint 2.5: Illustrate through multiple media	The teacher supports understanding by identifying patterns not only in text but also in the environment of the classroom, school, etc. *Technology:* Drawing tools
Checkpoint 3.1: Activate or supply background knowledge	Teachers analyze or pretest students for key preskills and background knowledge. *Technology:* Computer-scored assessments
Checkpoint 8.4: Increase mastery-oriented feedback	In cooperative groups, students may receive feedback from the teacher and from peers. *Technology:* Blogs
Checkpoint 7.1: Optimize individual choice and autonomy	Students are assigned to one of three groups tiered by difficulty; all students are working on the same task but with varying supports. *Technology:* Digital pen
Checkpoint 8.2: Vary demands and resources to optimize challenge	Varied supports in the working groups alter the level of independence and difficulty in solving the task. *Technology:* Interactive whiteboard

Note. Adapted from Hall, Vue, Strangman, and Meyer (2004, p. 17).

incorrectly thought of the graph as a picture, a common misconception for younger children but one that can linger with some older students. Ms. Jackson pointed out that graphs are representations of data rather than, for example, a picture of a mountain (with an ascending and descending line graph; Garcia & Cox, 2010).

Using the ADAPT framework described in Chapter 1, Ms. Jackson knows that the task she will teach and assign to her students is to create graphs when given points for x and y. As Ms. Jackson thinks about the prerequisite skills for this task, she considers Tiffany's strengths and struggles in relation to the prerequisite skills. Ms. Jackson knows that Tiffany understands that points lie on x and y axes; that the points can either be positive, negative, or 0; and that a line can be drawn that connects the points. These skill areas have been a focus of Tiffany's Tier 3 intensive intervention for the past 2 weeks, and she has been responding well based on her weekly progress monitoring results. However, in yesterday's lesson, when graphing data points, it became evident that Tiffany was not transferring what she learned in Tier 3 to Tier 1 or core classroom instruction. Tiffany struggles with finding the data points on her worksheet and placing the points where they belong. Tiffany understood the concept but struggled with the implementation. Ms. Jackson decided to adapt the instruction for Tiffany by providing her with a graphing calculator, which is an example of an Instructional Material category from the ADAPT framework. Ms. Jackson knew that, after providing instruction and pairing students to promote conversations about the graphing task, she would have to work individually with Tiffany to provide more instruction (Instructional Delivery category example from the ADAPT framework) on graphing data points and on how to use a graphing calculator. Tiffany then would have to work through one or two examples with Ms. Jackson. Only when Tiffany was able to complete the examples successfully would Tiffany then be ready to work independently or with a classmate to solve the remaining problems. As she plans her adapted lesson for Tiffany, Ms. Jackson considers UDL checkpoints and knows that her adapted, differentiated lesson, which is an example of an Instructional Activity from the ADAPT framework, will match up to Checkpoints 2.5 (Illustrate through multiple media), 8.2 (Vary demands and resources to optimize challenge), and 8.4 (Increase mastery-oriented feedback), among others. By applying her adaptations mindset using the ADAPT framework to Tiffany's instruction, Ms. Jackson has identified ways to help her learn the lesson's objective. To learn more about UDL, readers can access detailed information at *www.udlcenter.org/aboutudl/whatisudl/3principles* and refer to Noono (2014) regarding six ways to engage every learner using UDL at *https://thejournal.com/articles/2014/12/03/6-ways-to-engage-everylearner-using-udl.aspx*. In the next section, we discuss computer-assisted instruction as a means for intensifying interventions.

Technology Application 2: Computer-Assisted Instruction

For decades, *computer-assisted instruction* (CAI) has been a popular tool for teaching mathematics to students with disabilities. CAI and software programs have helped students learn mathematics content through the use of traditional computers (e.g., laptops) and, in recent years, mobile devices (e.g., tablets). Anyone who has walked into an elementary, middle, or high school classroom has probably seen teachers and/or students using laptops and tablets as part of instruction. Using educational software and/ or mobile device apps, teachers can implement CAI as a standalone teaching resource or as a supplemental support tool for traditional teacher-led lessons (Devisir & Kalaimathi, 2016). Also, CAI is often used to provide additional independent practice opportunities for students with MLD, and for students who are receiving Tier 2 or Tier 3 mathematics interventions who are in need of more repetition and practice to master skills (Bouck & Flanagan, 2009). Importantly, for students who struggle learning mathematics, CAI has been shown to help improve their motivation and attitude toward mathematics (Okolo, 1992). So, CAI can serve as a valuable instructional resource for general and special education teachers to support students who are experiencing difficulties with mathematics at the elementary, middle, and high school levels. In this section of the chapter, we offer two questions to consider answering: How can CAI mathematics programs be selected to match individual student needs? How can CAI programs be integrated into Tier 2 and Tier 3 interventions?

Tips for Selecting CAI Mathematics Programs for Individual Student Needs

For CAI to be of value, teachers must be able to recognize and choose appropriate CAI programs (e.g., software, apps) and to use those programs to improve the mathematical outcomes for all students, including those students who show difficulties with mathematics instruction. However, it is important to note that simply using technology does not guarantee positive results. It is equally important to understand the instructional design of mathematics software and apps. Thinking back to Ms. Jackson's interest in differentiating and adapting instruction for her struggling students, she needs to be familiar with effective instructional components that have been proven successful for teaching struggling students important mathematical concepts and skills and, thus, should be embedded in CAI programs. Ms. Jackson must also know how to implement CAI to supplement or support teacher-led lessons (Vrasidas & Glass, 2002). One problem teachers often face is sorting through the vast number of CAI programs on the market and selecting effective, evidence-based mathematics CAI programs that can help their students. Some teachers select CAI programs only after looking at the price tags (e.g., free or inexpensive) or checking for popular CAI programs (e.g., What are the "best sellers"?). These approaches for selecting CAI programs, while somewhat easy to do, can be problematic because CAI programs that do not contain key evidence-based instructional components may not be useful for improving the mathematical knowledge of students who are struggling with an array of concepts and skills that they must master.

To assist teachers in selecting CAI programs, researchers have provided a number of tips to facilitate the identification of appropriate programs that align with their individual student's needs (e.g., Ok, Kim, Kang, & Bryant, 2016). We highlight three of these tips. The first tip relates to the importance of understanding that "one size does not fit all"—programs that may be useful for some students may not be a good match for other students with different needs. The instruction–student match is particularly important when selecting programs for struggling students who require intensive intervention. With this in mind, the student's characteristics (e.g., needs, preferences) first need to be identified and learning objectives need to be identified that align to specific CCSSM or state standards, and IEP goals and objectives for students with MLD (Powell, 2016).

The second tip focuses on searching for CAI programs via search engines (e.g., Google, iTunes) using key words (e.g., specific mathematics skills such as fractions) that might be options as good matches for an individual student's mathematics objectives. Teachers can use CAI program review websites to gain specific information about perceived educational value, program features, whether the program contains violent depictions, and so on. Readers can access the list of example review websites at *https:// tinyurl.com/yxarwrtr*. Some review websites also provide objective expert reviews and/or allow teachers to search programs aligning with the CCSSM, state standards, IEP goals, and grade levels. Be aware, however, that not all "objective" reviews are worthwhile. For example, some program publishers may have solicited reviews of their products with a slant on providing positive reviews. Other reviews may have been conducted with typical learners in mind, rather than struggling students. Once the search process has been completed, teachers can compile a list of potential CAI programs that seem to fit their classroom needs. When possible, request a free trial of the program.

The third tip relates to evidence-based instructional components. For CAI to be most effective, teachers must select CAI programs that meet a particular student's individual needs and learning goals while at the same time include effective, evidence-based instructional components. Teachers should carefully examine a software program or an app for the presence of effective instructional components for successfully teaching specific mathematics concepts and skills to their students. Figure 10.2 provides an evaluation form containing a list of instructional components to consider and a rubric to determine each component's quality, which teachers can use to assess various CAI mathematics programs. Evaluating programs using a rubric can help teachers compare programs that were initially selected to find the one(s) most well designed and effective. As you can see, the evaluation form has three sections. The first section is used to identify basic information about the program, such as name, specific mathematics skills examined, and content/graphic level. The second section is used to evaluate whether the program includes instructional components and practices that have been proven to be effective for students with disabilities. These effective instructional components include general instructional strategies (e.g., modeling, teaching an instructional strategy or strategies), mathematics-specific instructional strategies (e.g., visual representations), and technology-specific variables (e.g., customizable settings, easy navigation). After Section 2 is completed, Section 3 can be used to compute a total percentage score for the program. Remember, however, any program's effectiveness for particular students can be determined only as it is being used by those students, which is the topic of the next section.

Section 1. Identifying Information

Check for basic information of the CAI program you select.

Name of CAI program			
Publisher		**Price**	
CCSSM Domain	☐ Counting & Cardinality ☐ Operations & Algebraic Thinking ☐ Number & Operations in Base Ten ☐ Number & Operations–Fractions ☐ Measurement & Data Geometry ☐ Ratio & Proportional Relationships ☐ The Number System ☐ Expression & Equation ☐ Functions ☐ Statistics & Probability *If the application overlapped several areas, check all that apply.* Specific CCSSM #: _____		
Mathematics Skills	☐ Early Numeracy/Number Sense ☐ Calculation ☐ Reasoning/Problem Solving ☐ Vocabulary/Concepts ☐ Other (_____)		
Objectives			
Content Level	☐ Primary ☐ Upper Elementary ☐ Middle School ☐ High School Specific Grade Levels: _____		
Graphic/Theme Level	☐ Primary ☐ Upper Elementary ☐ Middle School ☐ High School		
Type of CAI Program	☐ Drill and Practice ☐ Game Lecturing or Tutoring ☐ Simulation ☐ Supplementary Tool for Learning		

Section 2. Evaluation

Select the appropriate score of each category like ☒ or ☑.

Category	Description	Score	
Objective	Clearly stated and easily identified		3
	Easily identified although not clearly stated		2
	Difficult to be identified		1
Strategy	Strategies are provided for doing the work, and skills are broken down		3
	No strategy is provided, but skills are broken down		2
	No strategy, and skills are not broken down into small steps		1

(continued)

FIGURE 10.2. CAI mathematics program evaluation form. From Ok, Kim, Kang, and Bryant (2016). Adapted with permission from Sage Publications.

Category	Description		Score
Examples	Students are given three or more examples for each concept/skill		3
	Students are given one or two examples for each concept/skill		2
	No examples are given for each concept/skill		1
Practice	Many (e.g., at least five) practice opportunities are provided before moving on to the new skill/concept		3
	Some (e.g., one to four) practice opportunities are provided before moving on to the new skill/concept		2
	No practice opportunities are provided before moving on to the new skill/concept		1
Multiple Representations	Multiple representations including visual representations (e.g., graphs, pictures) were used to teach the target math skill		3
	Visual representations were used to teach the target math skill		2
	No visual representation connected to the target math skill was provided		1
Vocabulary	Vocabulary related to the target math skill was taught explicitly		3
	The definitions of vocabulary related to the target math skill were provided		2
	No vocabulary learning related to the target math skill		1
Error Correction and Feedback	Students are notified of correct/incorrect response and are given the correct answer		3
	Students are notified of correct/incorrect response, but not given the correct answer		2
	No notification and no correct answer given		1
Error Analysis	A record is kept of the types of errors that the student makes, and the analysis is reported		3
	A record is kept of the types of errors that the student makes, but nothing is reported		2
	No error analysis available		1
Progress Monitoring	Total points are provided, and progress is detected by the CAI program of tracking system		3
	Total points are provided, but no tracking available		2
	No total points are provided, nor is tracking available		1
Motivation	Keeps students engaged in learning		3
	Engages students at first, but loses their attention soon		2
	Little to no engagement		1

(continued)

FIGURE 10.2. *(continued)*

Category	Description		Score
Navigation	Easy/simple navigation and easy to get help		3
	Easy/simple navigation but difficult to get help		2
	Not easy/simple navigation and difficult to get help		1
Visual and Auditory Stimuli	Background image and sound are not distracting, and sound can be turned off		3
	Background image and sound are not distracting, but sound cannot be turned off		2
	Background image and/or sound are distracting, and sound cannot be turned off		1
Font	Font size is sufficient and modifiable, and font type is easy to read		3
	Font size is sufficient or modifiable, but font type is easy to read		2
	Font size is not sufficient nor modifiable, and font type is not easy to read		1
Customized Settings	Can be customized easily for an individual student		3
	Can be customized but is limited for an individual student		2
	Cannot be customized for an individual student		1
Content Error and Bias	The content is free of errors, up to date, and free from bias (e.g., race, gender)		3
	The content is free of errors and up to date but is not free from bias (e.g., race, gender)		2
	The content is not free of errors, is dated, and is not free from bias (e.g., race, gender)		1

Section 3. Grading

A	Number of score 3 (_____) × 3 = (_____)	B	Number of score 2 (_____) × 2 = (_____)
C	Number of score 1 (_____) × 1 = (_____)		
Total	(A + B + C [_____]) ÷ 45 × 100 = (_____)%		

A (90–100%)	B (80–89%)	C (70–79%)	D (60–69%)	E (< 60%)

FIGURE 10.2. *(continued)*

Tips for How to Integrate CAI Programs Successfully into Tier 2 and Tier 3 Intensive Interventions

After selecting CAI programs, it is important to carefully plan how CAI is going to be integrated into an instructional routine in a Tier 2 and Tier 3 intervention. We provide several tips for integrating CAI programs into interventions. The first tip is taken from Bryant and his colleagues (2015) who determined that CAI is most effective when combined with teacher-directed instruction. For example, when teachers are preparing to provide explicit instruction for teaching multiplication facts to their struggling students, they should administer teacher-directed lessons that have explicit modeling and guided practice, and use CAI programs, for instance, during a warm-up activity to review prerequisite skills and, later, to provide independent practice opportunities. For Tier 2 and Tier 3 interventions, CAI programs can provide students who require intensive interventions with additional review and practice opportunities that are needed to master the skill being taught.

The second tip relates to differentiating instruction based on how students respond to and interact with the CAI programs. Teachers can customize the settings of a CAI program (e.g., set up individual goals, pace, difficulty levels) to meet the needs and preferences of a particular student. For example, teachers can vary the learning pace to accommodate those students who need more "slowed-down" instruction in order to learn and practice the mathematics. The second tip refers to *scaffolding,* which is a process in which teachers provide temporary, additional supports for students in order to enhance their learning. Some CAI programs allow teachers to select and provide more scaffolding (e.g., using multiple representations such as a number line), which is an important aspect of intensifying and individualizing intervention.

The third tip for integrating CAI programs into interventions focuses on progress monitoring and assessment data. These tools can help teachers determine each student's areas of difficulty and provide more intensive instruction on the skills when needed or select an easier or more difficult skill to ensure that instruction is tailored to student performance and to ensure that students are benefiting from using the CAI program.

Tip 4 cautions teachers about the learning characteristics of some students with disabilities and those who are receiving Tier 2 or Tier 3 interventions. These students may have short attention spans and engage in off-task behaviors. Some of them might get bored easily when using the same CAI program. When this is the case, it may be useful to have two or three additional CAI programs available to keep students engaged during learning (Cumming & Rodriguez, 2013).

The fifth tip refers to a means for managing student use of the CAI program. For instance, if using an Apple product (e.g., iPads) to deliver CAI, teachers can use the Guided Access feature to lock the app while students use it. Students cannot leave the app assigned to them and use other apps or the internet unless teachers insert a passcode. It is important to remember that although technology has benefits for boosting students' learning and motivation, the positive effect will occur only when the technology is used effectively. As stated earlier, technology is best used as a supplementary tool for instruction, combining effective teacher-direct instruction with invaluable student interactions between students and teachers. Examples of CAI programs for intensifying Tier 2 and Tier 3 Mathematics Interventions for early numeracy, whole-number computation, advanced mathematics skills (e.g., algebra, fractions), and functional mathematics skills (e.g., time, money) are noted in Table 10.2. Review websites, which were previously discussed, can be used to identify highly recommended CAI programs. However, all CAI programs listed should be evaluated using an evaluation form and rubric, such as what we provide in this chapter, to ensure that the programs are appropriate for individual student learning needs and IEP goals and objectives. In the final section of this chapter, the use of virtual manipulatives is discussed as another means for intensifying interventions.

Technology Application 3: Virtual Manipulatives

Virtual manipulatives (VM) are a relatively new technology that obviously combines the terms *virtual* and *manipulatives*. "Virtual" indicates not being physically existing and appearing on a computer or touch screen. "Manipulatives" are physical objects such as algebra tiles and geoboards. Thus, VM are simulated objects that users can move and manipulate virtually. Representations such as number lines are commonly used as ways to model the mathematics for students who struggle learning mathematical concepts and skills. Multiple representations are so important that the NCTM (2014) highly recommended using mathematical representations as one way to promote students' successful mathematics learning. Recently, with the development of online educational resources, virtual formats of manipulatives and other representations have become available via websites and apps. VM can replace or supplement the use of concrete manipulatives for teaching mathematics. For example, thinking back to Ms. Jackson's need for additional instructional materials to teach graphing data points, she can consider using VM as another way to demonstrate how to graph data points. Ms. Jackson can also use the evaluation form and rubric for examining VM choices to ensure that there is a good student–technology match. As noticed in a Google Trends analysis between 2004 and 2018 (*https://trends.google.com/trends/explore?date=all&q=virtual%20manipulative*), interest in the use of VM has grown for teaching mathematics and are now available for various devices, including computers, tablets, and smartphones (Shin, 2017). Shin and her colleagues (2017) noted that VM can be implemented in various instructional groupings. Instead of, or in addition to, using concrete manipulatives, teachers can implement VM during Tier 1 whole-class instruction by using interactive Smart Boards. Teachers can also integrate VM in their Tier 2 or Tier 3 small-group instruction using a variety of platforms. For example, students can get immediate positive or corrective feedback on their responses directly from web- or app-based VM.

According to Reimer and Moyer (2005), such self-generated online verbal and written feedback allows users to actively engage in their learning and to track their progress, which can be motivating for students who exhibit mathematics difficulties or who have MLD. We pose three questions for consideration in this section of the chapter: What

TABLE 10.2. A List of Mathematics CAI Programs

Name (type)	Grade Level	Mathematics Skills (CCSSM)
Early Mathematics Skills		
• Toddler Counting 123 (app) • Number Concepts 1 by IntelliTools (software) • Jump Numbers (app) • Montessori Number Land I Learn to Count (app)	K–elementary	Counting (K.CC)
• Elmo Loves 123 (app) • Introduction to Math, by Montessorium (app) • Dexteria Dots—Get in Touch with Math (app) • Park Math by Duck Duck Moose (app) • Love to Count by Pirate Trio (app) • Todo Math (app) • Bugs and Numbers (app) • Monkey Math School Sunshine (app) • Moose Math by Duck Duck Moose (app) • SwitchIt! Early Math with Spider and Friends (software)	K–elementary	Various early mathematics skills (K.CC, K.OA, K.NBT, K.MD, K.G)
Whole-Number Operations		
• Pet Bingo by Duck Duck Moose (app) • Motion Math: Match (app) • Mystery Math Town (app) • Math Evolve (app)	K–elementary	Addition, subtraction, multiplication, division (1.OA, 1.NBT, 2.OA, 2NBT, 3.OA, 3.NBT)
• Math Blaster HyperBlast (app & website) • Math Drills by Instant (app) • Reflect Math (website) • Show Me Math by Attainment Company (software) • Quick Math—Multiplication Table & Arithmetic Game (app)	Elementary–secondary	Addition, subtraction, multiplication, division (3.OA, 3.NBT, 4.OA, 4.NBT)
Advanced Mathematics Skills		
• DragonBox Algebra 5+ (app)	Elementary	Basic algebra (3.OA, 5.OA)
• DragonBox Algebra 12+ (app) • Get the Math (website) • Algebra Touch (app) • Basic Algebra Shape-Up (software)	Secondary	Algebra (6.NS, 6.EE, 7.NS, 7.RP, 7EE, 8 EE, HS-A-REI)

(continued)

TABLE 10.2. *(continued)*

Name (type)	Grade Level	Mathematics Skills (CCSSM)
Advanced Mathematics Skills *(continued)*		
• Slice Fractions (app)	Elementary	Fractions (3.NF)
• Motion Math: Fractions! (app) • MathTappers: Equivalents (app)	Elementary–secondary	Fractions (4.NF, 5.NF)
• Doodle Math Shape (app) • Montessori Geometry (app) • Dragon Shapes: Geometry Challenge (app) • The Land of Venn—Geometric Defense (app) • Cyberchase 3D Builder (app)	Elementary	Geometry (1.G, 2.G, 3.G, 4.G)
• Crafty Cut by Touch Press Games (app)	Secondary	Geometry (6.G, 7.G)
Functional Mathematics Skills		
• Motion Math: Pizza! (app) • Jungle Coin—Learn Coin Math (app)	Elementary	Money (2.MD)
• Counting Bills & Coins (app) • Attainment's Dollars & Cents (app & software) • Next Dollar Up (app)	Upper elementary–secondary	Money (2.MD, 4.MD)
• Jungle Time—Learn How to Tell Time (app) • Todo Telling Time (app)	Elementary	Time (1.MD, 2.MD, 3MD)
• MathTappers: ClockMaster (app)	Elementary–secondary	Time (1.MD, 2.MD, 3MD)

Note. Grade level was determined for both content and graphic level.

resources are available on websites and for mobile devices for supporting mathematics instruction? How can VM be integrated into small-group, intensive interventions? What are considerations for using VM successfully in mathematics interventions?

Examples of VM for Mathematics Instruction

Website

As is well known, a *website* is a collection of webpages, each of which holds a specific uniform resource locator (URL) that is accessible via the internet. Beginning in the early 2000s, websites introduced VM aligned with NCTM content standards. For example, the National Library of Virtual Manipulatives presents VM aligned with number and operation, algebra, geometry, measurement, and data analysis and probability standards (NCTM, 2000) in PreK through 12th grades. More recently, NCTM's Illuminations present VM aligned with visual tools recommended by CCSSM (NGA & CCSSO, 2010) as well as NCTM principles and standards (NCTM, 2000). One of the Standards for Mathematical Practice by CCSSM is modeling with mathematics (CCSS.MATH. PRACTICE.MP4). Meeting this practice standard, NCTM's Illuminations provide various ready-to-use diagrams or visual games that present students' problem-solving situations and help them find solutions using VM. A list of example VM, including summarized information on the features of VM (e.g., device compatibility, price, related mathematic topics, and visual models), can be found at *https://tinyurl.com/y5a7ybf7*.

Mobile Web Apps

Mobile web apps are defined as internet-enabled applications that educators can access via a mobile device's web browser. Today, users can directly access mobile content without downloading or installing any apps. Thus, they can access and use VM using the internet regardless of device compatibility. VM websites have been recently developed and updated, such as The Math Learning Center and Illuminations, which provide mobile-friendly web apps. Students can use mobile web apps–based visual tools (e.g., number line, geoboard, dot) for a number of relevant mathematics topics (e.g., fractions, money, perimeter, area) during their Tier 2 and Tier 3 mathematics instruction. In addition, students can get corrective feedback and repeated practice opportunities using a wide range of multiple representations built into the apps.

Mobile Native Apps

Mobile native apps, smartphone applications that provide fast performance and a high degree of reliability, can be downloaded and stored on mobile devices through such providers as the App Store or Google Play. One of the benefits of these mobile native apps is that they provide easy access to the installed apps without requiring internet access in classrooms or in environments where Wi-Fi access is restricted (Bouck, Working, & Bone, 2018). Websites, such as Conceptua Math and Illuminations, are also available as mobile native apps, although the types of available VM on the native apps are not the same as those available via the websites. For example, Illuminations offers a greater variety of options for interactive activities using VM on its website than on its mobile native apps. ABCya.com's Virtual Manipulatives! is another example of a mobile native app, which is available only for iPads.

Application of VM for Intensifying Small-Group Interventions

Teachers can implement VM in Tier 2 or Tier 3 interventions with a small group of three to five students. The following are tips for using VM to intensify small-group instruction. First, when teaching mathematics using VM, teachers should explicitly demonstrate how to manipulate visual tools. Teachers can use a *think-aloud strategy* (i.e., asking students to say out loud what they are thinking about when solving and representing mathematical problems) to model how to change the visual shapes, colors, and quantities of VM as multiple representations.

Second, after demonstrating how to use VM, teachers should periodically monitor whether students understand what they have been shown and can independently make alterations. For example, teachers can ask students guiding questions such as "Why did you move the fraction bars? Why did you move the number on the number line?" Providing guiding questions helps students to actively engage with the VM (Sayeski, 2008). Responding to teachers' questions, students can self-monitor, which is an important form of *self-regulation* (i.e., the ability to control one's problem-solving process).

Third, teachers can create new mathematical problems on many VM programs that allow such action. Teachers can create specific types of problems that are challenging for students who have difficulties and require increased opportunities to practice. Providing multiple practice opportunities as part of Tier 2 and Tier 3 interventions is one way to intensify interventions to help students master targeted mathematics concepts and skills.

Fourth, for students receiving intensified interventions, VM programs can be customized so that students can select their personal preference for colors and shapes of dynamic images. This "customizing" feature can potentially increase students' interest, motivation, and engagement in their mathematics learning, all of which are critical factors for struggling students (Moyer-Packenham & Westenskow, 2013).

Fifth, aligned with CCSSM (NGA & CCSSO, 2010) for Mathematical Practice, students can use VM to "represent" and "map" mathematical relationships using built-in visual tools. Students can easily manipulate graphs or number lines on the screen to find their answers, rather than physically drawing those diagrams. That is, students who struggle with mathematics can use VM as dynamic visual representations, which can help them translate mathematics problems into more meaningful mathematical solutions (Shin & Bryant, 2017). Consider, for example, a student who uses a VM area model to solve the following problem: "I eat ½ of a loaf of bread per day. How much bread will I eat in 2 days?" The student can use a VM area model representation to conceptualize the mathematics as an aid in problem solution.

Finally, students use built-in VM functions to receive immediate feedback on correct and incorrect answers, which is another critical feature for intensifying interventions. Shin and Bryant (2017) give an example of students who selected an incorrect answer for a word problem involving multiplying fractions. When this happened, students received immediate feedback for an incorrect answer. Students then went back and retried the problem using VM.

Considerations for the Successful Use of VM as Part of Interventions

Although VM can be used as alternate visual tools in the classroom when teaching mathematics to students with mathematics difficulties, or MLD, it is important to carefully plan how to integrate VM into intensive mathematics interventions. Many experts, such as Bouck and colleagues (2017) and Shin and colleagues (2017), have expressed concerns that should be considered when using the tools. The first consideration is that simply using VM does not guarantee that students will develop conceptual understanding (Moyer-Packenham & Westenskow, 2013). Importantly, the NCTM (2014) highlighted the need to help students engage in connecting mathematical representations to deepen their understanding of mathematics concepts and procedures. For example, although students may select correct answers while solving mathematics problems using VM programs, the process does not guarantee that students fully understand the reason behind their solutions. Thus, teachers should monitor and check whether students can explain the relationship between quantities and visual representations shown on VM programs.

The final consideration, as discussed in the CAI section, is the importance of selecting appropriate VM programs that are aligned with (1) IEP goals and objectives, (2) mathematics domains as indicated from the CCSSM, and (3) students' individual learning needs. It is critical that teachers evaluate the features of VM to determine which websites and apps are most effective for teaching mathematics to their students. When evaluating VM apps in particular, teachers should consider instructional interface, interactive features, and interactive questions. Interface questions can include "Do the font color, type, and size meet students' needs?"; "Does the function of the presented screen work correctly?" Instructional features can be evaluated through a series of questions such as "Is the content error free?"; "Does the VM program offer demo videos showing how to use VM?"; "Are there multiple opportunities for students to use the VM program to learn each mathematical concept and skill?" Finally, interactive questions could include "Can the student receive error correction and feedback?"; "Can the teacher create new problems and model features?"

Conclusion

This chapter provides information regarding how to use the UDL framework, CAI, and VM to intensify mathematics instruction and interventions. Applying UDL can help teachers reduce barriers to accessing the curriculum and provide flexibility in intensive instruction. Using appropriate CAI and VM can provide students who have mathematics difficulties and MLD with enhanced, differentiated mathematics learning opportunities. We recommend that teachers consider using these technology tools for effectively intensifying mathematics interventions for struggling students.

REFERENCES

Assistive Technology Act, 29 U.S.C. § 3 (2004).

Bouck, E. C., Bassette, L., Shurr, J., Park, J., Kerr, J., & Whorley, A. (2017). Teaching equivalent fractions to secondary students with disabilities via the virtual-representational–abstract instructional sequence. *Journal of Special Education Technology 2017, 32*(4), 220–231.

Bouck, E. C., & Flanagan, S. (2009). Assistive technology and mathematics: What is there and where can we go in special education? *Journal of Special Education Technology, 24*(2), 17–30.

Bouck, E. C., Working, C., & Bone, E. (2018). Manipulative apps to support students with disabilities in mathematics. *Intervention in School and Clinic, 53*, 177–182.

Bryant, B. R., Ok, M. W., Kang, E. Y., Kim, M. K., Lang, R., Bryant, D. P., & Pfannestiel, K. (2015). Performance of fourth-grade students with learning disabilities on multiplication facts comparing teacher-mediated and technology-mediated interventions: A preliminary investigation. *Journal of Behavioral Education, 24*(2), 255–272.

Bryant, D. P., Bryant, B. R., & Smith, D. D. (2019). *Teaching students with special needs in inclusive classrooms* (2nd ed.). Los Angeles: SAGE.

Cumming, T. M., & Rodriguez, C. D. (2013). Integrating the iPad into language arts instruction for students with disabilities: Engagement and perspectives. *Journal of Special Education Technology, 28*, 43–52.

Devisir, K., & Kalaimathi, H. D (2016). *Effect of CAI on the achievement of information technology.* Raleigh, NC: Lulu.

Garcia, G. G., & Cox, R. (2010). "Graph-as-picture" misconceptions in young students. In A. K. Goel, M. Jamnik, & N. H. Narayann (Eds.), *Diagrammatic representation inference* (Lecture Notes in Artificial Intelligence No. 6170, pp. 310–312). Berlin: Springer-Verlag.

Hall, T., Vue, G., Strangman, N., & Meyer, A. (2004). *Differentiated instruction and implications for UDL implementation.* Wakefield, MA: National Center on Accessing the General Curriculum. Retrieved from *https://sde.ok.gov/sites/ok.gov.sde/files/DI_UDL.pdf.*

Higher Education Opportunity Act of 2008. Public Law 110-315, 110th Congress. Retrieved from *www2.ed.gov/policy/highered/leg/hea08/index.html.*

Individuals with Disabilities Education Act Amendments of 2004, Public Law 108-446. (2004). Retrieved from *www.gpo.gov/fdsys/pkg/PLAW-108publ446/html/PLAW-108publ446.htm.*

Kennedy, M. J., Thomas, C. N., Meyer, J. P., Alves, K. D., & Lloyd, J. W. (2014). Using evidence-based multimedia to improve vocabulary performance of adolescents with LD: A UDL approach. *Learning Disability Quarterly, 37*(2), 71–86.

Maccini, P., Gagnon, J. C., & Hughes, C. A. (2002). Technology-based practices for secondary students with disabilities. *Learning Disability Quarterly, 25*(4), 247–261.

Moyer-Packenham, P. S., & Westenskow, A. (2013). Effects of virtual manipulatives on student achievement and mathematics learning. *International Journal of Virtual and Personal Learning Environments, 4*(3), 35–50.

National Council of Teachers of Mathematics (NCTM). (2000). *Principles and standards for school mathematics.* Reston, VA: Author.

National Council of Teachers of Mathematics (NCTM). (2014). *Principles to actions: Ensuring mathematical success for all.* Reston, VA: Author.

National Governors Association (NGA) Center for Best Practices & Council of Chief State School Officers (CCSSO). (2010). *Common Core State Standards for Mathematics.* Washington, DC: Authors. Retrieved from *www.corestandards.org/assets/CCSSI_Math%20Standards.pdf.*

Noono, S. (2014). 6 ways to engage every learner using UDL. Retrieved from *https://thejournal.com/articles/2014/12/03/6-ways-to-engage-every-learner-using-udl.aspx.*

Ok, M. W., & Bryant, D. P. (2016). Effects of a strategic intervention with iPad practice on the multiplication fact performance of 5th grade students with learning disabilities. *Learning Disability Quarterly, 39*(3), 146–158.

Ok, M. W., Kim, M. K., Kang, E. Y., & Bryant, B. R. (2016). How to find good apps: An evaluation rubric for instructional apps for teaching students with learning disabilities. *Intervention in School and Clinic, 51*(4), 244–252.

Ok, M. W., Rao, K., Bryant, B. R., & McDougall, D. (2017). Universal design for learning in pre-K to grade 12 classrooms: A systematic review of research. *Exceptionality, 25*(2), 116–138.

Okolo, C. M. (1992). The effects of computer-based attribution retraining on the attributions, persistence, and mathematics computation of students with learning disabilities. *Journal of Learning Disabilities, 25*(5), 327–334.

Powell, S. (2016). Choosing iPad apps with a purpose: Aligning skills and standards. *Teaching Exceptional Children, 47*(1), 20–26.

Rao, K., Ok, M. W., & Bryant, B. R. (2014). A review of research on universal design educational models. *Remedial and Special Education, 35*(3), 153–166.

Reimer, K., & Moyer, P. S. (2005). Third-graders learn about fractions using virtual manipulatives: A classroom study. *Journal of Computers in Mathematics and Science Teaching, 24*(1), 5–25.

Rose, D. H., & Meyer, A. (2002). *Teaching every student in the digital age: Universal design for learning.* Alexandria, VA: Association for Supervision and Curriculum Development.

Sayeski, K. L. (2008). Virtual manipulatives as an assistive technology support for students with high-incidence disabilities. *Journal of Special Education Technology, 23*(1), 47–53.

Shin, M. (2017). An analysis of mobile virtual manipulatives apps for the teaching of elementary school mathematics. *Journal of Korea Multimedia Society, 20*(6), 935–949.

Shin, M., & Bryant, D. P. (2017). Improving the fraction word problem solving of students with mathematics learning disabilities: Interactive computer application. *Remedial and Special Education, 38*(2), 76–86.

Shin, M., Bryant, D. P., Bryant, B. R., McKenna, J. W., Hou, F., & Ok, M. W. (2017). Virtual manipulatives: Tools for teaching mathematics to students with learning disabilities. *Intervention in School and Clinic, 52*(3), 148–153.

Shippen, M. E., Morton, R. C., Flynt, S. W., Houchins, D. E., & Smitherman, T. (2012). Efficacy of a computer-based program on acquisition of reading skills of incarcerated youth. *Remedial and Special Education, 33,* 14–22.

Vrasidas, C., & Glass, C. V. (Eds.). (2002). *Current perspectives on applied information technologies: Distance education and distributed learning.* Greenwich, CT: Information Age.

Index

Note. Page numbers in italic indicate a figure or a table.